DO LUNCH OR BE LUNCH

DO LUNCH OR BE LUNCH

The Power of Predictability in Creating Your Future

HOWARD H. STEVENSON

with
Jeffrey L. Cruikshank

Research Assistance by
Mihnea C. Moldoveanu

HARVARD BUSINESS SCHOOL PRESS
Boston, Massachusetts

Printed in the United States of America
02 01 00 99 98   5 4 3 2 1

Library of Congress Cataloging-in-Publication Data

Stevenson, Howard H.
    Do lunch or be lunch : the power of predictability in creating your future /
Howard H. Stevenson, with Jeffrey L. Cruikshank : and research assistance
by Mihnea C. Moldoveanu.
        p.   cm.
    Includes bibliographical references and index.
    ISBN 0-87584-797-8 (alk. paper)
    1. Business forecasting.   2. Industrial management.   3. Corporate
culture.   I. Cruikshank, Jeffrey L.   II. Moldoveanu, Mihnea C.   III. Title.
HD30.27.S84   1997
658.4'0355—dc21   97-12470
                                                                         CIP

To my ancestors, both genetic and intellectual,
who gave up certainty to create predictability.

To James,
    With appreciation of
the challenges you face,
    with hope that you
find this useful and
    with anticipation of
a great future!

                    Sincerely,

                    Howard

contents

preface

Let me begin on a personal note.

I am currently on my third tour of duty as a professor at the Harvard Business School. Between academic stints, I've worked in a variety of businesses, ranging from a midsize paper company to a from-the-ground-up investment management firm. I've served on the boards of several dozen corporations. I've written or cowritten cases about some 200 companies. In recent years, with several of my academic colleagues, I've puzzled over the difficult field of entrepreneurship, trying (I think with some success) to make sense out of this rambunctious, highly individualistic field.

Throughout my checkered career, I have been looking for a useful way to interpret all of the disparate things I was learning, in a wide variety of contexts. And I had a growing conviction that there was a pattern that cut across and unified much of the behavior within the many human organizations in which I found myself, in one capacity or another.

In the notion of predictability I think I've found that pattern.

And you, the reader, might well ask, "So what?"

I can give several partial answers, which are intended to encourage you to read on. Certainly, I'm writing this book in part to share my observations about some of the interesting things I've observed. (Academics are inclined to do this.) But I have two far more important goals for this book.

The first is to provide a useful lens for people to interpret their own lives. Prediction is a powerful tool, and predictability is a powerful attribute—hence the subtitle of this book. But mastering and applying the art of prediction, and getting to be a predictable entity, are not easy tasks. I have some ideas about how to do this, which I share in the later chapters of this book.

The second is, frankly, to sound an alarm. I see a number of trends in our society, particularly in business organizations, that give me great cause for concern. As these trends intensify, so does my concern. Many of the very organizations that we have created to help us bring about our desired futures are now acting in ways that undermine this critical goal. They are undercutting the meanings and values that are the indispensable underpinnings of predictability. When business executives excuse their arbitrary dismissal of capable long-service employees in the name of short-term bottom-line improvement, I cringe—not just because of the inhumanity of the deed, but also because of its shortsightedness. And when people say that self-interest (read "greed") is the best decision rule, I cringe again—not just because of the pure immorality of such a worldview, but also because of what it says about our ability to act in concert to accomplish vital goals.

My readers should understand that I am an unabashed, enthusiastic, lifelong capitalist. I've made good money, for myself and others, wearing that hat. But I have no patience with companies (or, for that matter, governments) that consciously or unconsciously adopt policies that undermine their own legitimacy. I dread the convulsions—social, political, and economic—that are sure to result when large numbers of people reach the conclusion that the corporations and other institutions we have created to make our lives better are in fact making them worse.

In recent years, businesses have tended to favor short-term profits over long-term predictability. Politicians are into short-term, feel-good measures rather than the difficult work of long-term thinking and investment. In this book, I propose to turn the telescope around and look through its other end. I argue that predictability is a powerful tool of management—perhaps the most powerful. Conversely, I argue that the organization that embraces unpredictability is not only inhumane, but incompetent.

As I sat down to commit these ideas to paper, I realized almost immediately that I wouldn't be satisfied speaking to the relatively small audiences that normally pay attention to books by business school professors. I therefore resolved to speak to my readers in the same voice that I use to connect with people in business—in the context of a Harvard Business School reunion, or a Young Presidents' Organization event, or a company-sponsored seminar. I hope that I have succeeded in making these ideas accessible without making them seem trivial.

If I've succeeded in the task I set out to achieve, this book will offer you an analytic framework and the tools necessary to understand predictability and to use it well. Maybe some of you who try on this new lens will find, as I have, that it brings your world into sharper focus. If so, I'm sure you can find ways to improve on it and become leaders in helping people cope with change.

introduction

Habit is habit, and is not to be flung out the window by any man,
but coaxed downstairs a step at a time.
Mark Twain

In a sense, this is a book about habits. It is a book about the patterns that people and organizations invent (or fall into) so that they can conduct their business and go about their daily lives.

But this is not a book about the past. My premise is that, in terms of taking action in our lives, there is no such thing as the past. In fact, there is no such thing as the present. There is only the future. Yes, we reflect on our experience; we review precedent to help us predict the consequences of our decisions. But then we must *act*, in the here-and-now, minute to minute, in order to get what we want or need. Without exception, our actions are aimed at a *future*. It may be a future that is only minutes ahead of us, or one that is years ahead of us, but in every case we are trying to shape a future. The reason why we set the alarm clock every night, and then get out of bed the next morning, is to create the future.

This is what makes Mark Twain's observation about habit so interesting. Why *shouldn't* habit be flung out the window? Why should it be coaxed downstairs a step at a time? Is it because we are sentimental creatures who can't bear to leave our vanished past behind? Or are we hard-wired in such a way that we naturally default to the status quo?

I don't think it's either. I think habits help us look into our futures. The most durable habits—the ones that may seem most stuck in the past—often turn out to be very useful predictive tools. The explanations we make out of what has occurred in the past often lend insight into how we think about our options and guide our attempts to predict our futures. It is the need to *predict* that finally persuades us to coax our habits downstairs. Habits, along with other tools and techniques, help us choose our futures.

And this need to predict seems to be the essence of being human. One by one, under the scrutiny of science, all of the other characteristics that supposedly separate us from our fellow creatures on earth have fallen by the wayside. We are not the only builders and wielders of tools. We are not the only species with opposing digits. As sociobiologist Edwin O. Wilson has demonstrated, we are not the only altruists.[1] We are not the only animals with advanced communication skills. We have already been humbled by porpoises, and there is mounting evidence that we are about to be embarrassed again—this time by whales, which seem to have the ability to communicate across vast stretches of ocean without any technological assistance whatsoever.

We may not even be the only species that has a concept of "future." The next time you are awakened at dawn by a screaming crow, walk outside and get the offending bird's attention. Then pick up a rock, look the crow in the eye, and very slowly cock your arm. It's very likely that your crow will act upon its prediction about the future and take cover.

No; what seems to distinguish us from every other species is a single, odd, invaluable trait: the ability to contemplate *multiple* futures, over varying time frames. From childhood, we are constantly, relentlessly, trying futures on for size. Sometimes we consciously indulge ourselves by doing so: "When I grow up, should I be a firefighter or an astronaut?" But, far more often, we predict in order to survive and prosper. To modify Descartes, I predict, therefore I will be.

It is not hard to imagine where this drive to predict came from. Back in the distant past, one of our low-browed ancestors saw a flurry of movement behind a nearby rock. Into his brain flashed two equally valid interpretations: *Eat! Get eaten!* But which is it? Quick! Which future lurks behind the rock? In the days of saber-toothed tigers, woolly mammoths, and the like, the question probably came up on a regular basis, and with great urgency.

If Darwin was right, the creature who answered the question correctly ate lunch, and the creature who didn't *was* lunch. Of course, every 65 million years or so, a large meteorite might roll into town and give *everybody* a really bad day. But, in general, the good predictor—the one who identified alternative futures and picked the right one—survived and procreated. The others didn't. Over many millennia, this led to us: you and me.

Today we face entirely different challenges of survival. We've bested the mammoths, only to encounter AIDS, hypertension, terrorism, deforestation, and a thousand other plagues. (Everyone has his or her own list.) But our mindsets and our skill sets remain largely unchanged from those of long ago.[2]

Which future lurks behind the rock? A basic premise of this book is that, consciously or unconsciously, we organize our lives in ways that will help us answer this all-important question more effectively. We continually try to hone our predictive powers and put ourselves in situations in which those powers will be enhanced (and in which they have already demonstrated their usefulness). In some cases, we even sacrifice comfort and personal gain to safeguard our ability to predict the future.

First big point: in this book, I will help you understand the tools that are available for honing your *individual* predictive powers. The application of these tools—observation, categorization, calculation, and others—should make it easier for you to identify alternative futures, assess them and choose among them, and then steer toward the one that seems the most promising. And it should help you avoid the misery of steering toward, and enduring, the wrong future. In other words, this book should help you *act*, and act effectively.

Second big point: whenever possible, we humans try to put ourselves in situations that enhance our predictive powers. If this is true, then one can argue that human organizations, *especially* business organizations, exist in part to enhance predictability. That is one reason why we organize them and why we join them. Another reason, as I discuss in later chapters, is to do complicated things that we can't do as individuals. And economists offer many other explanations—for instance, the maximization of shareholder wealth. But, to my mind at least, economic explanations fall far short of human reality. The real truth is that we establish and join organizations to predict (and, even better, to create) our futures.[3] In other words, we work for both bread *and* predictability. And, in the long run, I argue, my life cannot be predictable unless I help to make your life predictable.

Let's bring this discussion down to earth. In January 1996, AT&T announced that, for competitive reasons, it would lay off 40,000 of its 300,000 workers within the next three years.[4] Although the scheme had been in the making for quite some time, it took most observers inside and outside the company by surprise. AT&T's stock began to rise almost immediately. Wall Street was happy.

But other interested parties were not. In an interview on National Public Radio (NPR), the president of the Communications Workers of America energetically took the company to task. The company had absolutely no plan or schedule for actually *effecting* these cuts, he complained. Therefore, AT&T's

dramatic announcement served no purpose except to put the entire company on edge and to leave the employees wondering if and when the ax would fall on them.

NPR's next interviewee was an AT&T public relations staffer, one of 900 such staffers companywide, none of whom was slated to be laid off. "Well, there's something to that," he said, in effect, of the union president's complaint. "I guess this does make everybody's life a lot less predictable over the next few months."

By its words and deeds, AT&T was saying, "We can live with huge doses of unpredictability if enough money drops to the bottom line as a result." But this is corporate misbehavior, pure and simple. The misbehavior lies not so much in laying off 40,000 people—which AT&T hasn't actually done, as of this writing, and in fact may never have intended to do—as it does in acting unpredictably, even capriciously. By introducing high levels of unpredictability into people's lives and taking a series of highly public steps that only prolonged the suspense, AT&T undercut its own legitimacy as a human business organization. True, it may have made the announcement with the best of intentions: being candid and so on. But the net effect of the way it was done was to impose high costs on both those fired *and* those who remained.

"May you live in interesting times," went the ancient Chinese curse. AT&T's actions certainly made life more interesting for many thousands of people. And it will almost certainly come back to haunt the company. Change the rules in midgame, take away predictability, and see what happens. "The whole issue of loyalty has evaporated," one manager (who was not in peril) commented. "As far as loyalty goes," said another, lower-level manager (also not at risk), "you can forget about that."[5]

A recent cover story in *Business Week* featured Scott Paper's Al Dunlap—by all accounts, a "successful" manager. But Dunlap has an interesting nickname: "Chainsaw Al." He has earned this nickname by aggressively slashing the payroll (and other costs) at a series of companies that he has headed.[6] Ask not for whom the chainsaw roars, O hapless employee; it roars for thee.

The power of predictability is derived, in part, from behaving ourselves. "Do unto others as you would have them do unto you," Jesus said.* Would you like to work for someone named Chainsaw? (Would Al Dunlap like to have someone named Chainsaw working for him?) I believe that leaders at all levels of human organizations can see the benefit of the Golden Rule by looking through the lens of predictability: being predictable to others is a good thing. Valuing and emphasizing organizational predictability is a good and doable thing.

In this book, I argue that managers and organizations enhance their effectiveness by being more predictable. I try to make the case that individuals who manage people have a special obligation to act honestly, humanely, and effectively—and that, most often, this translates into acting predictably toward those with whom they deal. And I offer suggestions as to how individuals can work toward mutual predictability in the context of human organizations.

Individuals gaining control over their futures, and organizations succeeding through providing what is expected of them—predictability is power.

---

*Think of the effective individuals you've worked with, and the effective teams you've served on. Wasn't predictability a key contributor?

DO LUNCH
OR
BE LUNCH

chapter one

Predictability: The Good, the Bad, and the Ugly

*What lies hid is unknown,
and there is no desire for the
unknown.*
Ovid

A pop quiz. Quick! What do the following actions and attitudes have in common?

- **Building a strong culture**
- **Staying attuned to the customer**
- **Building technological expertise**
- **Creating clear performance guidelines**
- **Promoting employee involvement**
- **Promoting employee empowerment**

They're all about how companies invent their future, right? They're an old-fashioned list of virtues. It's the Good Old Days, in bullet form. It's the kind of stuff that, in so many words, managers and owners of businesses used to say they stood for. And it's the kind of stuff that people used to look for when they were embarking on their business careers and had the luxury of picking one company over another.*

Building a Strong Culture. Of course, way back when, they didn't use words like *culture, involvement,* and *empowerment.* But they lived those concepts every day. Take culture, for example, and consider the examples of John Patterson's NCR, Tom Watson's IBM, Irwin Miller's Cummins Engine, Dave Packard's and Bill Hewlett's proud offspring, the De Pree family's Herman Miller, and others. My pairing of individuals with each of these companies is deliberate. These are organizations that grew out of the values of an individual or a family, out of a particular social context, and out of a specific moment in time, and which transformed their legacies into an enduring culture. These leaders imagined a future, made it believable to others, and then, engaging their compatriots in the process, set about creating that future. I argue in this book that these are companies that recognized and solved the conundrum of being culturally consistent— *predictable*—without becoming rigid, or ponderous, or unwelcoming to new kinds of talent.

Staying Attuned to the Customer. Some on this list, and many others not necessarily known for their cultural savvy, also prided themselves on being exquisitely attuned to their customers. Sidney Weinberg's (and later John Whitehead's) Goldman, Sachs, the head-and-shoulders-above-the-pack star in its own field, deserves special mention here. So do Sam Walton's Wal-Mart and Frank Perdue's Perdue. Being fanatically obsessed with the customer is a very useful test for employees to measure new

---

*Now *that* sounds antique! It's hard to remember that, back in the 1950s, the heads of major corporations were anticipating a shortage of managers at every level and were scheming to "lure" unsuspecting college kids into the ranks of industry.

ideas against: *What would Frank do in this situation? Would he honor the money-back guarantee, or would he stall?* And, not inconsequentially, it provides just about the best job security in a tumultuous world. The customer who is happy today is likely to be there for you tomorrow. Predictability![1]

Building Technological Expertise. Building technological expertise is a way to harness what Joseph Schumpeter, Harvard economist and entrepreneurial historian, used to call "creative destruction." No matter who you are or what business you're in, there's a tidal wave of change headed at you. You rarely have the choice to stay dry; most often, you have the choice of which way you want to get wet. The best way to stay ahead of changing technologies is to change them yourself. There's a parallel in whitewater rafting: when you hit those scary rapids, your first impulse is to backpaddle and slow things down—but often the right thing to do is paddle *forward*, as hard as you can.

I've heard two different corporate statesmen, in very different industries, say almost exactly the same thing about technological change. Bill Foster, founder of Stratus Computer, is fond of telling those in his organization that, if they don't obsolete their own product, someone else will. And Irwin Miller at Cummins Engine has been saying very much the same thing for several decades. It's interesting that thoughtful leaders in two such different industries (computers and diesel engines) would invoke the same technological mantra.

And it's unfortunate that more industrial leaders (outside of Japan, of course) haven't arrived at the same conclusion. The decline of the American auto industry in the 1970s and 1980s was particularly painful to track if you knew something about American business history. Back in the nineteenth century, when this country's industrial muscles and sinews were being put in place, business leaders were absolutely committed to technological innovation. Andrew Carnegie, for example, once ripped the guts out of a nearly brand-new steel production facility because his first lieutenant, Charles Schwab, confessed that there was a slightly better way to configure the plant. John D. Rockefeller's relentless quest for perfection pushed his Standard Oil Company into unlikely innovations, including the invention of the railroad tank car (to eliminate the loading and unloading of wooden barrels in and out of boxcars).

One last technology-and-water metaphor: whenever I hear about a levee breaking somewhere along the Mississippi, I think about Henry Ford. Ford was a brilliant designer of cars, but he was even more skilled at using other people's innovations in productive new combinations. The Model T, introduced in 1908, was one of the most astonishing technological accomplishments of this or any other century. But Ford, of course, never had the benefit of hearing the Foster-Miller dictum about obsoleting one's own products. And his blind passion for his beloved Model T—which by the 1920s had been obsoleted by the upstart General Motors line—almost killed the Ford Motor Company. Piling up sandbags in the face of rising water is a self-limiting strategy. Water (like technology) eventually goes where it wants to go, with or without your help, and history suggests that you're better off helping it than hindering it.*

Creating Clear Performance Guidelines. The importance of clear performance guidelines seems self-evident, but I'll take a minute to state the obvious. Like B. F. Skinner's pigeons, people need to know what they're going to be rewarded for and what they're going to be punished for. This is a point that you'll encounter

---

*Change is scary, but the alternative to change is scarier. CBS in founder Bill Paley's heyday was absolutely fearless. As Paley declined, so did his network. Except for timidity, there's no reason why CBS shouldn't have invented and launched *both* CNN and MTV (they had the resources, including Columbia Records, the world's best news agency, and cable TV assets) and leapfrogged ahead of the competition for another few decades.

regularly in this book: I'll only play this game if the rules are clear in advance. General Electric has had its shortcomings and weaknesses in the years under Jack Welch, but lack of clarity in performance guidelines has not been one of them: "Be number 1 or number 2 in every industry we're in—period."*

Promoting Employee Involvement and Empowerment. Employee involvement and empowerment are two sides of the same coin. I'm on the board of a company that recently adopted the practice of inviting union members who have done a particularly good job identifying and solving a problem at the mill to attend a board meeting and be recognized. I'll never forget the first such meeting I attended. A ramrod-straight, grey-haired line worker not far from retirement age came in, sat down, and listened impassively to our speechifying. When we had finished, he looked up and down our long table and said, "I'm 63 years old. I'm the third generation in my family to work in this mill. And this is the first time management has acknowledged that I might have some idea about what needs to be done here. Or *anybody else in my family,* for that matter." An eloquent condemnation, if I ever heard one!

Good management has learned (sometimes only after several generations have come and gone) that the guy out on the shop floor knows perfectly well what's breaking down, how often, and probably even *why* it's breaking down. And even if the engineer up in the air-conditioned control room understands more or less the same things, he probably doesn't understand the reality of *living* with that problem. To him, up there in splendid isolation, a production snafu is mostly a threat to his monthly production figures. But, down on the floor, it may well be a

---

*This guideline worked so well for GE that Emerson Electric—the opportunistic St. Louis–based manufacturing giant—stole it. In fact, so many companies appropriated GE's dictum that it wound up creating niche markets for a zillion smaller companies.

threat to life and limb—a sword of Damocles hanging over Joe's, Frank's, and Sandy's heads. So Joe, Frank, and Sandy live with a terrible level of unpredictability, despite the fact that the problem may require only a $500 fix.

This is the lesson of Eastern Europe, brought home to the factory floor: centralized control can't deal with a changing world. Unless the lines of communication are open, and unless using them is as easy as not using them, management doesn't hear about the no-brainer $500 fix—and life stays stuck in a bad spot. The point is not to goose management to provide a perfectly safe workplace. (It can't.) The point is to get management to say, "We'll do everything we can to help our employees work safely." This puts the shoe on the right foot. And, by so doing, it helps employees know what's going to happen to them. By extension, it will help you learn what's going to happen to *you*.

■ The Wrong Stuff

OK, here's our second pop quiz. Quick! What do the following practices have in common?

- **Reengineering**
- **Continuous improvement**
- **Matrix management**
- **Strategic restructuring**
- **Managing by stock price**
- **The virtual organization**

Easy, right? These are all the things you're *not* supposed to do, if predictability in the workplace is your goal. It will look to some like I've just swept all contemporary methods of change off the table. Do I suggest that we not change? Absolutely not. We *must* adapt, and often—as the valuable lessons of Carnegie, Rockefeller, and our other patrons of successful industry illustrate.

Before we implement a new practice that will change all the rules, though, we want to know how that change will manifest, and at whose expense. In other words, we want predictability, which the methods above don't deliver. As I say in my road shows, "Reengineering means that the rules are changing. Continuous improvement means that the rules are going to *continue* to change. Matrix management means that there are two sets of rules, and we won't tell you which one you were supposed to have followed. Strategic restructuring means that, even if you follow the rules, you may be dogmeat. Managing by stock price (maximizing the price of a share) means that all the other rules are probably there just to be broken. And the virtual organization means that there aren't any rules anyway."

Scope of the problem: the World Wide Web is an increasingly good barometer of what's on whose mind—and also an indicator of information overload. Let's look on the Web for numbers of mentions of these unmentionables. Reengineering: 47,976 (uh oh!). Continuous improvement: about 10,000. Strategic restructuring: 99,428 (yikes!). Matrix management: about 400 (an idea whose time has passed? hope so!). Managing by stock price: 0 (not surprising, given the accurate, but awkward, phrasing I've settled on, but rest assured—"shareholder value" comes in at about 3,000). The virtual organization: about 800.

So, if the Web is to be believed, the biggest contemporary threat to predictability in business comes from the would-be strategic restructurers and the reengineers. The matrix managers seem to be leaving the field, and the virtual organizers seem to be keeping their powder dry.

Now, let's slow down and be a little more even-handed, if only briefly, calling on the Web to help make our points.

Reengineering. It is true that reengineering, *done right*, can be a powerful tool for positive change. For example, it's one way to push responsibility down to the level where it belongs, to where empowerment can take place. But, done wrong, it's the worst kind of arbitrary deck shuffling. Think of how often Scott Adams, the creator of the "Dilbert" comic strip, tees off on the more unsavory side of reengineering.[2]

Or follow this fad as it inflates and deflates in the pages of *Business Week*. A *Business Week* review of Hammer and Champy's *Reengineering the Corporation* in the spring of 1993 begins with the following promise: "Here's one idea that's going to last a lot longer than you can hold your breath: reengineering. It's the hottest management concept since the quality movement." Now, the reviewer *does* quote Hammer and Champy to the effect that reengineering fails to achieve "any results" in seven out of ten companies where it's tried. But when it works—hey, it *really* works. And it seems to evoke travel metaphors: Hallmark Cards (according to Hammer and Champy) took "The [Reengineering] Journey," while Taco Bell took what it called a "voyage of discovery."

"Ultimately," the review concludes, "reengineering means doing more with less—not only less time but fewer people. That means individual hardship. But in these tough times, it's an idea that's bound to endure."[3]

But stay tuned! The arrival of a new book by Champy—now a solo artist—early in 1995 makes us wonder whether we shouldn't have tried harder to hold our breath. Remember, by this point, almost 2 million copies of *Reengineering the Corporation* had been sold, evidently to interested managers around the world. (And, ominously, the book had been printed in 14 languages.) So how does Champy open his new book? "Reengineering is in trouble." Uh oh! It emerges that, with some notable exceptions (Federal Express, Bell Atlantic), reengineering has been more or less a fizzle. Champy lays the blame for this mess at the feet of management, but a 1995 *Business Week* reviewer pointedly observes that Champy himself effectively ignores the huge initial challenge of bringing employees along for the Reengineering Journey. "Managers awash in the ugly chaos of tearing apart their companies will find guidance and consolation here," the reviewer concludes.[4]

One more time, then, to make sure I've got it. Reengineering (done wrong) is an effective tool for creating ugly chaos in which workers are ignored and managers wind up needing guidance and consolation? Driver, stop the bus! My friend Dilbert and I are in search of predictability!

Continuous Improvement.   Done right, continuous improvement is the answer to the problem of technological and economic change. It's one way to get the right answer to the question "Where will the world *be*, when we get there?"—and people are unwilling to embark on a journey when they haven't a picture of either the destination or the journey. It puts an appropriate emphasis on customer satisfaction, especially through increased product (or service) quality and dependability. It can even be arranged so that it doesn't come mainly out of the hides of one group or another, presenting the future in bite-sized and equitable (read "predictable") chunks.

For example, Georgetown Steel Corporation and the United Steelworkers of America recently formed a continuous-improvement partnership, which is designed to create a "workplace environment characterized by innovation, pride in workmanship, safety, and job security."[5] (It's interesting to note that innovation and job security are not seen as necessarily antithetical by either management or the union.) The federal Department of Health and Human Services in 1994 went so far as to suggest that its recently initiated continuous-improvement program would also "foster better job satisfaction" among HHS employees.[6]

We need to wish them well, because, done wrong, continuous improvement is reengineering in sheep's clothing.* It either does bad things or just doesn't do much at all.[7] Only about one-quarter of the companies pushing for continuous improvement in the early 1990s reported "significant results"—meaning that, in three-quarters of the reported cases, whatever unpredictability was injected into the corporation was unproductive.[8] And here's another one of those "fad flags" we keep coming up against: in 1990, 97 companies applied for recognition under the Baldrige Award program, which singles out companies for successful quality-improvement programs, often based on continuous improvement. In 1991, 106 applied. But then, in 1992, the number of applicants dropped to 90.[9] Uh oh! Is our executive attention wandering again?

I think it's fine to have a Baldrige Award, despite all the process and paperwork that seems to be involved, and the companies that win them certainly deserve applause for their accomplishments. But I also think about all those companies (75 percent!) whose programs go nowhere. The workers in these companies are first subjected to unpredictability when management embraces continuous improvement. And then they're again subjected to unpredictability when management loses interest and moves on to the next fad.[10]

Matrix Management.   I personally have a little more trouble being friendly toward matrix management (I've been matrixed, once or twice), but let me try. Matrix management recognizes the fact that we *have* to cooperate and that, in most cases, we *can't* prosper by pursuing a single, uncomplicated set of goals. In fact, complexity is the reason we blundered into matrix manage-

---

*Words are powerful. How many of us would sign up for a program called "chronic tinkering" or "incessant reengineering"?

ment in the first place. Corporations were justifiably criticized for pursuing strategies that were too static and simple-minded, or too much derived from "functional silos." In response, they cooked up truly ornate strategic plans and then invented a complex "matrix," which mandated multiple inputs into most key decisions, to carry out the plan.

And some good things resulted. Under a matrix management system, it got to be a little harder than it used to be to just say, "Oh, hell. Let's just believe what marketing is telling us, and blow off engineering." Shaping the future involves striking a balance ("Let's settle on something that's innovative at a low price and is needed by current or easily identifiable prospective customers"). Ideally, matrix management helps strike that balance. Done right, as my colleagues Chris Bartlett and Sumantra Ghoshal have pointed out, it involves more of a *mental* construct than a formal organizational structure. Many Japanese companies have prospered with matrixlike systems, in large part because these systems were imposed as conceptual constructs *before* the fact, and not superimposed onto an existing system.

Done wrong, of course, matrix management means that no one important is accountable for anything, and that it's the hapless workers down in the organization who will be judged after the fact, according to a set of rules that they could not have anticipated.[11] In my own experience, it often means losing sight of the *ends* (happy customers! sales!) and focusing on a dreary, mechanistic *means* to those ends: "In keeping with this company's stated goal of cross-functional interpollination, the policy of this company is to have you work for two bosses." If I'm a customer, am I served by and do I care about this alleged interpollination? Not likely! Once-proud and once-market-sensitive Unilever hit the skids in the mid-1990s in part because its management structure had been matrixed into a hidebound, customer-proof kind of unaccountability. What do you say to a $45 billion business in which profit-and-loss responsibility rests with 90 (count 'em—90!) regional, product, and financial managers?[12] How about, "Ugh!"

Both Unisys and Digital Equipment Corporation (DEC) have recently dumped their matrices. "We have cast aside matrix management and instituted clear accountability for revenue, profits, cash flows, and assets within our business units," wrote DEC's CEO, Robert B. Palmer, in his somewhat embarrassed president's letter for 1994—the year in which his company lost $2.16 billion. "We are eliminating the costly infrastructure associated with the previous management system."[13] (Read "Heads will roll.") Unisys, for its part, explained that it hoped to save $400 million annually as a result of its dematrixing, mainly by "reducing the infrastructure overhead and administrative costs associated with the previous highly interdependent matrix structure."[14] (Here again, read "Dead bodies in the hallways.")

Once again, think of the rhythms of predictability (or, in this case, unpredictability). Some smart guy invented these systems after the fact and imposed them on thousands and thousands of people. For as long as they lasted, these matrices created ambiguity and anxiety for many of those who labored under them. Then they got blown up, and, in their wake, enough people had to be axed to realize half a billion dollars in Death-of-the-Matrix savings.

Strategic Restructuring. Ben Rosen at Compaq would tell you that his restructuring of that company helped keep it in the game, and he would be correct. The reason there are tree pruners is that a conservative pruning now and then can help keep a tree alive.

The problem is that restructuring usually occurs in a crisis situation. It is prompted by the fact that people *haven't* been taking care of business, and now they're deep in a hole. Failed to improve continuously, have we? Failed to prune deadwood and fertilize the tree's roots? Well, then, let's kill a division or two. (But don't necessarily remember this carnage when it comes time to vote new stock options to top management.)

We might as well stay with Unisys and DEC, as these are two companies that can't seem to keep out of the restructuring business. Unisys has gone through five restructurings in seven years.[15] DEC goes for less frequency but more punch. Having penned the abovementioned letter to the shareholders and employees, Robert Palmer then flew to Europe and addressed a meeting of the company's justifiably anxious European customers. "Think of us as having to take apart a large, older building that was in danger of falling down," Palmer told the gathering, "while reconstructing a new, more modern building, on the same site, on the same strong foundation, with the occupants in residence, and at the same time."[16]

Well, yes and no. The implication of Palmer's speech is that the building's occupants *survived* this masterful facilities up-grade. In fact, some 31,000 of them (25 percent of the payroll) did not.

Does restructuring "work"? Again, it depends on what measure you choose to employ. According to a survey of major firms that "downsized" between 1989 and 1994, about 30 percent experienced increases in worker productivity—whereas 34 percent experienced productivity *decreases*. And that's one of the more reassuring measures. For example, although a solid 2 percent of the workers in these companies reported improved morale (thank God for diehard company loyalists!), another 86 percent reported that morale had been damaged.[17]

Done wrong, restructuring involves no subtle decisions, either customer by customer or employee by employee. It's like using dyna-mite on your front door when you forget your housekey. I have a friend who used to work for DEC. He was a highly talented manager. DEC, picking up on his competence, made him the head of a struggling division. And, when DEC zeroed in on that division during an early round of strategic restructuring, my friend was fired—out of the company. Smart! One possible take-home lesson: don't do good enough work to get yourself promoted.

But there are ways to restructure that aren't death-dealing. When Xerox decided to put its house in order in the early 1980s, it somewhat nervously accepted its unions' demands for job security throughout the restructuring process. The gamble paid off, and Xerox recovered much of its lost market share. "People won't contribute to your organization unless they're secure in their livelihood," explains Ronald Blackwell, a union economist involved in the Xerox restructuring. "They're afraid of change if it's going to threaten their livelihood. Grant them security and they're not afraid to contribute their ideas."[18]

Thoughtful managers, casting an eye toward predictability, can also build a reasonably benign kind of "restructuring" into the daily machinery of the workplace. This is the corporate equivalent of tree pruning. The consulting firm of McKinsey and Company moves out the worst-performing 10 percent of its consultants every year. This is not a warm and fuzzy process, by any means. But it's one that's understood and signed onto by everyone who enters the firm. The voluntaries are indistinguishable from the pushouts. It's ruthless, but in a predictable kind of way.[19]

Managing by Stock Price.   I know I promised to be fair-minded in this run-through, but managing by stock price is another thing that can't be done fairly, sensibly, or in a way that enhances mutual predictability. It is, in fact, one of the great business crimes of the century. It is the neighborhood where Chainsaw Al Dunlap—whom we met back in the Introduction—lives. The CEOs and CFOs who dabble in this stuff earn a bad name for all their peers.[20] A cynical few victimize the gullible many.

Let's let Chainsaw—who fired 11,000 people at Scott Paper, drove the company's stock price up by 225 percent, and then sold it to a competitor—speak for himself. "The responsibility of the CEO is to deliver shareholder value," he commented in a recent forum. "Period. It's the shareholders who own the corporation. They take all the risk. And how does the CEO maximize value? He does that by focusing on profit. But how does he get profit? By making the best products, by building the best facilities, by having the best workforce, by globalizing his company. And, yes, sometimes you have to get rid of people."[21]

Well, there you have it in a nutshell. The shareholder takes all the risks, and all the other parties take their lumps.* The trouble is that *real* value in a corporation is often overlooked in the process of "managing up" (some would say "manipulating") its perceived value. And the great escape hatch in managing by stock price is that there is no time frame associated with the practice. If I jack the price up into the stratosphere for one nanosecond, is that "success"? Of course not. Well, how about if I jack it up by 225 percent just long enough to sell it? That's gotta be success, right? Especially if I'm pretty confident that no one is going to come along behind me and calculate the costs associated with all those vanished jobs.

The brutal fact is that most things (pigs, cows, companies) are worth more dead than alive. It's always possible to take short-term actions that will improve a company's operating results, especially if you're not concerned about the long-term consequences of those actions. In Utah, they used to tell a joke about a farmer who decided he was going to make his mule more

---

*Later in this same discussion, Chainsaw said that he personally had taken an "enormous risk" when he had invested his own money in Scott Paper, the company he had taken over. "Yes, I made a lot of money," he acknowledged. "But I created six and a half billion dollars. I got less than 2 percent of the wealth I created."

Some employees might argue that, by investing in skills and knowledge most useful for Scott and moving to some pretty isolated places, they, too, took risks. But who wants to argue with a man named Chainsaw?

efficient. So, one day, he cut that mule's grain ration. And every day for the next month, he cut that mule's grain ration a little bit more. One day, a neighbor asked him how the experiment was going. "Not so good," admitted the farmer. "He got more and more efficient, and things were looking great. Then he up and *died* on me."

To be fair, I should say that much of the pressure for managing by stock price comes from outside the corporation. In fact, it comes from people like me and you, or our investment managers. Companies know full well that most publicly held stocks are now owned by pension funds and institutional investors—a reversal of circumstances from the 1950s, when individuals held most stocks. But, in this new ownership environment, assets like employee know-how get slighted or ignored entirely; sugarplums get polished up and served.

The Virtual Organization.   I've left the virtual organization until last, in recognition of its recent arrival on the unpredictability landscape.* Let's see. We need to say something even-handed here. Well, not every company needs to be permanent, or even "real." Some tasks are time bound and should be structured as such. The Rolling Stones' 1994–1995 Voodoo Lounge tour, for example, was no small enterprise, involving $140 million in "venture capital," 250 full-time employees, and estimated revenues of over $300 million. The stage set required four days to assemble, three different stage sets were built, and the group spent many months leapfrogging around the countryside. Almost all aspects of the enterprise, from logistics to sound systems, were contracted out. Voodoo Lounge was a creature of fax machines and hotel rooms. And, when the tour was over, the "company" just vanished.[22]

---

*Here's an interesting coincidence: the phrase *virtual corporation* was coined by a manager at DEC.

And it's certainly true that a company needs to focus on its true competence—say, pretzel making—and it needs to get out of all the other nutty stuff that it may have drifted into, including tending lawns, booking plane tickets, cooking burgers, and so on. Kinko's, the once-humble copying company that's now gone nearly national, is good at this: focusing on an appropriately narrow (and sufficiently wide) range of business services.

Not so good at this, though, are the zillions of small software development firms that don't build enough of a core to create a critical mass and vanish mysteriously, usually just when you need them. True, many of these companies derive great benefit from minimizing overhead and being acutely opportunistic. But they risk ending up like Gertrude Stein's Oakland, with no *there* there. It's voodoo of the bad kind. There's no water cooler, no shared learning, no passing along of corporate culture and experience, and no building of mutual confidence and trust.[23] When your assets go out the door every night, you can't afford to let them make the transition from being "real" to being "virtual."[24]

■ The Importance of Being Unsurprising

For a variety of reasons, I often find myself surrounded by people who are interested in business strategy. At other times, I'm surrounded by people who either are negotiation theorists or are themselves crack negotiators. And a third group with whom I commonly mingle is made up of technowizards—people who push technologies forward (or their handlers, who pay to have them pushed forward).

I'm often struck by a common theme that the people in these three groups like to sound. They listen politely as I ramble on about predictability, and then they lean forward conspiratorially. "Howard," they tell me, "your heart's in the right place. But let's face it. The way you *win* in this world is by surprising your opponents."

The strategists usually go a step further. "I'll buy this predictability stuff up to a point," they tell me. "In fact, it's a hell of a good strategy. But past that point, predictability is for losers. Play by the rules until you're sure you can deliver a knockout blow, and then . . . *pounce!*"

I'll go along with this up to a point. "Yes," I say wearily, "but pounce very judiciously. And make sure you do so in a large world, in which you won't come across the pouncee in a dark alley, and make sure that your suppliers and employees don't come to think of you as the kind of manager who can't be counted on," and so on, and so on.

The most effective counterargument I've found to the proponents of strategic unpredictability is to carry the strategic approach to its logical extreme. Thieves are good strategists: they pounce, they make a good living, and the most recent set of crime statistics I saw suggested that there's only a 3 percent chance of going to jail for stealing. Well, if I can steal $30,000 worth of stuff a year, for each year of projected jail time, stealing is worth $1 million to me. Isn't this an interesting way to look at the world? It's the purest of market lenses, and it permits—even encourages—one to commit mayhem. And the mayhem may hurt just a few victims (the individual you mug) or thousands of people (the company you mug).

In a complicated society, where mutual cooperation is critical to simple functioning, it's important to be as unsurprising as possible. I once asked one of my cousins if I should go ahead on a deal with someone with whom he worked. "Well," he said after thinking for a minute, "if you're known by the company you keep, you don't want to be seen with that guy."

In the short run, pouncing hurts the pouncee and makes a mess on only one, isolated rug. But, assuming that the pounce has visibility, it also has broader implications. It makes the rest of us wary. It negates our instinct for cooperative action. Then things can't, and don't, work as well as they have to.

And so, how do we make complex organizations predictable? Essentially, by making the components of these organizations—us—predictable in them. We start by understanding our individual desire, even need, for predictability, and we build from there.

chapter two

Predictability Important? Says Who?

Every year, if not every day,
we have to wager our salvation
upon some prophecy based upon
imperfect knowledge.
Oliver Wendell Holmes

In the beginning, human existence was pretty simple, right? You're walking through the jungle, and there's a flash of motion in the bushes next to you. You ask yourself the Big Question:

Am I lunch, or is it lunch?

You ask this question because you know that, either way, action is required. If you want lunch, you have to act. And if you want to avoid being someone else's lunch, you also have to act.

But human actions are rarely the expression of pure animal instinct. Much more often, they involve both a more-or-less conscious look into the past and a look into the future. We look back to say, "What have I seen before that looks like this, and what does that suggest about what I should do now?" And we look forward to say, "If I do *X*, what's going to happen?" and "What do I *want* to have happen?"

■ Getting on the Same Page

These future-oriented questions have a number of similar-sounding words associated with them, and it probably makes sense right up front to get both the writer and the reader—me and you—using the same words to mean the same thing. The words are *prediction, predictability*, and *projectability*.

Prediction. Let's admit right off the bat that we *fin de siècle* humans are very ambivalent about the notion of "prediction."

On the one hand, the word has fallen into serious disrepute, mostly because of the crystal-ball connotations it has acquired. When we hear the word *prediction*, we think of the Psychic Friends Network on cable TV, seances, palm readers with gaudy kerchiefs on their heads, and those hole-in-the-wall fortune-tellers who tend to set up shop near bus stations. Our guard is up. We're no fools!

On the other hand, businesses pay hundreds of millions of dollars each year for economic projections. (*Projection*, as far as I can tell, is a sort of soft word for "prediction"—it generally means, "Tomorrow will be just like today, only more so.") MIT runs a standing-room-only, $950-a-day conference on the future of the Internet. The late Jeanne Dixon's annual predictions issue of the *National Enquirer* practically sprinted out of the supermarket. The *Boston Globe* and other reasonably reputable newspapers print daily horoscopes, presumably because people read them.*

But *prediction* means, literally, a foretelling based on observation, experience, or reasoning. At least as Webster defines the word, there is no flimflam or hocus-pocus involved. In fact, prediction is an absolutely critical survival skill, one that has been imprinted on our mental wiring over many millennia.

---

*The *Globe*, like lots of other newspapers, hedges its bets by putting the horoscope on the comics page—but not dropping it altogether.

What's going to happen next? When we answer this key question, we make a prediction. Without prediction, we don't have a clue about which actions to take or even which outcomes to value. *If I take action X, how will that influence what's going to happen to me next?* This is the me-lunch/it-lunch question. Most often, it puts the person asking the question in the middle of the prediction—it is me-focused—and, very often, it involves one or more other people. As you will see in later chapters, putting other human beings into your prediction greatly complicates things.

For the purposes of this book, I want to sharpen our use of the word *prediction* still further. My grandfather used to say that horseraces happen only because people agree on one thing and disagree on another. They agree that they should be betting on horses in the first place, but they disagree on which horse will win. In this book, we won't focus on which horse is going to win (or which stock is going to rise, or which day next week would be favorable for a career move). Instead, we're going to ask, "Should you bet on a horse?" And, if so, "How should you do it?"

Predictability. *Predictability* means the likelihood of things happening in the way we expect they'll happen: *How sure can I be that outcome X will result from a certain action?* This has both good and bad connotations. *Predictable* is almost always used as a pejorative, but it's a word that I use almost exclusively in the positive sense. In fact, *predictable* and *predictability* badly need to be rescued from their unhappy limbos, because they are the only words that really capture what I want to talk about in this book.

Suppose someone says to you, "Jeez, that Mary is predictable!" Sounds bad, doesn't it? But when I say, "Jeez, that Cummins Engine Company is predictable!" I'm paying it an unqualified compliment. In the later chapters of this book, I argue that more companies should be so predictable, and suggest ways to get there.

Projectability.   This is a word that's guaranteed not to get past your spell checker, because I just now made it up. It's a word that will prove useful for our purposes in this book, because it implies not only prediction (what's going to happen next), but also an estimation of how I will *value* that predicted future. In other words, if outcome X actually comes to pass, how am I going to *feel* about it?

Is this a detour? No. In fact, it's a main thread in this book. It doesn't do you much good to sharpen your prediction skills if you can't know which future you *want* to aim at, and how you and others will feel about *achieving* that future. As the Caterpillar said to Alice, if you don't know where you want to go, then any road will get you there. Projectability means being able to assess *today* how you're going to feel about something that can't happen until *tomorrow*. Complicated, difficult, but absolutely crucial— and we do it all the time.

■ Five Predicaments

Now that we're all on the same page, I'm going to ask you to evaluate a couple of situations. The first four are fictional; the fifth is a true story. (Warning: they get a little trickier as you go along.) As you answer these hypothetical questions, ask your- self *why* you're answering the way you are. Think about predic- tion, predictability, and projectability.

Situation 1.   You're broke. You've squandered your last dollar on a lottery ticket. Now you learn that there's a 50-50 chance that your ticket is worth either $1 million or nothing. I glide into the room with an inscrutable look on my face and offer you

$500,000 in cash, on the spot, for your ticket. Here's the cash right here, as a matter of fact, in this bulging Naugahyde attaché case.

Do you sell?

Situation 2.   You have to make an important business trip to Quandaree, a new nation that has just been carved out of the Indian subcontinent. You have two airlines to choose from. One is MalAir, a wretched U.S.-based carrier with rotten food, on which you've racked up half a million frequent-flier miles. MalAir's saving grace is that it has the best on-time arrival record of all U.S.–based carriers. It spends three times the industry average on maintenance and one-third the industry average on food service.

The other choice is Air Quandaree, the new national airline. You can find out nothing about Air Quandaree except that its planes have recently been repainted. Someone said there's an interesting curry entrée in first class.

Which airline do you choose?

Situation 3.   You're the new CEO of my company. I'm the chairman of the board. We on the board don't know you very well, and you don't know us. I propose two different bonus arrangements for you. The first is simple—you get 10 percent of the profits, period. The second is a little more interesting. The board will award you anywhere from 0 to 25 percent of the profits, depending on how well it thinks you're doing your job. That decision will be entirely subjective. The board will hold you up to a standard of their own devising, which it may or may not reveal to you.

Which plan do you pick?

Situation 4.   You're corporate counsel for a utility with old, regional roots. Decades ago, under pressure from Washington, your company sold off its gas companies, and the bills of sale explicitly stated that the buyer assumed all responsibility for environmental problems. Now your former subsidiary has gone belly up, and the EPA is asking you to pony up funds to help clean up the site—and, if you refuse, they threaten to take you to court to foot the entire bill. Do you want to "voluntarily" hand over $1 million today, or go to court and risk paying $10 million somewhere down the road?

Pay now, or take your chances?

Situation 5. Let's turn now to the real world for a true story about two companies and their respective unions in the early to mid-1990s. You'll note that, when we venture into the real world, the story gets much more complicated.

The first company is Caterpillar, Inc., the huge, Peoria, Illinois–based earthmoving equipment manufacturer. A contract between the company and its union, the United Auto Workers (UAW), expired in 1991, and more than 12,000 workers went on strike. Most eventually returned to work without a contract, but in 1994 the line workers again struck the company. This time, Caterpillar hired replacement workers, infuriating the UAW and greatly raising the stakes. Peoria became the most dramatic battleground between management and labor in America, with both sides playing hardball.

After a year and a half, and after exhausting a strike fund of $30 million, the UAW gave up and returned to work—with no concessions from Cat, and still without a contract.[1]

The second company is Cummins Engine Company, based in the small city of Columbus, Indiana. In 1993, Cummins entered into contract negotiations with the independent Diesel Workers Union (DWU), which had organized the company some six decades earlier. Although relations between Cummins and the DWU had been generally positive over the decades, a bitter strike had erupted in the early 1970s over job security. Now it looked as if that episode might be replayed under even tougher circumstances. In the face of a shrinking southern Indiana job base at Cummins, the DWU was demanding job security.

For its part, the company was asking for major changes in how engines would be made in the Columbus area. This would necessitate large-scale revisions in work rules. Cummins was also seeking significant increases in employee contributions to health plans, from both the active workforce and retirees.

The two sides began their talks far apart, and the discussions were far from tranquil. But, after four months of difficult negotiations, a surprising conclusion was reached: Cummins and the DWU announced agreement on an 11-year contract. Concessions had been made on both sides. For its part, the company gave lifetime job security to all active employees in the bargaining unit. This was a risky and potentially expensive gamble, if productivity did not increase as much as projected.[2]

Caterpillar and Cummins both made the same product—diesel engines. The membership of both unions wanted the same things: higher wages, better working conditions, job security. Both companies wanted givebacks from their workforces, in terms of benefits and work rules. Both situations were characterized by uncertainty, fear, rising tension, and frustration—the attributes of most protracted negotiations.

Which outcome do you like better? Based on only this evidence, which company would you rather work for? As a manager, or as a shop-floor worker? Why? Do your answers touch on either predictability or projectability? If you couldn't predict or project, how would you choose?

◼ Searching for Predictability

Let me answer my own questions about these five situations. See if you agree with my conclusions and, more important, with my logic.

Situation 1. The lottery ticket that may or may not be worth something. Are you kidding? I *sell*. Gimme that attaché case! I can't risk ending up with nothing; there's nothing I can do to make me believe more in my chances for the full $1 million. A half-mil will do me just fine, thank you.

Situation 2. Choosing an airline. A little tougher, but not a close call. It's back into the wretched skies of MalAir for me—can't afford to miss the meeting, and I'd like to live to see my grandchildren.

Situation 3. Picking a compensation plan. Well, a 25 percent bonus sure sounds good, but, if I can't figure out the rules of the game, I don't think I want to play. I'll take that 10 percent, Mr. Chairman.

Situation 4. Me and my deep utility pockets. I'll grumble about the unfairness of it, but I'll pay a little now rather than risking a big hit (and lots of lawyers' fees) later on. Or worse: I don't know what kind of a crazy jury I might draw, if this goes to court, and I sure don't want my kids reading about their father being found "guilty" of acts committed long before I joined the company.

Situation 5. Caterpillar versus Cummins. Let's see. On the face of it, Cat got the better deal. Its workers threw in the towel and took their places back on the line. Cat bet that it could break the union, and it won.

Meanwhile, Cummins was making some very expensive concessions to its workers. But I'd argue that Cummins got the better deal. For one thing, in terms of labor costs, the company now has a pretty good handle on its labor costs well into the next century. And, for another, it has a workforce that got what it most wanted—job security—and that presumably will be working *with* (and not against) the company for the duration of the contract.

In other words, both sides in the Cummins settlement made their lives more predictable. And, assuming that a satisfied workforce is a key determinant of product quality, the 11-year contract also stands to make the lives of Cummins's customers more predictable

Not so at Cat, where one UAW worker predicted, in the wake of the workers' capitulation, "It's going to be an angry work-force." Cat made its life predictable by imposing its will. But this is a leaky and short-lived kind of predictability—the pre-dictability of dictatorship. "A year after the Caterpillar strike ends," as the *Wall Street Journal* put it, "the company-union feud simmers."[3] People who live under a dictatorship (corporate or otherwise) act predictably only until the dictator leaves a flank exposed. While they're waiting for that mental lapse, they engage in a thousand small mutinies. Lights get left on. Things get lost. Warranty costs inexplicably begin to creep up. Then, when the downtrodden get their hands on some power—which sooner or later they always do—they turn the tables with a vengeance. At this point, even the semblance of predictability is gone. The tumbrels begin to roll toward the center of town.

If you agree that Cummins got the better deal, the next logical question to ask is "Why?" I'd argue that things came out the way they did in Columbus because the two sides had spent decades learning to be predictable to each other. (It's like those world-class tango dancers you see on TV. Good outcomes come about only when you know each other's moves.) Not so in Peoria, where Cat and the UAW were more often at crossed swords with each other. Yes, relations were "predictable," but only in the sense that each knew that, if the other sensed weakness, it would pounce. (Cat also went through a management transition, which rarely enhances predictability.)

Again, my point is *not* that companies have to avoid tough decisions or refrain from the kind of midcourse corrections that today's rough-and-tumble competitive environment demands. Nobody loves a company that goes broke trying to be predictable. In the decade between 1983 and 1992—that is, the decade preceding the 11-year contract between Cummins and the DWU— Cummins closed more than 40 plants, warehouses, and office facilities, and cut its Indiana-based workforce almost in half.[4] So it wasn't so much *what* Cummins did, but *how* it did it, that made the difference. The difference was predictability.

■ Why *Is* Predictability Important?

When analyzing businesses and their strategies, it's all too easy to forget the humans who make up those organizations. It's all too tempting to uncomplicate those people as we search for a "macro" vantage point, to the extent that managers and employees cease being humans and start being "inputs," "variable costs," or—most damning of all—"overhead."

But this is a little like trying to say that a snakeskin is a snake. A snakeskin is only a snake if there's *snake* inside it. An organization is only an organization if there are *humans* inside it. If we want our human organizations to work better, we need to understand what makes people tick and find a way to give them what they need.

What they need—what *we* need—is predictability.

To take productive action in today's complex contexts—to find the right mate, to build a satisfying career, to make our way home safely at night on unfamiliar city streets—we need a bigger repertoire than our hunter-gatherer ancestors had. We need to make the best predictions possible. These predictions therefore must be based on a clear and competent view of the world, which

29

may grow out of education, real-world experience, or both. And then we have to make that future come true.[5]

There are two ways to get to a preferred future. The first is to pick a high-percentage outcome and hope for the best. The second is to make your prediction come true. But this second path is available only if you get the other people around you to want what *you* want and work with you toward realizing that future. This is a fundamental trait of leadership. It's why George Bush's confession that he'd always had trouble with the "vision thing" was so damaging to his presidential campaign. Going back two centuries to another George: "I'm not going to freeze my butt off all winter at Valley Forge, for little or no pay, if that guy with the white wig and the wooden teeth can't tell me (1) what's coming next, and (2) why that'll be better for me than sticking with the status quo."[6]

As you'll see in subsequent chapters, there's almost no aspect of organizational life that can't be interpreted through the lens of predictability. Why do we have seniority systems, and why are they defended so tenaciously by the unions? It's because the unions' membership will go to great lengths to limit arbitrary (read "unpredictable") actions on the part of the owners of the business. Why are salaries in Japanese businesses cohort based? It's because the Japanese perceive great societal advantage in discouraging members of a given age cohort from stabbing and betraying each other. And, for the most part, they don't. This is a strength that has served them well in the past and will again in the future.

Why *is* predictability important? Another way of answering this question is to turn it on its head. What happens in the absence of predictability? Would you want to be a supplier to an unpredictable organization? an employee of such an organization? a customer? a stockholder? a resident of a community that hosted such an organization? If every stakeholder says "no" to this question, then there's surely something to this notion of predictability.

Like the two sides in the Cummins negotiations, we humans—in business organizations and elsewhere—have to find ways to be predictable to each other. We have to acknowledge and counteract the increasing number of forces that, at the turn of the century, are pushing us all into unpredictability.

chapter three

Where Prediction and Predictability Live

Fortune is arbiter of half our
actions, but she still leaves the control
of the other half to us.
Niccolò Machiavelli

The challenge of making an accurate prediction and taking an effective action has driven human behavior almost from day one. Those were the Bad Old Days, when rude primeval circumstances—the law of the jungle—forced us to answer the do lunch/be lunch question. Biology ruled, one way or the other.

In subsequent millennia, despite the decline of the saber-toothed tiger, our interest in prediction has only intensified. This has happened in part because our social and economic organizations have become immensely more complicated. This is mostly a good thing. It was the piling up of surpluses, after all, that first gave us the time to sit down and become philosophers. But the orchestration of more complex societies has put much more pressure on human predictive capabilities.

On a closely parallel track, our frontal lobes were getting a bit overdeveloped.* There's nothing like a souped-up brain, capable of asking itself big, open-ended questions—*How did it happen? What does it all mean to me, and to you, and to us? What have we learned? Is that all there is? Will it happen again?*—to focus us on issues of predictability.

And, toward the end of the nineteenth century, a new discipline with important implications for prediction crept out from under the skirts of philosophy—psychology. (Let's say the crucial year here was 1890, when William James—trained in anatomy and physiology but, for almost two decades prior, a Harvard philosophy professor—published *Principles of Psychology.*) When you get down to what makes people tick in the late twentieth and early twenty-first centuries, this is a good field not to overlook.

In the good old days, the presence of food prompted only one response: the biological: *See it, grab it, eat it.* But along came the big-brained babies, and we had to start worrying about societal needs: *Save some for Junior.* This in turn raised philosophical dilemmas: *Why favor Junior over anyone else?* And no sooner did the philosophers settle on a decision rule for allocating food ethically than the psychologists came along and cast doubt on its meaning: "Junior represents your unfulfilled wishes." So today, as we take action to affect future outcomes, we have to acknowledge multiple obligations.

Let's look at each of these realms—biological, social, philosophical, and psychological—to figure out why and how, over the course of human history, they have lent urgency to the challenge of prediction.

---

*Many anthropologists now believe that it was the emergence of the big-brained infant, with relentlessly high metabolic needs, that forced the creation of pair bonding, families, complex social units, and other predictive mechanisms.

■ Biology and Predictability

The biological case for predictability is probably the easiest to make. Start with the key question introduced in the Introduction: "Am *I* lunch, or is *it* lunch?" Can I find clues in my environment that enable me to sit at (not arrive on) the table?

Every animal faces these challenges, although not usually on the conscious level. *Can I fly? If I can't fly, how far can I jump? Can I make it from this tree to that tree?* (Wouldn't it be fascinating to tap into a squirrel's brain as it is making this assessment?) But humans raise this internal dialogue to a rarefied level. Instead of *Getting colder, shorter days. Find and bury nuts*, we have the luxury and the burden of asking, "Which nuts? Why bury them— why not store them in some cool, dry place? And, as long as we're going into the food storage business, why don't we think about something more interesting than nuts? How about grain? *Which* grain?" These are the kinds of questions that differentiate us from all other animals.

A word about instinct: I'd like to suggest that what we call an "instinct" is simply a prediction that has become hard-wired into our brains over the eons. Some of these serve us very well, by minimizing time-to-action. When my peripheral vision picks up something winging toward my head, I flinch. This is a good habit that our low-browed forebears picked up, and it continues to serve us well. *Object approaching? Duck!*

Other instincts shade out toward irrelevance or even pose risks to you and me in the twenty-first century. The Falling Dream that you and I have every now and then seems to be designed to help us hold on tight to our tree branch while we're napping— not so helpful today, with so few predators running around down below us, but not too harmful either. It probably keeps us from falling out of bed every now and then.

Ever watch a not-so-hungry dog attack a dish of chow? This is the eating instinct: get it while you can, because it might not be here tomorrow. Unfortunately, we humans have the same instinct programmed into us: if you can catch it, you'd better eat it. This instinct definitely hurts us, in an age when most of us are surrounded by a relative abundance of food.

But, again, this is where we humans can set ourselves apart. We don't *have* to act instinctively, based only on what our genetic programming tells us about the future. Instead, we can contemplate alternatives, place a value on them, pick one, and aim for it. I now understand that, if I keep eating at the age of 50 at the same rate that I did when I was 16, I probably won't live to see those grandchildren I was worrying about in Chapter 2. If I'm smart—or at least not totally obtuse—I adapt my behavior and start denying myself all kinds of fun and fattening foods. Why? Because I assess potential futures and, based on that assessment, take action.[1] I decide that I'd like to be skinnier and livelier, rather than the alternative.

Some of our recent advances in medical science have raised the biological predictability stakes even higher. In fact, they're providing us with exquisite new dilemmas. If your family has a history of Huntington's chorea (Woody Guthrie's disease), you can now take a genetic test to discover if you're one of the male offspring who has inherited this terrible ailment.

This is a fairly clean decision: do I want to know my medical future when it can be foretold with great certainty? I have a friend whose father died of Huntington's chorea who has decided that he doesn't want to take the test. He has also decided that, as a result of choosing *not* to know, he can never get married. The fact that some people say "no" to this question doesn't undercut the importance of predictability. Rather, it underscores the importance of projectability. Many people can't stand the prospect of projecting themselves into an unacceptable future. If you have a 50-50 chance of gaining information that would make tomorrow intolerable, why predict?[2]

The choice gets even tougher when a particular genetic test can only indicate probabilities—60-40, 70-30, or whatever. Suppose a certain test indicates that I have a 60 percent chance of developing breast cancer sometime in my lifetime, and suppose there's a surgical procedure that, if performed today, might improve my long-term chances of survival by 20 percent? On the other hand, if I'm *not* precancerous—of which I can't really be sure—this surgery will have been a traumatic and unnecessary intervention. These are very new kinds of quandaries, and we haven't even begun to develop the intellectual and emotional tools needed to make these kinds of calculations.[3]

We're also entering an era in which predictive information will have to be guarded much more scrupulously. Surely we don't want other people to be equipped to make better predictions about us than we ourselves can make! The Department of Defense recently ran up against this problem when two recruits refused to give DNA samples to a central repository. The army routinely banks genetic materials for the gruesome but necessary task of identifying mangled bodies—in other words, the DNA equivalent of dogtags. But the two soldiers feared that this data could be abused sometime in the future. If insurance companies gained access to the information, for example, they might deny medical coverage to individuals with genetically detectable problems. The army said it had no such plans in mind but inexplicably refused to *guarantee* confidentiality. Faced with this level of unpredictability, the soldiers balked.

■ Sociability and Predictability

I use the word *sociable* here in its scientific sense; that is, inclined by nature toward companionship with others of the same species. Sociability has deep biological roots, onto which we graft years of cultural indoctrination. We learn at a very early age that, in order to be healthy, happy, and even safe, we need to interact with other people, win their love, and win their support for the things we want to accomplish.[4]

The sociable case for predictability is clear and compelling. Human society is not the only one that works toward bringing about a particular future. (So do ant colonies, wolf packs, and all other functioning societies.) But, as noted earlier, we seem to be the only animal that contemplates alternative futures and then acts on that contemplation. We may be the only creatures who persuade others of our kind to act in concert with us— depending, of course, on how you define the word *persuade*. We are certainly the only beings who worry about how *others* of our kind will react to the future that ultimately arrives.

This raises a sequence of more or less inescapable questions, working from the individual outward:

- *How am I going to feel about my future, when it arrives?* This is the challenge of projectability, defined in Chapter 2. When I'm 12, I define a perfect future as the day I complete my collection of baseball cards. But, by the time I'm 16, I've lost all interest in baseball cards, and now I dream only of the day when I no longer have a curfew imposed on me by my parents. When I'm 25, I've come to terms with my parents, but I become fixated on the idea of how simple life would be if I were rich. And then, when I'm 60 and successful, I think about how simple life would be if I *weren't* rich. Because these are one-person questions, they aren't technically the basis of sociability—until I take my answers and attitudes out into the world, that is.[5]

- *How are you going to feel about my future?* If I'm successful, are you going to be jealous of my success? There is a Russian folktale in which the main character gets three wishes and uses the first two of them to wish trouble on his friends.

Envy and jealousy determine much of human behavior.[6] "The nail that sticks up gets hammered down," as the saying goes. This dictum seems to underlie a lot of the tearing down of heroes that so characterizes our culture today. So how much responsibility do I have to take for meeting *your* needs, at the same time that mine are being met? The answer is, a *great deal* of responsibility, and not only for reasons of self-defense.

• *How are* you *going to feel about* your *future?* The old proverb warns us to beware of making wishes, lest they actually get granted. What if you don't like the future that you and I have jointly brought about? If I live in your family, or on your block, or maybe just in your culture, I might wish I hadn't contributed to a future that makes you unhappy.

• *How am* I *going to think about* your *future?* Will I admire you or hate you for your success? Will I like you in spite of it or respect you because of it? I'm just as prone to envy and jealousy as you are, after all.[7] But, in certain cultural contexts, I may be thrilled if your future is gratifying to you. Many Jewish and offshore Chinese communities operate on the assumption that an honor for one member of their group is an honor for all. When I was a boy, we Utah-based Mormons derived great satisfaction from the success of J. Willard Marriott and other prominent Mormons. We were taught to believe that a Latter Day Saint accomplishing something more or less heroic was probably good for all of us.

In fact, heroes serve a useful purpose in all societies. They provide leadership and inspiration, and the singular vision that they impress upon the culture helps move the culture forward. But heroes can emerge only in a reasonably coherent cultural context. Collectively, we *allow* heroes to step forward, often to fill a leadership void. Think of the famous example of Franklin Delano Roosevelt's leg braces, which were studiously ignored by the reporters of his day. At least in the past, when our culture was more coherent, we were prepared to overlook someone's weaknesses if he or she was providing a valuable service to society. And this, in turn, gave us a measure of predictability. Especially in those troubled times, we wanted to believe that we had someone in charge who could tell us what was around the next corner.

The downfall of Richard Nixon presents an interesting twist. By the early 1970s, there were many camps—and not just vengeful Democrats and newspaper reporters—who were willing to accept a measure of unpredictability to get rid of Nixon. But, when Spiro Agnew's sordid past started to surface, this raised the impending unpredictability of the social order to new heights. What would happen if we got rid of both a sitting president and a vice president?

The solution that emerged in Congress was to get rid of Agnew first—which was accomplished in record time, as I recall— protect the line of succession (predictability) by appointing the dull-but-clean Gerald Ford as vice president, and then go after Nixon.

Heroes emerge from cultural consensus and then reinforce that consensus. By so doing, they make our lives more predictable. John F. Kennedy proclaimed to the nation in his stirring 1961 inaugural address that we were going to put a man on the moon within 10 years. This was an absolutely outlandish prediction when he made it (ask any NASA engineer), yet it turned out to be true. Leadership in that case meant envisioning a possible future and dragging a skeptical nation along behind. And the reward to the nation came in the terrible summers of the late 1960s, when almost everything else in the social fabric seemed to be unraveling, and (plodding, predictable) NASA closed in on its target.

I have concentrated on political illustrations of the importance of prediction in the realm of sociability. But businesses, which are neither more nor less than organizations of people trying to get to a jointly defined future, provide countless additional illustrations that are just as powerful. On May 5, 1932, Konosuke Matsushita called a meeting of his coworkers at Matsushita Electric Industrial Company, the company he had founded exactly 14 years earlier.[8] Matsushita told his workers of a chance encounter he had recently had with a tramp on an Osaka street. The tramp was filling a tin cup at the public water fountain. Matsushita was struck by the fact that a system had been created that could provide a vital good—free water—to a penniless vagrant. Why couldn't a manufacturing company achieve a similar scale and efficiency to make household goods available to the masses at minimal cost? That day, Matsushita announced a 250-year plan to create just such a company—probably a modern-day record for imposing a predictive grid on human activities!*

■ Philosophy, Psychology, and Predictability

We also have the *philosophical* case for the importance of predictability. Fortunately, there are lots of signposts to help make this case.

The first of the cardinal virtues, for example, is prudence, which could be defined as the ability to take action in light of predicted consequences. This is one of the main things this book is about—taking the right action based on what you think is going to happen.

Philosophers make this point in different ways. Hegel argued that an individual's worth is determined by the opinions of

---

*In the spring of 1982—with Matsushita himself still a force in the company's affairs—the company announced the successful completion of the first of five 50-year subplans, and the beginning of the second.

others. Therefore, we must predict the effect of our actions on others' opinions of us. And Kant stressed the notion of duty, which certainly enables others with similar values to understand and intersect with your own actions.

Wittgenstein said that words acquire their meaning through use and that therefore language is inherently a record of history and culture. Habermas wrote of communicative action and argued that agreement should be the primary goal of communication. Coordinated action—the logical next step after agreement—is the second major focus of this book. The other person's view of my actions allows him or her to predict, coordinate, and act with me to effect agreed-upon futures.

This philosophical view shades inevitably into the realm of psychology. The psychological case for the importance of predictability is also fairly easy to make. We live in a world of great complexity and uncertainty. In such a context, the great trap is to set your mind on a single, specific, low-percentage outcome and bet the farm on that prediction's actually coming to pass. It's not that taking a risk is a bad thing in and of itself. In fact, most risks grow out of the need to *act*—to take steps to deal with the future—and an action-oriented person has to take risks. At the same time, it's unwise to take big risks with no sense of the probable outcomes, or to bet on a single outcome when the odds are long.[9]

It makes perfect sense to say, "Now, let's see. I could be either a fireman or a baseball player. Let me go down the road until I get to that fork, figuring out whether I've got what it takes to play in the majors. And then, if I don't, I'll head down the fireman road." This is versatile, adaptive thinking, which builds prediction into multiple outcomes.

By contrast, it makes almost no sense to say, "Mary is the only woman I'll ever love. If she doesn't marry me, I'll choose a life of solitude." The unhealthiness resides not in the risk taking, but in a kind of prediction and assessment of futures that closes off options—and often turns out to be cruelly self-fulfilling. At least in my experience, when Mary hears that particular plot line, she won't respond too positively.

We have to understand our own psychologies before we can predict an outcome, project ourselves into that future, and then act. The human condition is to push, to explore, to look over the next mountain, to want *more*. Few of our animal cousins seem to share this acquisitive streak, which takes numerous forms. Some forms of this acquisitiveness are positive; many more are destructive.

For instance, some people gamble. I live in Massachusetts, which runs a lottery called Megabucks on Wednesday and Saturday nights. I've learned to avoid going to convenience stores between six and eight o'clock on those nights, because the lines of amateur gamblers make it hard to pick up a loaf of bread quickly. And, as a former mathematician, it pains me to see people betting their money on hitting a specific group of six numbers between 1 and 48. The odds of succeeding at this are about 12 million to one.* What does that mean? Well, put positively, those odds are about the same as flipping a coin and having it come up heads between 23 and 24 times in a row. Or, if you're a February baby, they're worse than the odds of walking into a room full of randomly selected people and discovering that the first six people you bump into have the same birth month as you.** In terms of the more manageable numbers that govern our daily existence, these are hopelessly long odds. For all practical

---

*Mass Millions, the other big-payoff game, is worse. And my son once calculated that the popular Powerball game presents the same odds that would result if someone laid pennies edge to edge from Little Rock, Arkansas, to Boston and challenged you to pick the particular one he was thinking of. Again, don't bet the farm against long odds.

**1 in $(48 \times 47 \times 46 \times 45 \times 44 \times 43) = 1$ in $1 \times 2 \times 3 \times 4 \times 5 \times 6 = 12,276,512$, to be precise.

purposes, buying a lottery ticket doesn't make you more likely to win than *not* buying a lottery ticket.

Of course, I'm not saying it's a shameful thing to trust Lady Luck and take a flier with a dollar every now and then. But this is (or *ought* to be) the predictive equivalent of indulging a pinball habit, or of pitching pennies at the traveling carnival: a guilty pleasure with no expectation of great return. Besides, there is some short-lived pleasure in projecting one's self into the future and imagining how good life would be if your number hit. Many of us get more pleasure from a vicarious visit to a strange land than from enduring the hassle of really getting there. Spending a buck a week is OK, if it's for fun—and if you're not dipping into the rent money to do it. But, when we have major life decisions to make, we can't afford to play the slots; we have to exercise real predictive skill.

Meanwhile, experimental psychology is telling us that there are clear limits on our cognitive powers (that is, on how we understand the world). Because we misunderstand what our eyes see, we wind up coping with optical illusions. Do those railroad tracks really converge out there on the horizon? No, but it sure looks that way. Even if we get the inputs right, our powers of analysis are equally befogged. "Look at all those sweepstakes winners on TV," we say. "I'd better fill out that Publisher's Clearinghouse entry form. And maybe I'll just subscribe to a magazine or two to help me fall into the right bin." Because we frame questions inadequately in our minds, as Tversky and others have demonstrated, we make fundamental interpretive errors.

So, to recap: we humans are inherently acquisitive, we see phenomena incorrectly (or misinterpret a correct perception), we ask the wrong questions, and then we make computational errors. (No wonder we wind up playing Megabucks!) Our facile minds and our great emotional range—the building blocks of our psychologies—equip us to predict poorly and set us up to fall into predictive traps.[10]

■ Dodge That Bus—or Don't?

So predictability is driven by multiple forces in our lives: biological, social, philosophical, and psychological. I won't surprise you when I argue that, despite its importance, prediction is not easy. (Even palm readers stress how difficult their art is.) But, if you want to exert a positive influence in one or more human organizations—which most of us do, at one point or another—you have to worry about issues of predictability, which means touching the bases in each of these four realms.

Each of these realms also comes to bear on issues of *projectability*. Should I take action without knowing what my hoped-for future is likely to mean to me? I will argue that the answer is "no." And what happens when more than one person is doing the projecting, and multiple viewpoints and value systems come into play? Should I take action without knowing what my hoped-for future is likely to mean to *you*? Or what *your* future is likely to mean to you? Again, the answer is "no." As I argue in later chapters, these are absolutely critical questions in the context of human organizations.

Let's look at two examples—one individual, the second collective—to underscore the point. The light changes, the "WALK" light beckons, and you step off the curb. When you're halfway across the street, you look to your left and spot a bus coming directly at you. *Fast*—50 feet away, 40, 30—closing *fast!* What do you do? Look to see if the bus driver is in distress or slumped over the wheel? Check to see whether the stoplight is indeed signaling him to stop? Calculate whether the bus still has room to stop in the remaining patch of road between you and it? Not likely. Your hard wiring kicks in and makes the crudest of predictions—*Yow! Death imminent! Jump out of the way!*

In real life, time is always limited. We can never do enough observing or calculating to act with complete confidence. In fact, as you'll see in Chapter 6, many useful things turn out to be incalculable. This escapes the attention of bad economists and drives good economists crazy. Events overwhelm the logical sequences of the laboratory. When that bus is careening toward you, it *has* to be a case of "ready, fire, aim." You leap to a conclusion (you predict), and then you leap for the curb (you act).

Biology has spoken. Given the pace at which events were unfolding, sociability, psychology, and philosophy didn't really come to bear. But let's slow down time—and that bus—enough to inject a few interesting predictive complications.

Take projection: if the two alternative futures are (1) get squashed and (2) don't get squashed, most people find the task of projection to be an easy job. But now the bus is in slow mo. Suppose I can contrive to get winged by the bus, dramatically but not too painfully, and this sets me up for a huge financial settlement from the city. Nursing my feigned disabilities, I retire happily and live off my windfall.

Hmmm. This sounds pretty good. Assuming no real pain or damage, it may even sound a little better than leaping into that fetid grey-and-brown pile of waste over by the curb there *(projection)*. But it's going to be a tough trick to decide just where to stand to get winged just a little but not too much *(prediction)*. I think I'd rather be sitting in that pile of waste shaking my fist at the back end of the bus—unharmed except for my pride—than really badly winged *(projection)*. Staging a car crash on the freeway, at rush hour when things aren't moving very fast, is probably a better way to get winged just a little bit *(prediction)*.

Complicated, right? And, as suggested several pages back, there are at least a couple of other forces swirling around in my mind that will probably come to bear on this slow-mo decision. For example, if I grew up in a household where taking any money from any governmental authority under any circumstance was anathema, then I probably won't entertain any pain-and-suffering scenarios (*projectability* and *sociability*). If I'm a charter member of the suicidist school of thought, I'll be fighting back that impulse to jump (*philosophy*, of a sort). And, if I'm in one of my manic phases, I may just decide to race the bus to the next corner (*biology and/or psychology*).

Now, let's take a minute to escalate this exercise to a collective activity, to illustrate how quickly these predictive processes get complicated in real life. For example, how should the over 100,000 employees of General Electric—with their unique biological, social, philosophical, and psychological attributes—think about a prospective nationwide rise in interest rates? And, assuming (1) that you could make such an assessment and (2) that corporate policy should reflect majority opinion (not always a great assumption!), what should corporate policy be?

Well, in real life, the company's Capital Services group (GECS) would probably argue for a rate increase, which would increase its margins. But the company's manufacturing subsidiaries would argue against such an interest rate increase, because higher financing costs would almost certainly cut into their sales. *They* would request that GECS hold the line and help the manufacturers grab additional market share.

This may be an unfair example, given GE's almost unmatched hugeness and diversity. But it illustrates some of the complexities of taking effective action with other human beings around. Sure, *I* want to get out from in front of the bus, but do my 100,000 colleagues? Maybe there isn't a single, or even a dominant, answer. The one employee who's highly leveraged on margin in the interest-rate futures market, for example, will disagree with the consensus.

The Elasticity and Linearity of Time

Our bus example illustrates how much trouble the city treasury would be in if time could be slowed on cue. The passage of time is *not* within our human control, but that doesn't mean that time is fixed. It would be very helpful, for the purposes of prediction and action, if our brains always perceived time the same way. But, in fact, as noted above, our cognitive skills are less than perfect, and our ability to interpret what we see and hear is sometimes suspect. Our perception of the passage of time is highly elastic and therefore suspect. Those last three seconds before you leap for the curb seem like an eternity. ("I saw my whole life pass before me.") Conversely, those late-night hours you spend curled up in bed with a good book flash by at an astonishing clip. You glance at the clock and discover it's way, way past bedtime. ("I lost track of time.") Different cultures, moreover, perceive the passage of time very differently, which again underscores the importance of sociability and socialization to prediction. The perception of time varies not only with activity and culture, but also over the course of a single lifetime. Think of how long summer vacation lasted when you were a child, contrasted with June, July, and August of last year.

Well, not surprisingly, this elasticity wreaks havoc with pro-jectability. How can we pick and aim for a future if we can't be sure our time sense isn't playing tricks on us? How long is June going to *feel* next year, based on decisions I'm making today? How long will I *want* it to feel?

Meanwhile, of course, time is also linear. Choices made today make some things possible in the future but also make many other things impossible. We predict today in order to give ourselves a shot at good options in the future. But, for the most part, those options are mutually exclusive. If I decide to study brain surgery, I probably can't also become a world-class violinist. Opening one door, as it turns out, closes many others.[11]

Putting time's elasticity and linearity together underscores the complexity of making good predictions and projections, and then taking good actions. When we are young, we predict that we will always like mocha-chip ice cream and hate artichokes. Maybe we then take more or less permanent steps to get far away from artichokes—only to discover in adulthood that it's *fun* to wrestle with the prickly things. They taste good and make other things taste good, too. Or, more likely, we childishly refuse to learn a language at a time of life when our brains are still capable of it, only to find many years later that having learned to speak Italian fluently would have greatly enriched this visit to Tuscany. Or we lock ourselves (financially, emotionally, and socially) into a northern climate, only to discover to our chagrin that Aunt Ethel was right and that our aging joints would be far better off somewhere out in the desert.*

■   **Looking Ahead**

A young friend of mine recently shared with me a dilemma she was facing. She had received a job offer from an Israeli company. From her point of view, the circumstances looked promising. Among other things, the potential employer had a record of taking good care of his fast-track managers, awarding them equity positions of 5 percent on average if they performed well in their first two years with the company.

On the other hand, my friend told me, she would be the first American (and the first woman) hired onto this track. She would be highly visible, and her work would be scrutinized carefully—

---

*For my pressed-for-time CEO types who have bought into predictability and now want the action steps, you can now jump to Chapter 8. Think of it as a secret passage, or shortcut. I hope you'll then go back and see what you've missed.

inside and outside of the company. Her question to me was, should she take the job? And did I see any hidden pitfalls?

Maybe because my head was full of Wittgenstein and Habermas that week, I first advised her to get her terms straight. Among other complicating factors, crossing the American-Israeli cultural divide argued for clarity. If the equity position depended on her both *performing* and performing *well* in her new job, then surely those two words demanded a clear definition. And, assuming that she displayed a reasonable amount of tact in seeking this clarification, her potential employer would appreciate her thoroughness and her willingness to build a basis for coordinated action.

I asked her how much time she had to make the decision, and she said that her potential employer wanted a response by the end of the month—about three weeks away, at that point. I suggested that, despite this time limit, she should think as creatively and rigorously as she could about the possible futures that seemed to lie ahead of her, especially in light of everything that she knew about herself. If she failed, how would she feel about failure? How would her massively overachieving family feel about failure—and would that matter to her? (My guess was that it would.) Conversely, based on what she knew today, how would she feel about success? How would owning 5 percent of a company half a planet away two years from now fulfill her needs— biological, social, philosophical, and psychological? What more would she have to find out (about the job, about the company, about herself) in order to answer these questions with a high degree of confidence?

A week later, she phoned me and told me that she had turned down the job. She had spent several days learning about Israeli society and had decided that it was not for her. Her prediction about herself was that she would succeed at her job and enjoy that, but would fail in other aspects of her life—and that the success in the professional realm would not compensate adequately for unhappiness in other realms.

What emerged clearly from her self-analysis was that she wanted *variety* as well as predictability.

But aren't those two goals directly contradictory?

The answer, as you will see in the next chapter, is "yes and no."

chapter four

Variety versus Predictability

One wants to know what is
going to happen tomorrow.
Will the lady in the mauve frock
be more amiable than she is today?
Such questions keep human beings alive.
H. L. Mencken

Now that I have you fully focused on the importance of prediction, I'm going to introduce a parallel argument, which will at first appear to undercut that premise. It's clear, at least to me, that all of human history revolves around a single, inescapable tension: between our desire for predictability—for all the reasons I articulated in the previous chapter—and our concurrent need for *variety*.

In the past century, biologists have articulated what they call the "law of requisite variety." Simply put, a species that experiences no variety from generation to generation is very likely to become extinct. Why? Evolution, we've learned, works through the processes of variation, selection, and retention. Mutations pop up more or less at random. If they "work" in the context of a changing environment, they're selected and retained. Bad mutations aren't retained. And, when the environmental change is rapid and radical enough, unchanging species are also left behind. It's a small paradox, but one with lots of implications for this book: the continuity of life depends on change. Preserving life over time, in a changing context, requires change. And preserving the capacity for coordinated action requires predictability. Neither variety nor predictability can be allowed to win this tug of war.[1]

There's also a deeply rooted *individual* imperative for variety. The reader can supply his or her own illustration of the point. Think of your favorite piece of music, or flavor of ice cream, or hobby. Now, imagine an unrelenting diet of that pastime or that consumable. Sooner, rather than later, you'd go crazy. When we say, "Everything in moderation," we mean, in part, "Don't hurt yourself through excess." But I think we also mean, "Keep it special." Allowing for a varied diet keeps special things special. Variety, we say, is the spice of life.[2]

Think about this same issue from the societal standpoint, where the contributions of the individual and the group come together. The group requires variation (through the individual) and retention (on the societal or species level). The great advantage that the human species and human societies have over others is their ability to retain and disseminate the knowledge gained through successful variation. When one farmer introduces a productive new strain of rice, we don't kill off all the rest of the world's farmers. We teach them to grow the new strain, too. (The same retooling notion also underlies most kinds of executive education.) We relentlessly ask ourselves, "What's working? What's not?" This book attempts to persuade you that the way we answer that question—whether we know it or not—is to look at a phenomenon and determine whether it's enhancing predictability or diminishing predictability across our human societies.[3]

Another great advantage that we have, as a result of our capacity to envision multiple futures, is trying a given future on for size. If it works, great; if it doesn't, well, we can reverse it. What would the nation be like with no (legal) alcohol? Let's try Prohibition. What happens? We experience a host of social evils that are collectively worse than the disease we were trying to cure. OK, failed experiment; let's repeal it. This is a kind of experimentation that the dinosaurs never got around to—and when the Big Meteor arrived, they paid for it dearly.

Sooner or later, cultures desperately need the individual who can call the status quo into question by seeing the world differently and not seeing the same cause-and-effect relationships as everybody else. The rare (I would even say mythical) exception would be a culture that existed in a context of absolute stability—perhaps on an idyllic South Seas island. But what happens, even in this context? Sooner or later, something changes. The local volcano erupts, or the big ships arrive from the Place Where the Sun Rises, or the fish stocks mysteriously dwindle. This is when the oddball is needed. In a vacuum, it doesn't much matter whether or not the emperor actually has clothes on. But, when the crunch comes, we need the clear-eyed little boy who laughs at the naked emperor. Some cultures revere their mentally unbalanced members as precious resources—mystics and prophets who have a special capacity to deliver an unvarnished kind of wisdom. In the land of the blind, as the saying goes, the one-eyed man is king.[4]

But wait a minute. Isn't there also a countervailing tension? When it comes right down to it, none of us really *likes* the whistleblower. We have a sneaking suspicion that this self-defined loner, swimming against the societal tide, is somehow not playing by the rules. It's disconcerting, maybe even destabilizing, to have someone running around calling a spade a spade. Of course it's a good thing to have Ralph Nader ridding the highways of dangerous cars and cutting imperious companies down to size. But would we really want Ralph Nader to be president? And would he know how to build something?

The emperor appreciates it when we suspend disbelief. And when we're totally honest with ourselves, we admit that we *like* making the emperor happy—or at least we like what happens to us when the emperor is happy.[5] We get predictability. The naked emperor who thinks he is clothed actually can lead us, if we set him up to do so. Conversely, we sometimes take steps to make sure that the troublemaker (rather than General Motors) is cut down to size. This is because we don't want our predictive models demolished gratuitously. "Engine Charlie" Wilson told us that what was good for GM was good for America. Demolishing that decision rule without providing a replacement feels like vandalism to us. In the land of the blind, therefore, the one-eyed man sometimes winds up in the zoo. Or someplace worse.

So let's agree on the need for variety—at the level of the individual, the species, and the culture. Variety provides the *content* of innovation, the stuff of action. But we've already agreed on the need for *predictability*, which gives us a *context* within which innovation and action can occur. It's something like a sentence. We all agree on the rules of syntax; that is, sentence structure, so we can be understood (predictability). And we allow each other to vary the content of the sentence as creatively as possible (variety).[6]

Continuously, as effectively as we can, we need to make decisions and move forward. On an individual level, this means acting in order to meet our physiological needs and repair the disorder caused by natural processes. On a societal level, we do the same sorts of things on a grander scale. We defend our borders, strengthen our economy, build and rebuild our cities, write laws, build moral codes, prepare for war or peace—all in the name of improving our lot.

In short, we know that the future will arrive, and we know that we will have individual and collective responsibilities in that future. In all cases, we need to act in the present based on what we think the future holds for us. Our paradox emerges: to make good predictions, we want a context of predictability, which means having a model of the world in which X leads to Y, and X_1 leads to Y_1, but *not* one in which X can lead to either Y, Y_1, or

Z at random. But, to ensure that we have enough good options to choose among, and also to protect ourselves from the tricks that time almost inevitably plays on the calculation of our preferences, we demand variety. We've got to have a way to surface change agents *and* to create a context of predictability, so that change can be recognized, foretold, and accommodated.

■ Magic and Humor

I promised at the beginning of Chapter 2 that there would be no magic involved in the types of prediction that this book addresses. But let's use an example from the realm of magic to examine the tension between variety and predictability, and to begin to explore the importance of shared experiences and common frames of reference. As I've already hinted, shared experiences and common frames have important implications when it comes to predictions and assessments that are made by more than one person; that is, most of the important decisions in life.

Let's imagine that David Copperfield, celebrated magician, is on the big stage in Las Vegas. In front of thousands, he announces that he's going to make this penny disappear! Right from between his fingers, right before our eyes! There's a drumroll, a puff of smoke, and Copperfield throwing his arms out wide, hands empty, waiting for the applause to roll over him.

Well, frankly, we're not impressed. How magical was *that*? I could probably do that myself. Pretty predictable (in the bad sense of the word).

Now, let's imagine that Copperfield does the same thing, but this time it's an airplane that vanishes in the puff of smoke. *Now* we're impressed. This is new, spicy, different. It's not exactly unexpected—in fact, he told us he was going to do it—but it plays on our previous life experiences (we know a plane is heavy and hard to hide!) and throws us a curve. We make a prediction: no way can he make those many tons of metal and plastic disappear. When he does, we're tickled.

We're also a little bit relieved. Our other prediction was that he *would* succeed at this trick. (Otherwise, why would he try it in front of all these people?) Can he pull it off? He does! It's variety and unpredictability, within well-defined bounds. It's "unexpectedly predictable." After the fact, you can get comfortable with it.

One last example in the same vein and venue: Copperfield announces that he's going to *dewilp* a *pflorg*. He puts a nondescript object on the table and waves his wand. There's a little movement along the edge of the object and maybe a muted noise. Copperfield again extends his arms triumphantly. As in the case of the penny, we don't respond very well, although this time for different reasons. What exactly happened up there? How much magic was involved? We have no frame of reference, and we aren't in a position to be astonished. Maybe pflorgs always dewilp when they detect movement. And besides, as in the case of the penny, this seems pretty insignificant. Who gives a damn?

Humor has some of the same qualities and inherent limits. Humor is a surprise within acceptable bounds. The successful joke writer and joke teller play by the rules, the most important of which states that the punch line has to be plausible and has to fall somewhere within the audience's zone of experience. In other words, we want predictability with a twist. Knock-knock jokes are only the most obvious example:

> *Knock, knock.*
> Who's there?
> *Boo.*
> Boo who?
> *Oh, quit your sniveling.*

It simply wouldn't do to lead people through this extremely ritualized pattern only to thwart them at the end. The punch line has to be something that could have been predicted, but wasn't. "Your mother" or "The instrument of your death" wouldn't be fair. The punch line has to surprise us a little bit, but not too much.

Coordinated Action

Why this digression into magic and humor? Because, as I said, we attach great importance to shared experiences and common frames of reference. We have to act—not only as individuals, but also as groups of individuals—but, as our philosophers warned us, we usually need to settle on *meanings* before we can settle on actions.

A recent story in the *Atlantic Monthly* told of an elderly Chinese couple who had finally completed the first translation of James Joyce's *Ulysses* into Mandarin. This was an absolutely herculean job, at the end of which the translators confessed to some concern. Puns, jokes, and plays on words—the soul of Joyce's masterpiece—don't translate well. Had they even begun to capture the spirit of the book? Can the reader in Peking understand the writer in Dublin, through the screen of even the best translator? How much is lost? Too much?

The fact is, we can't share humor with groups we don't know very well. It's hard: a key symbol may be meaningless across a cultural divide. Or worse, it may be inadvertently offensive. Don't clap an Arab on the back convivially or give him the circled-thumb-and-forefinger "OK" sign! There's not enough of a shared base of meaning.

The same holds true for action involving more than one person, which I've already introduced as *coordinated* action: you will do this, and I will do that, and together we will achieve our larger end.

For example, you and I have to get that refrigerator down this steep flight of stairs and out the front door. Before I'll volunteer for the bottom end of the job, I need to have confidence that you won't act randomly. I need to believe that you'll carry through on your commitments and that you won't take advantage of my commitment in some unexpected way. I need to predict your behavior—just about as much as you need to predict mine when it's your turn to be on the bottom.

Coordinated action, based on a foundation of predictability, is what allows societies to form, to grow, and to prosper. Coordinated action is the only real justification for human organizations, especially *business* organizations. Now, I'll quickly grant that churches, PTAs, and even the occasional business school often engage in coordinated action in order to serve some higher purpose. But companies are *only* about coordinated action. In legal terms, a corporation is an individual that has been "incorporated" (that is, given a body) for the purpose of performing certain specific tasks—and, in most cases, this means coordinated action on the part of the incorporators.

Companies exist so that people can take actions together, and to far better effect than if they acted as individuals. Because companies exist, a vast array of very complicated goods and services can be produced. For those of you who don't know a lot about how businesses work, imagine a one-person baseball team or orchestra. Can't be done. The core activities—offense and defense, symphonies and operas—are unimaginable without the contributions and coordinated actions of a large number of specialists.[7] And, just like you and me on the staircase, committed to each other (and maybe to the refrigerator), these specialists are all making excellent predictions about each other's behaviors.

Prediction is important because, by allowing coordinated action, it makes companies and societies possible. Looking at it from the other end of the telescope, companies are useful—you might even say they are "good"—because they help make our lives predictable. A good organizational environment is one that is predictable.

■ Connecting the Maps

Magic and humor illustrate the importance of operating within a shared context of experience, so that our predictions can be either artfully rewarded or artfully frustrated. We have to make sure that we're speaking the same language, in every sense of the word, or the refrigerator may wind up killing one or both of us.

Now, imagine having to take a complex action, in conjunction with other people, based on this kind of information. As anyone who has worked in a large corporation knows, this is an only slightly exaggerated version of a daily challenge. Coordinated action depends on our *understanding* each other and making good predictions about each other. As specialization increases, this task becomes more and more difficult. And, although we struggle to understand and pass along our understanding, as soon as we cross functional boundaries and other demarcations of specialization, we begin to lose things in the translation.

Similarly, we lose things as we cross hierarchical boundaries. Think of how maps are used in warfare. The private is hunkered down in a foxhole with his own map of the front lines. It's a spare and to-the-point document, a very good representation of that private's reality. It shows this tree, that rock, the minefield, the chow line, the latrine, and, at its far eastern boundary, some sort of river.

The colonel, meanwhile, has a map of the local theater. It shows his battalion, several nearby base camps, the closest landing strip, and the directions from which both friendly and unfriendly tanks are most likely to come.

Far away in some secure bunker, meanwhile, the general is looking at his wall-sized map of the world. Each plane represents an entire bomber group. Each ship represents a convoy. Large arrows, sweeping unimpeded over every type of terrain and across national boundaries, indicate the progress of the opposing armies over space and time. After pondering the strategic situation, the general issues a command: "The Second Army should flank the enemy by pushing eastward."

Down the ladder goes the order. From the colonel, it passes along by radio down the chain of command, to the sergeant, who takes the word out to the front lines: "Move out to the east!" Our private climbs out of his foxhole and warily starts moving eastward. Within 500 yards, he arrives at a watery ravine, made impassible by the recent destruction of a bridge. The advance stops.

What's gone wrong here? Several things. First, the strategic understandings at the various levels of command are not sufficiently linked to permit coordinated action. It's not that everyone can be, or should be, working off the same map. The general can't be responsible for small details, and the private can't be responsible for holding the grand overview in his head. But the various maps absolutely have to be coordinated. East always has to be east. As the maps go up and down through various scalings, information essential for the next level of command must be preserved.

But let's go a step further. What the private *really* needs, today, is a map of what the ravine region is going to look like when he gets there tomorrow. When the private arrives at the cliff edge, it will be easy (and painful) to talk about what *was*. But it would have been better to spend the time a day earlier deciding what *should be*, and what is most likely to be. If a bridge is going to be where there isn't one today, a whole bunch of people are going to have to coordinate action.

My father's job during most of World War II was to land on enemy shores with the second wave of invasion forces. He was unarmed, mainly because he had something like 60 pounds of radio gear to haul through the surf and up onto the beach. My father had to have faith that the agreed-upon sequence of coordinated actions—*soften up beach defenses with bombardment, hit beach with first wave, dig in and hold a position, hit beach with second wave*—would all go off without a hitch, so that he'd have a reasonable chance of making it alive onto and off of the beach. And "faith," in this case, meant believing his own predictions and the predictions of his superiors.

Large-scale military campaigns are coordinated actions in their purest form, but they are certainly not unique. Most businesses face vast challenges of communication across functional lines, as well as up and down the hierarchy. People working in those organizations are using the tools of prediction and projection to take coordinated action—more or less effectively, depending on how successfully their "maps" have been coordinated.

Why Culture Counts

Culture is a human invention. It is, I suggest, an agreement on how we will feel about different outcomes. It is the foundation of projectability across large numbers of people. Sharing a culture lets us take collective action and is therefore the foundation for our individual well-being. Culture building (and therefore projectability building) is the most compelling reason to form human groups in the first place.[8]

But culture today is under assault. My contention is that, if we continue on the path we're on today, in the closing years of the twentieth century, the stability and longevity of society will be at risk in the twenty-first century. This will happen in part because we will lose the predictive value that culture is supposed to provide to us.

The assault on culture comes from both without and within. Because most of the external threats have been discussed extensively in the press and in scholarly circles, I'll touch on them only briefly here.

I remember vividly when, in 1962, I first encountered Rachel Carson's masterpiece, *Silent Spring*. This was the book that introduced the idea that our hubris in altering the natural environment was having unexpected and dangerous consequences. I also remember the skepticism with which Carson's book was treated, at least initially.[9] The idea was silly: how could DDT in the fields hurt eagles on the mountaintops? Surely, more than three decades after that seminal event, and a quarter-century after the first Earth Day, I don't need to belabor the point that resources are finite. We will either conserve and use them prudently, or we will not. If we choose the former course, we will be acting (wisely!) on a prediction about our collective future.

In addition to acknowledging resource limitations, we must recognize the fact that the world has gotten smaller. A century ago, it simply didn't matter to the larger world if someone in a jungle somewhere helped a new virus enter a human host. Today, with jet travel and relatively permeable national borders, the emergence of new and virulent diseases matters immensely. Similarly, if a bank went bust in Singapore 100 years ago, that failure would have had no impact on people outside of a small economic elite. It would have taken months for the news to reach us, if in fact it ever did. Today, a 26-year-old British national working in Singapore can bring down a 200-year-old bank singlehandedly, and in the process pose a real threat to the international economy.

Economic dislocation also puts pressure on the culture. The massive restructurings that have taken place in the 1980s and 1990s have severely undercut the notion of security and trust in the corporate context. Issues of "right" and "wrong" aside—at least for the moment—we can agree that a former bulwark and anchor of society is no longer there. Even the phone companies and the utilities, once the soul and embodiment of stability, are now going through convulsive changes.

The collapse of outdated geopolitical structures also raises the stakes for cultures around the world, and illustrates how quickly cultural consensus can dissipate. As countless observers before me have noted, the end of the Cold War liberated some people but confused and terrified many others. Marshal Tito leaves the world stage, the artificial construct he leaves behind in Yugoslavia crumbles as if it had never existed, and a disastrous civil war ensues in the region. We watch the on-again, off-again instability of our neighbors to the north and south, and take steps (like NAFTA) to shore them up. Farther afield, we hold our noses and surreptitiously back the likes of Hafez el Assad in Syria, Saddam Hussein in Iraq (even the post–Desert Storm variety), and other thugs around the world, mainly because we fear the collapse and fragmentation of the rickety states over which they rule more or less despotically.

To protect our predictive capabilities, we always take the devil we know over the devil we don't. Gorbachev is the favorite of the Western world until we figure out what Yeltsin is all about. Yeltsin is our favorite until we decipher the next plausible, *predictable* Russian leader. (No doubt the Russians feel this far more acutely than we do.) Incumbents are reelected in such overwhelming numbers not only because they control money and media, but also because we know what to expect from them—even when we don't expect much.

There are also increasing numbers of internal factors that are putting intense pressure on our culture in the United States. Many of our central cities are marooned islands of despair, in which gangs provide the greatest measure of predictability. When a member says his gang is his family, he is implicitly pointing to the predictive power that the gang affords him: do this, and that will happen. At the other end of the spectrum—out in newly notorious places like Idaho and Montana—bands of armed libertarians deny the authority of federal and state governments. They, too, provide predictability to their adherents, while they make the rest of us nervous.

These are anticultural manifestations that present a great peril to our society. We devalue each other and, in the process, make ourselves less predictable to each other. Example: I'm a 40-year-old lawyer living in the Central West End of St. Louis. My kids attend private school. Both my husband and I have good jobs and a growing portfolio. The block I live on—once a wealthy neighborhood, then a declining neighborhood, and now on the rebound—has just voted to "take the street private." We're opting out of our neighborhood and, by extension, out of our city and our culture. From now on, the police function on our street will be performed by a private security force.

Or we write off the future: I've got mine; the hell with whatever the rest of you want. The result is an ever-diminishing ability to take collective action and to protect the "common wealth." If I don't perceive any overlap between your needs and mine, I'm perfectly willing—maybe even within my rights—to throw you and your kind overboard.

This is not a new phenomenon, of course. There are myriad examples in our past. The Plains Indians adopted an attitude of stewardship, even reverence, toward the buffalo, which provided their tribes with the food and clothing they needed for survival. The white man shot the buffalo for sport, or for the incidental delicacy that could be stripped off the carcass, and thereby pushed the animal to the brink of extinction. Our immigrant ancestors—including mine, who first tried farming in the rocky hills of New England—were similarly irresponsible toward the land. Plow it up; use it up; and when it starts to become unproductive (or, worse, blows away), move on. These offenses took place within, and were blows against, a larger culture.

Today, the write-'em-off impulse takes different forms, but it is still very much with us. The blatant greed of the money-changers at their worst (captured in novels like *Bonfire of the Vanities* and movies like *Wall Street*) waxes and wanes, but continuing economic uncertainty sustains the drawbridge mentality. I've got mine; the hell with those coming behind me. But it's not just callow yuppies who are at fault. Example: I'm 80 years old, retired in Florida, and my investments have turned out to be good ones. My Social Security check arrives on time, and, so far, when I cash it, it doesn't bounce. Truth be told, I don't need the money, but hell—I kicked in all those years, and so what if I'm getting back 40 times my investment? Do I really have to worry about whether they're putting enough money into the Social Security trust funds for 40 years from now?

I would say "yes"—you absolutely *do* have to worry about what will come next, if only for your grandchildren. As a society, the consequences of blowing off the future are growing dramatically more dangerous. It's a genetic disaster to wipe out the buffalo (and the peoples that depend on them); it's a disaster of another order of magnitude to wipe out the ozone layer and perhaps render the planet uninhabitable for our species. Inexorably, the future is closing in on us. Depending on what we do today, which future we point toward, the future will be either a field of opportunity or a killing field.

I believe that we face a future of increasingly constrained resources. With skillful application of technology and entrepreneurial initiative, the pie will continue to get marginally bigger—but many more people will be expecting to earn or grab a piece of it. (Think of the consequences in terms of both prices and pollution if over a billion Chinese start to use energy at the same per capita rates as those in the United States.) Those who got away with selfishness in the past were able to do so because of the sheer munificence of our resource-rich democratic and capitalistic society. Today, in an age characterized by declining natural resources and alarming government deficits, most would agree that the remarkable cornucopia that was nineteenth-century America is gone forever.

Meanwhile, there are pressing issues on which we desperately need to reach consensus, which we can't even discuss productively. It's hard enough for me and my suburban neighbors to talk through an issue like gun control. What if we added a beleaguered inner-city resident and a self-styled "militia man" to our discussion group? But topics that can't be discussed don't go away; they go underground. If we don't encourage discussion (at least) of new, exotic, and morally dubious gene therapies, those manipulations will happen in Switzerland and will be available only to the rich. Cloning—a scary genie now loosed from its bottle—holds the potential to further rend the social fabric, making it tougher for us to jointly envision the future.

To return to the theme that opened this chapter—variety versus predictability—I argue that we have to let the "common weal" determine how far our public discourse must range. For variety's sake, the answer *has* to be "The farther, the better." But the kinds of inward-directedness and selfishness that beset our society when times are flush and scary (the 1920s, the 1980s) are inimical to genuine debate and experimentation. These times are long on fads (odd dances and "creative" financial instruments) but short on true innovation. Conservatism reigns: *all I want is to protect my own.*

And perversely, in this same flush-and-scary climate, predictability declines. If all you want is to protect your own, then I can't trust you farther than I can throw you. Both variety *and* predictability sag, as the rich get richer.

Is all of this tub thumping only a case of my Mormon heritage getting the better of me? Maybe. But, as I read it, all of human history suggests that, when a big enough gap opens up between the haves and the have-nots, that gap is highly unstable. The have-nots have very potent ways of getting even.

"Après moi, le deluge," as Louis XV put it.* And, in retrospect, this was an excellent prediction.

---

*I was pleasantly surprised to learn recently that Louis's wife, Marie Antoinette, did *not* advise the starving peasants to eat cake. She was 11 years old when the phrase first appeared in Rousseau's *Confessions*. But it certainly *sounds* like something that a queen with bad powers of projection might have said.

chapter five

Predictability in the Past

Whether you like it or not,
history is on our side.
We will bury you.
Nikita S. Khrushchev

What do we do when we have a task at hand and a choice of tools with which to do it? Easy: we pick the best tool. But what *is* the best tool? In any given era, the authoritative answer comes from the institution best able to say what lies ahead (predictability), and, even better, best able to help me envision what that future will mean to *me* (projectability). The more I know about how the currently reigning institution came into favor, and where it sits in the ever-shifting balance of power that is complex society, the better my ability to pick the right tool to lead to my projected goal. A little historical background can substantially improve my predictive abilities.

Alfred Chandler, one of my Harvard colleagues, dates the rise of the modern managerial class to the second half of the nineteenth century, when the increasing complexity of business created the need for new kinds of organizational structures, which in turn had to be populated by new kinds of managers.[1] More than a century later, this managerial culture is now so deep in our subconscious sense of how the world works that it's hard to imagine what life was like before it was invented.

But the great corporations that arose in the United States after the Civil War presented a radically new context for individual affiliation and "embeddedness." When John Patterson founded National Cash Register in 1882, he not only set out to corner the cash register market, but he also deliberately set about creating a cradle-to-grave corporate culture, the likes of which hadn't been seen before in the United States. He was highly successful at both. The Justice Department tried to put him in prison for anticompetitive practices; meanwhile, life in the city of Dayton, Ohio, became more predictable than almost anywhere else on earth.* Dayton loved National Cash Register.

By the 1920s, and for most of the subsequent half-century, large numbers of Americans were "company men." This phrase has become loaded with negative connotations, but it essentially defines the window through which long-time corporate employees view their world. For the company man, the corporation provided predictability, and in the context of a world that (even then) was changing rapidly, predictability was a good thing. "The AT&T escalator only goes up," they used to say.

And, even when the fundamental reality of the particular corporation was constant change and upheaval, the company man knew what the cards held for him. Back in the good old days, for example, long-time IBM employees liked to grumble that IBM stood for "I've Been Moved." This could be read as a plea for increased predictability: "Stop moving me around!" But I think it meant exactly the opposite. I think the seemingly discontented IBM company man was saying, "I can live with the disruption and inconvenience of regular relocations, because I know what the future holds for me."

---

*It was only an unpredictable turn of events that kept Patterson out of jail. When Dayton was flooded in 1913, Patterson led his company's efforts to bail out the city, and the grateful city fathers persuaded Justice to leave him alone.

Not so today. The rules have changed, and not necessarily for the better. We've already seen what happened to the AT& T escalator in 1996. For 40,000 or so people, it stripped its gears as it rumbled into reverse. And this is now the rule, rather than the exception. If you're an up-and-coming young executive at IBM headquarters in Armonk, New York, and the company says that it wants you to become head of sales in Topeka, you've got to ask yourself a few questions right off the bat: *What happens if they downsize again? Do I get left high and dry in Topeka? Will they even send me plane fare home? Even if I'm sure I can get home, what about my ophthalmologist spouse, who may have trouble getting invited into a practice in Topeka? Or my aging parents, whom I'll have to persuade to move to Kansas on the assumption that I'll be there for a while?*

People bet on people—especially when they're trying to evaluate and shape their futures. This is both an instinctive need and the most practical strategy for survival. Corporations are a real good way for us to make each other more dependable. Yes, we join corporations because we have to pay the bills. But, more important, as noted in the last chapter, we join them to enhance the predictability of our lives. Corporations tell us the rules, assure us that there's a continuing market for our services, and buffer us from the cruel winds of the economy. These aren't "nice-to-haves"—they're necessities.

When corporations suddenly stop providing us with these vital goodies, we become disoriented. Sometimes we acknowledge our anger and strike back, whether through sabotage, whistleblowing, or plain old clock punching. Sometimes, if we're flexible and optimistic enough, we start looking to embed and affiliate ourselves elsewhere. And sometimes we simply give up and conclude that predictability is a pipe dream.

And, although my heart is in business, I could easily make the same point in the political realm. We crave the measure of predictability that "the United States of America" seems to embody; we are justifiably anxious when something or someone makes us wonder whether we've been betting on the wrong horse.[2]

For example, I suspect that few people under the age of 50 can appreciate the wriggly chills that went down American spines in November 1956, when Premier Khrushchev made his famous prediction about burying us. Back in the 1950s, in the days of Red Scares and duck-'n'-cover nuclear alerts, it was almost impossible for us not to take him literally. The specter of an overpowering Red Tide—legions of Communists with shovels relentlessly throwing dirt over our decadent station wagons and barbecue pits—was a powerful one.

Only after the fact did Khrushchev recognize the power of his prediction. He had not set out to rouse us to action—far from it. Khrushchev would have preferred for us to *sleep* through our burial. He was still explaining himself years afterward. "We believe that Karl Marx, Engels, and Lenin gave scientific proof of the fact that the system, the social system of socialism, would take the place of capitalism," he told the National Press Club in 1959. "That is why I said that looking at the matter from the historical point of view, socialism, communism, would take the place of capitalism and capitalism thereby would be, so to speak, buried."[3] So *relax*, already, America; forget about that particular peek into the future.

Well, as it turned out, this was not one of the great predictions of the century. (It was nowhere *near* as good as Louis XV's on the deluge!) Even by the sorts of measures that might have been applied back in 1956, it probably could have been identified as a long shot. Honestly, now, arriving from Mars on your first visit to Earth in the fall of 1956, which country do you think you would have bet on—the one with one indigenous language or the one with dozens? the one that controlled most of the major multinationals or the one that was hermetically sealed off from all outside forces? the one with the world's longest unde-fended border to its north or the one with a huge, angry, restless neighbor to the south? Better that Khrushchev had kept his mouth shut—or, failing that, that we hadn't paid him any notice.

Nevertheless, Khrushchev predicted, and we listened. And not just with our ears, but also with our guts. Why? Because he was hitting us where it hurt: in the soft tissue of our culture, where we go for reassurance about life's predictability. Here was a guy with an arsenal of nukes promising to bury us. And he sounded so *certain!*

Humans need to know what's coming at them—or, at the very least, to have the range of possible futures circumscribed. We don't necessarily need certainty, but we want to act with confidence that we're making an informed choice. We don't even demand that the news be good news; mostly, we want to know what's coming at us. "I have nothing to offer but blood, toil, tears, and sweat," Winston Churchill told the House of Commons in May 1940. (Imagine what a political opponent could do with *that* sound bite today!) "You ask —" he continued, "what is our aim? I can answer in one word: It is victory, victory at all costs, victory in spite of all terror, victory, however long and hard the road may be; for without victory, there is no survival."[4]

A stirring performance from one of the great orators of the century. Churchill predicted nothing but hard work and discomfort, but somehow managed to push "terror" out the door and roll "victory" in as its replacement. And, at the end, of course, he threw in that little zinger about "survival."

Survival is what prediction is all about. In this chapter, we take a quick and highly selective dash through human history. Some readers might think they hear their digression detectors going off. But bear with me. The aim of this chapter is, first, to demonstrate that human evolution (probably physical, and certainly social) has been about improving our predictive capabilities; and, second, that this process of improvement has been intimately linked to the accumulation of surpluses (wealth). Getting better at prediction has improved our lot in life. It has also made us much more interested in arranging the future in ways that will protect what we've already accumulated—and maybe even put us in a good position to accumulate a little more stuff.

Khrushchev and other throwbacks notwithstanding, we're slowly getting better at this prediction game. I believe that we'll have to get still better in the future, and manage our wealth better, if we are to survive as a species.

■ Hunting, Gathering, and Guessing

In the beginning, when we were resource-poor, we basically reacted to our environment. We were hunter-gatherers. We specialized in pouncing (and being pounced on).

We were pantheists, seeing gods lurking everywhere—under the rocks, behind the trees, up in the clouds. This was useful, because it allowed us to impose a crude story line on life. And life seemed pretty damned random back then. What are we supposed to make of the fact that Brother Urg, strongest and bravest of our clan, walked out of the cave into the Loud Wetness this morning and was obliterated by a crashing sword of fire from the sky? Let's see, now. We can parse this one out. Most likely, the God of the Fire Swords was jealous of Urg's great strength and bravery, and decided to get rid of him in a cowardly—but most impressive!—way. Possible take-home lessons: (1) don't be strong and brave, or (2) don't tempt the fire-sword god during Loud Wetness episodes.*

That's probably how we humans came to grips with lightning and other bolts from the blue. Over generations, Urg's descendants learned that it was still vital to be brave and Urglike, but that electrical storms were not to be trifled with. But what about events

---

*A few millennia later, H. L. Mencken (in his misanthropic *A Book of Burlesques*) described civilization as "a concerted effort to remedy the blunders and check the practical joking of God."

that we really wanted to predict with a bit more regularity and accuracy?

For example, how about eating regularly?

We started to eat better when we began casting animal bones into the campfire to direct the next day's hunt. (More on this in the next chapter.) A next level up, in terms of predictive capability, was to clean up that leftover carcass—maybe even treat it with some of that crystalline white stuff that the Great Waters leave on the beach—wrap ourselves up in the preserved hide, head down to the watering hole, stay downwind, and wait. Prediction: I can fool something into walking up alongside me and throttle it, sometime before I starve to death.

Up one more rung on the ladder of prediction: let's you, me, and the rest of our tribe start in these woods at the bottom of this hill, fan out, and—on a prearranged signal—start walking up the hill through the woods making just as godawful a din as we possibly can. Prediction: by so doing, we'll force all the deer in the woods to the very top of the hill, where they will run out of room, panic, and jump off the cliff to their deaths on the rocks far below, where the rest of our tribe will have been sharpening their stones and firing up the cook stoves.

This was a good strategy, as long as it wasn't overused. It sustained the Shawangunks, in what was later to become south-central New York State, for centuries, mainly because they had a really top-notch local cliff to work with. And, in a limited way, it foreshadowed the next phase of human development—cultivation—which depended far more on predictive capabilities. But, with all due respect to the Shawangunks, this was still essentially a reactive posture. "Animals in the neighborhood, thank goodness; now, what do we have to do to catch 'em and eat 'em?" Gathering had essentially the same low-prediction quotient. "Berries? Ripe enough? Not poisonous? Let's eat 'em."

Now, all of this may sound like the remote past, populated by Urgs and Shawangunks, and therefore irrelevant. The truth is that it's not. Think about the circumstances of today's migrant workers, for example, who constitute one of the world's truly invisible and oppressed populations. They go where they hope the fruit is going to be. If it's there when they get there, they pick it and are marginally rewarded. (And it doesn't much matter where you live in the United States; somewhere near you, at some point during the year, a migrant army is at work improving your standard of living.) Similarly with day laborers: they show up at the designated square in Port au Prince every morning at dawn, and a lucky few are taken away in trucks to perform the manual labor of the moment.

For these workers, life is still as Hobbes described it: solitary, poor, nasty, brutish, and short. The Shawangunks (especially those at the bottom of the cliff) actually had it better. The reality is that, at any given point in history, multiple stages of human social evolution may coexist. But this can have ominous implications for cultural cohesiveness, which we discussed in the last chapter. Two camps of people living side by side, one enjoying great predictability and the other feeling bumped and shoved at every turn—Louis XV hardly needed a crystal ball! Nor do we. I have a friend who lives in San Diego. His house has two burglar alarm systems—one for the screens and the other for everything else—and he sleeps with a hostile German shepherd in his bedroom and a gun under his pillow. I'd call this a predictable kind of unpredictability.

But, for the sake of narrative simplicity, let's assume that our evolution is indeed linear, moving from simple states of existence to more complicated states. My contention is that improving individual and collective predictive powers is what has made these transitions possible. My second contention is that, over time, the seat of predictive authority has shifted: from religion, to civil authority, to science. At the risk of offending all the clerics, kings, and physicists who pick up this book, let's think of churches, thrones, and laboratories as tools for controlling the future. Again, seats of authority have coexisted and struggled for supremacy more often than they have not. But for now, let's be linear.

■ Religion as an Enhancer of Prediction

We've already touched on religion as an enhancer of prediction. Humans have an instinctual need to explain the inexplicable, whether it's a calamity (flood, famine, disease, death by lightning) or a recurrent natural phenomenon (phases of the moon, the seasons, and so on). Equally, we have a need to rationalize outcomes, as in the case of the late Brother Urg. "Ah, *here* is the piece of the puzzle we were missing," we say. "Now it all makes sense!"

Pantheism—gods under every rock and behind every tree—gradually gave way to more systematic and hierarchical religions, but the focus always remained on explaining and predicting. The anthropomorphic Greek gods were a natural outgrowth of Urg's assassin. My personal favorite Greek myth is the tale of Persephone: a business deal gone haywire on a global scale.

You'll recall that Zeus gave Persephone to Pluto to be his unwilling wife in the Greek version of hell. Now, because Demeter, Persephone's mother, wasn't cut in on this arranged marriage, she left Olympus in a huff to retrieve her daughter. This particular angry mom happened to be the goddess of agriculture, fertility, and other key aspects of rural life; and she wandered around the mortal plains of Earth for a while, bestowing rewards and punishments and generally being, yes, *unpredictable*. But, when it became obvious that Demeter's zigs and zags were threatening the hapless humans with famine and extinction, Zeus decided to renege on his deal with Pluto.

Now, Pluto, who had made his deal in good faith, wasn't pleased when Olympian errand boy Hermes arrived to retrieve Persephone. What are contracts all about, if not predictability? Negotiations ensued, and a new deal was cut: Persephone could go home once a year, as long as she agreed to return to the nether world within the year. I see Zeus as being Japaneselike in his flexible approach to contracts, and Pluto as essentially American in his willingness to impose an eternal dumb deal on the entire world in the name of "fairness." In a world that changes, deals have to be flexible—and both sides have to recognize that reality.

For the ancient Greeks, Persephone's tale explained the mystery of the seasons. The springtime is Persephone escaping and Demeter being happy; the winter is Persephone being sent back to her unwanted husband and Demeter being unhappy. (Demeter, lashing out at an easy target, kicks the peasants around for a few months.) We can also infer, perhaps, that there was a specific historical period of great famine, which was rationalized after the fact through the story of Demeter's erratic search mission. "At least we won't have to worry about *that* episode again," the peasants told each other hopefully, once the rains resumed and the harvests came back. As for the seasons, well, the peasants were stuck with those, but at least now they had an explanation for them.[5]

The Jews took this kind of thing much more personally. Theirs was a jealous God, who tended to step in and hand out judgments liberally, both to them and to their foes. "Break those covenants, will you? Then into bondage with you! Mess around with my chosen people? Have some locusts. Engaging in odd sexual practices and other wickedness again, eh, you Sodomites? Watch what I do to you and your neighbors down the road in Gomorrah, Admah, Zeboiim, and Zoar." Again, there's an attempt to explain the general inexplicability of life—"Why are there locusts? Why are nice guys like us slaves?"—and probably an effort to explain the sudden disappearance of local metropolitan areas.*

---

*Arab folk tales and mythology include very similar tales of disappearing cities, suggesting that life around the Dead Sea was less than predictable.

In this tour through the religions of the world, I don't seek to minimize their profound differences. The Egyptian pantheon was naturalistic, with a functional blurring of the line between humans and gods. ("It's not much fun to haul these huge stones up these ramps, but at least we're helping our divine pharoah make his last ride in style, and that may be good for our own little afterlives.") The Norse gods were all-powerful and authoritarian—something like the Olympians without their redeeming streak of playfulness. The Buddha counseled acceptance of events in this earthly plane as the Almighty's will, not to be struggled against. But each of these ancient groups used their gods to explain the workings of a complex universe. Their texts—no matter if it's the Koran, the Bhagavad-Gita, or the Old Testament—are depicted by their adherents as the essential missing piece of the puzzle. "Here's what you've been looking for," they say, in effect. "Here's what you need to make sense of things and get by."

It's interesting to note that many myths and legends begin with the notion of a *quest*. Adam, Ulysses, and Siddhartha—all were searching for something. Siddhartha cut off his hair and spent ten years afoot, seeking to overcome ignorance. In Adam's case, the point of the quest was explicit: fruits from the tree of knowledge. The universality of this mythic theme of *searching*, often in forbidden realms, reveals how much importance we humans have always placed on knowledge. Knowledge of what? The future, of course. Adam didn't pluck that apple to find out where the Garden of Eden had come from. He wanted a sneak peek at tomorrow.

At the same time, many early religions, and most of the enduring religions in their early phases, featured a "cause-and-effect" underpinning. We see this in the widespread practice of making sacrifices to the gods. The sacrifices themselves varied widely, from material to monetary to personal, but the two principal motivations behind them did not. First, sacrifice was a mechanism for enforced subservience. Things aren't going too well? Maybe you should demonstrate a little humility by sacrificing that young lamb over there. But for the purposes of this book, the second motivation was a far more interesting one. This was the *transactional* approach to sacrifice. "OK, gods," the high priests would say. "We've done our part to ensure a productive hunt. We've sacrificed a young [fill in the blank]. Now you do your part."

Somewhere along the line, the high priests and priestesses started demanding a little predictability of their own. They wanted to know which cause led to which effect. After all, when you've persuaded your hungry coreligionists for the umpteenth time to make a sacrifice that they can ill afford to a god who has consistently failed to perform, your own credibility starts to come under increasing scrutiny. Let's face it. The first thing devout people usually ask is *not*, "Have we got the right god?" Much more often, they ask, "Have we got the right oracle?" Meaning you.

Imagine the power that accrued to that first Mayan priest who got the calendar right, or to the first Druid or Copt who pinned down the vernal equinox! Imagine the immense satisfaction that their followers derived when the rising sun threw a beam of light through a particular opening exactly when and where predicted—and *only* when and where predicted! To be sure, this was an authority that could be misappropriated by the individual sorcerer, and probably was, most of the time. But, hey, isn't it good to know that somebody in this fragile little settlement has a handle on something as mysterious as the sun and moon? No wonder the cults of priesthood sprang up to guard the secrecy of this knowledge!

The first thing that this kind of knowledge does is take away fear. If we know when the silver thing with the long tail is scheduled to arrive in the sky, we can celebrate its arrival (or, alternatively, we can choose to ignore it). If we know when the

Great Sky Beast is going to eat the sun, and how soon he's going to give it back, we can drink the juice of the grape or go about the business of piling up surpluses.

The second thing this kind of knowledge does is give us control over future outcomes—not so much in the case of comets and eclipses, but very much so in the case of the spring floods. "Time to put that [irreplaceable] seed corn in the ground," says the priest. And he's right. Thank the gods!

Religions have always had to strike some sort of bargain with their adjacent/competing predictive powers, which is sometimes science (when's the eclipse coming?) and sometimes the civil authority (you want to marry *whom*?).* The Mohammedans solved this problem simply by merging all predictive authority into one. In strictly observant Muslim countries, the Koranic law and the civil law are one and the same: the Sharia. This is part of the appeal of Islam, especially in turbulent times: the rules are crystal clear. If you do *this*, then you can be pretty sure *that* is going to happen.

Contrast this with Jesus' advice about rendering some things unto Caesar and other things unto God. Not quite as clear! Some students of religion have argued that it is this kind of loosey-goosiness that has enabled Christian cultures to adapt to change much more easily than their Muslim counterparts. Rather than "What does the Koran say about this?" it's more like "Hmm, well, we haven't seen anything quite like *this* before. Let's think up a response that renders a little unto Caesar and also steers a little bit toward this new guy." This is highly functional, inductive reasoning—one of the tools we will be picking up in Chapter 7—and I tend to think it actually is a great strength of Western cultures. But you could make the case that Jesus was history's

---

*There's the old joke about the priest who says to the judge, "Bah—you have no power. All you have the power to say is, 'You shall be hanged.' I have the power to say, 'You shall be *damned*.'" To which the judge replies, "Yeah, but when I say 'you shall be hanged,' we can be pretty sure it's going to happen."

first proponent of matrix management. And matrix management—as I argued in Chapter 1—is a particularly bad way to foster predictability in the workplace.

■ ## Civil Authority as an Enhancer of Prediction

The hunter-gatherers became cultivators only after two important things happened. First, they discovered something in the grain or vegetable food group that they really liked— probably hops or barley, or some other fermentable sort of thing—and decided that they wanted to have a reliable supply of this jolly-making stuff on hand. Second, they got reasonable assurances that they could eventually reap what they sowed. Way back in prehistory, therefore, the first agricultural surplus (after the seed corn was squirreled away) went toward setting up a rudimentary civil authority. Note the key role of *surplus*, which capitalists later would start to call "profit." Surplus, as we will see time and time again in our quick rush through history, is the mother of choice. In this case, the choice was to stop being nomads, claim a piece of turf, and settle down. And, in the parts of the world where the soil was marginal or better, people chose to settle down.

The civil authority protected us from outsiders. Whenever the Huns or the Visigoths arrived on the edge of town, we were able to retreat behind the city walls and wait for our expensive defense forces to bail us out. The civil authority also protected us from ourselves. It was always tempting to break into the seed corn, especially as the siege went on into its later phases and we started running out of food inside the walled city.

This raises an interesting dilemma. You have to give that civil authority enough power to affect outcomes, or you don't gain any predictability worth writing home about. On the other hand, if you give up too much authority, you risk winding up with an out-of-control tyrant, as about a third of the people in the British colonies of North America came to view King George III. And "out of control" means unpredictable. In real life, of course, almost no group manages to give up just enough power. Generally, they give up too much, and then either fight to get some of it back or suffer a new kind of capriciousness and unpredictability.

The Magna Carta is a wonderful illustration of human striving for predictability through civil authority. By the early medieval period, the barons of England had a pretty good life. Agriculture was getting more productive, the cows and sheep were getting fatter and tastier, and long-distance trade was just getting off the ground. Modest little surpluses were starting to pile up here and there. "Say," said the barons. "We've got a good thing going here. Let's invest a little more authority in those shabby Plantagenets and keep the ball rolling." Through this kind of self-interested fealty, the barons enhanced the predictability of their lives—countering the marauding and depredations of invaders and at the same time setting limits on their own commercial plundering of one another.

Well, it worked. And, because it worked, the monarchy accreted power to itself. Lo and behold, by the early thirteenth century, the once-shabby Plantagenets had begun using their newfound power in arbitrary and capricious ways, taxing and oppressing the very same feudal proprietors who had created them. (No one was worrying too much about the peasants at this point, even though it was their sweat that was racking up the surpluses, and even though, as noted earlier, peasants have a way of getting even sooner or later.) So the barons ran King John to ground and cut a thoroughly one-sided deal: no more arbitrary arrest or arbitrary taxation.[6] No more "scutages" (fees improvised by the king and imposed on the barons), except to ransom the king's body, make his eldest son a knight, or marry off his eldest daughter. No more arbitrary banishments or imprisonments. No more condemnations based only on rumor or suspicion. No more meddling with the Church.

Not a bad deal, if you can compel the king to sign it—which the barons did at Runnymede in 1215 and which their successors were careful to do to the next 32 kings of England.[7] Note the consistent theme in every concession that they wrung out of John: less arbitrariness, more predictability. One part of the Magna Carta that isn't often commented on is the commercial nuts and bolts that it detailed. "OK, your highness, here's the deal. We've gotta have London and other key ports free to conduct commerce without the threat of bizarre royal interventions. Our legal system has to function in fair and consistent ways. No offense, John, but these are the parts of our lives where we can't and won't tolerate unpredictability."*

The Magna Carta represented a great step forward for the predictive competence of the civil authority. But the importance of predictability and projectability in the political realm can also be underscored by examples of backsliding and retrenchment. If the present and future are simply too scary, we try to recreate the past. In December 1995, voters in both Poland and Russia gave large pluralities to the same Communist parties that had been thrown out of power only a few years earlier. Are these people stupid? No. Forgetful? Of course not. They know that the upside potential of a market-based economy is higher than that of a stultified, ossified, state-directed system. After all, they've had first-hand experience of that discredited system. But they also know that the uncertainty for them *personally* may be much higher in a swashbuckling capitalistic system. They've seen that one, too. Jobs go away. The price of bread goes up.

---

*Perhaps the current and future Congresses of the United States could glean a useful lesson from this. Although I'm a capitalist, I firmly believe that transactions can occur *anywhere*, under *any* set of rules, as long as that set of rules is knowable. Pop quiz. It's 1996. Would you rather buy Treasuries in the United States or securities in Russia? Why?

It's hard to play the democratic game if you don't know the rules. If you *do* know the rules, and those rules create uncertainty for older, less-skilled workers, you still won't play.

The life experience of most Poles and Russians has trained them to minimize uncertainty and personal exposure.* The recent elections signal clearly that unless something reassuring happens soon—something that restores a little predictability to life—the beleaguered citizens of those two countries will take the devil they know over the devil they don't.

■ Science as an Enhancer of Prediction

Meanwhile, as religion tries to make sunbeams come through the right window, things are marching along in the secular realm. Maybe it was a priest who figured out that nine parts of copper to one part of tin made a dandy metal, suitable for shields and daggers. But I don't think so. I bet it was a blacksmith, with some sort of soldier looking over his shoulder providing a strong motivation for both success and discretion.

The accretion of practical knowledge experienced many detours and interruptions over the centuries. In some cases, knowledge building was distracted by the civil authority. "You can make bronze?" asked the king. "Great. So now make something *really* useful—like gold, for instance." This was the birth of alchemy.

In other cases, religion intervened in counterproductive ways. A little bit of knowledge got combined with a lot of wishful thinking and sent the train of learning off the rails. Astrology, for example, must have had strongly religious roots, as well as

---

*This presents a clear contrast to China, where a more or less rickety state was overlaid on an extremely strong family structure. So, excepting disasters like the Cultural Revolution, when the Peking bureaucrats start to get unpredictable, your Chinese family is there to keep you on an even keel.

practical, agriculturally oriented ones. (For some, of course, it is still a type of religion today.) But a rudimentary knowledge of the stars was always at risk of being bent into mock predictive behavior. "Next Tuesday there will be a sign in the heavens that God is angry with you," says the priest who has a handle on what will someday be called Halley's comet. "This will mean that you are to hand over half of your earthly possessions to the Church."

But the knowledge that builds predictability comes from observation of the real world, which is only partially controlled by kings and priests. Over time, pebble by painful pebble, mountains of practical knowledge began to accumulate. We learned about metals and the stars. We also learned about mining, crop growing, animal husbandry, navigation, weather prediction, reading a landscape well enough to know what minerals it might hold, the physics of building and firing a catapult or a crossbow—all the realms of human activity where ideas were generated out of necessity and tested under fire. Gradually, those kings and priests who sought to contain, control, and distort knowledge (and thereby appropriate the powers of prediction to themselves) lost more and more ground.

We left the Middle Ages and entered the Renaissance, when we began to democratize the accumulation and "ownership" of prediction-enhancing knowledge and to exalt the *practical* applications of knowledge rather than the religious. To me, the two heroes and embodiments of this incredibly important process of transition were Galileo Galilei and Isaac Newton—of falling cannonball and falling apple fame, respectively.

In case you haven't thought about Galileo recently, he was one of the more systematic and productive thinkers of all time. For example, he proved that the oscillations of a pendulum were accomplished in equal times. He teased out the notion of specific gravity. He used the Leaning Tower of Pisa to prove that all solid bodies fell at the same speed (thereby infuriating the disciples of Aristotle), reinvented Aristotle's theory of sound (further baiting and aggravating the Aristotelians), made the correlation between atmospheric pressure and suction, confirmed Copernicus's odd notion that the earth revolved around the sun (thereby offending the Catholic church), concluded that the moon shone only by reflected light, and discovered four of the moons of Jupiter on the same night.

The fact that two popes in a row went after Galileo for pushing condemned doctrines shows that the religious hierarchies understood full well the troubling implications of his discoveries. If the sun didn't revolve around the earth, then it was very, very unlikely that Rome was the center of the universe.

The fact that they succeeded temporarily in shutting Galileo up illustrates another key point. Here was a guy who was making absolutely astonishing advances in practical knowledge, and the religious authorities managed to put a gag on him. Why? Because, in the mid-1600s, enough people still felt that the Church, with its over 16 centuries of credibility behind it, provided better predictive power than a lone astronomer with odd ideas. To revive an example from Chapter 4, if General Motors says the Corvair is safe, and some skinny geek says it isn't, who are you gonna believe?* But the popes were fighting a losing battle, because that lone astronomer had pieced together a model of the world with great predictive power.

Galileo died in 1642. Coincidentally, this was the same year that Isaac Newton was born. It was Newton who finally wrested predictive power out of the hands of the Church and delivered it into the hands of the scientists. The Newtonian laws of temperature, gravitation, and motion were a spectacular advance in human predictive power. "Based on my careful

---

*Just so I don't appear to be putting Galileo and Ralph Nader in the same league: they aren't. Nader got a demonstrably bad car off the roads. Galileo changed how humans understood the universe.

observations," said Sir Isaac, in so many words, "I predict that the radiation of heat from a body in a certain time will be proportional to the difference between its temperature and that of the surrounding media. I predict that every particle of matter will attract every other particle, and the stress between them will be proportional to the product of their masses divided by the square of their distance apart. I predict that, for every action, there will always be an equal and opposite reaction." And so on, and so on.

All science is about prediction: if X, then Y. When a scientific prediction works as well as Newton's did, it quickly becomes a "law." Newton's laws worked for nearly 300 years, and unless you do a lot of up-close work with subatomic particles, they still work today. It took a while for Newton's laws to find their way into practical applications, but when they did, science reigned supreme as the paramount source of predictive power. Think about the great credibility possessed by modern physicists, who make predictions about the tracks that particles will follow in exotic machines that have yet to be built—and then when these machines *are* built, the tracks show up, right on cue! Talk about the power of prediction![8]

Because of this great and growing reservoir of credibility, science for the most of the twentieth century was invoked to validate all sorts of odd propositions. Remember what Khrushchev told the National Press Club? That Marx, Engels, and Lenin had provided "scientific proof" that social-ism would replace capitalism.[9] Just as was true with the priests and kings, the predictive power of science was easily abused, and its hard-won wisdom was often put to bad uses. But it was powerful predictive medicine, all the same. And the people who figured out how to put it to work began generating surpluses—by now stored in financial instruments, rather than granaries—that surpassed the greed-soaked vi-sions of even the most grasping medieval monarch.

Sometimes the astounding successes of science create not predictability, but *un*predictability. When that happens, science gets into trouble. Take the example of the human genome project, which for the better part of a decade has been attempting to decode and "map" our genetic inheritance, strand by strand. This has got to be a good thing, right? If we know where everything resides, then we'll have the ability to rifle-shoot out all of the genetic flaws in our makeup. The future will be perfect, starting with our kids![10]

Well, maybe yes, maybe no, and that's why this particular scientific effort ran into unexpected opposition. The genome project portends to give us control (read "predictability") without any real sense of the *consequences* of that control. In this case, a gateway to knowledge feels like it might also be a gateway to unpredictability—or projectability into a known but very unpleasant future. When China imposed strict birth-control measures (one child per family), Chinese families who were hoping for male children evidently began drowning their infant daughters. How confident are we that the human genome map won't be used to accomplish even more reprehensible things in the future? We aren't. It's scary (read "unpredictable"). And so, we're having second thoughts.

■ Betting on People

We've looked briefly at three realms in which predictive power has been centered over the centuries: religion, civil authority, and science. My contention is that people have invested the most authority in the realm where they have found (or have expected to find) the best predictive powers, based on available skills and knowledge. In many cases, two of the three realms, or even all three, have joined forces to build predictability. The civil authority, for example, seeks out the moral sanction that can only be conferred by religion. Scientists like nothing better than a nice, tight patent, conferred and enforced by the civil authority. Religious leaders, as noted, call upon science to make sure that the sunbeam will indeed fall on the specified wall on the specified date. Property rights are protected by both the fear of jail *and* the fear of hell. Overlap is the rule; exclusive claims on the power of prediction are the exception.

So, now that I've introduced the notion of overlap, I can return to a parallel realm of human activity—one that underpins and overlaps with religion, the civil authority, and science. This is the realm of *human organizations*. I will focus most of my attention on business organizations, but at least a healthy minority of my examples will suggest how the urge for predictability applies to other forms of human organization.

Like the other three realms, human organizations at their best are quite good tools for making our desired futures come to pass. And, unlike the other three, human organizations are effective even when things aren't static. When they work, they are highly adaptable. This has made them increasingly valuable as life has gotten more changeable.

Earlier in this chapter, we visited the cave of Urg and his clan. Although still vulnerable to bolts from the blue, Clan Urg was already building a tiny measure of predictability inside their cave. Hierarchies were well established and rigidly enforced. Young Urgchins learned the ropes slowly, which gave them adequate time to let their brains and bodies develop, and thereby helped differentiate their species from most others. The old folks told and retold the clan's legends around the fire, using blackened sticks and daubs of mud to depict the cowardly but impressive God of the Fire Swords on the walls of the cave.

As long as Clan Urg had to deal only with itself and woolly mammoths, its limited predictive powers as a human organization weren't much of a liability. But things got more complicated. Other clans moved into the Urg territory, no doubt drawn by the fast-spreading reputation of the local mammoths as particularly flavorful and slow-witted.

What came next, in many cases, was war. War raised the predictability stakes dramatically. If you asked the wrong question—like "How defend Clan Urg against rocks?" rather than "How defend Clan Urg against bows and arrows?"—your whole tribe got wiped out. If you got the wrong answer to the right question, same thing. Even if you got the right answer to the right question, but just a tiny bit too late, same thing—wipeout. Not surprisingly, therefore, war brought forth the first book that is largely about organizing humans for effective action: Sun-Tzu's *The Art of War*. What did Sun-Tzu recommend as the surest way to control the future? The answer is not too surprising:

> *Know the enemy and know yourself; in a hundred battles you will never be in peril. When you are ignorant of the enemy but know yourself, your chances of winning or losing are equal. If ignorant of both your enemy and of yourself, you are certain in every battle to be in peril.*[11]

The old poet and warrior got very specific in his advice for waging war, down to the various conditions of the terrain that a warrior might encounter and the tactics that might be used under each condition. But what made Sun-Tzu's work so enduring was that he also previewed, in broad terms, almost every topic that would eventually become of interest to organizational theorists. As the above-quoted passage suggests, for example, *information* was absolutely critical to the art of war. This meant, in turn, that systems had to be developed for collecting, transmitting, and analyzing information, and subsequently for disseminating the knowledge that resulted. Controls, cross-checks, iterative loops, and so on all had to be invented. The psychological aspects of knowledge building had to be considered.

In short, Sun-Tzu provided a tidy package of prescriptions for controlling the future through human organizations. If you're going to war and you desire specific outcomes, here are the actions you should take. It was, in effect, an early argument for the scientific method: these conditions plus these actions yield this future. Victory! And, oh, by the way: a timely beheading here and there goes a long way toward reinforcing discipline, which in turn greatly enhances the predictability of your army.*

Look at Moses as a prediction enhancer in the organizational context. What are the Ten Commandments? They are a set of rules that say, "If you behave in these particular ways, then certain things will happen, and other things *won't* happen." This means that all of the interactions within the tribe will henceforth be predictable. We agree that we won't steal. This is good for the short and long term, because it means that I can be confident that I can hang onto my stuff today, and I can build for the future. We agree to honor our fathers and mothers. This is especially good for the long term, because it creates an intergenerational compact of support. First I'll sacrifice for you, and then you'll sacrifice for me. This takes our predictive powers out over two or three generations—not a bad trick at all, in an age when seas part and people turn into pillars of salt. And here's the really good news: because these rules come complete with the Divine Seal of Approval, almost everybody in our little tribe of believers is likely to obey them.

We've already worked King John over, and I won't exhume him for another round here. But, for most of the 2,000 years following the arrival of the Ten Commandments, much of humankind lived in settings where they knew *exactly* what was expected of them. Take my ancestors in Scotland. They accepted

---

*A certain king, Ho-lü, asked Sun-Tzu if the king's concubines could be used to demonstrate a troop movement. Sun-Tzu said yes, but when he tried to get 180 women to perform the drill, there was great confusion and laughter. So Sun-Tzu (to the king's dismay) beheaded two of the women. Subsequently, the drill went off without a hitch.

their lot in life more or less without question, because every force in their little universe was designed to achieve that outcome. If they broke the rules, they would have aggravated not only the local prince and the church, but most likely the whole community. In many cases, the rules were set up in such a way that the whole community was punished when one Son of Steven got out of line. So the *community* was a mechanism of enforcement, and quite an effective one. Prediction was a minor challenge, at best. Who's going to be the prince in 40 years? Why, the son of the current prince, of course. And what will your children and my children be doing in 40 years? Why, piling up rocks, of course.

Autocracies are a little bit like diving bells. They work fine up until the moment when a single seal springs a tiny leak—and then all hell breaks loose. Part of the "charm" of life on the moors in Scotland in, say, 1510 was the fact that the world was hermetically sealed. It was nasty, but it was very predictable: this is the way the world is and will always be. If you step out of line, you will get killed in one of those unpleasant ways you've already heard about in gory detail.

But what happens when the diving bell's seal lets go or the underlying technology changes dramatically?* First of all, people get a whiff of fresh air, a hint of the alternatives out there in the big world, all of which *have* to look pretty good when compared to the dreary present. But, in the same instant that these alternative futures start to get contemplated, the autocrat begins to implode like a defective diving bell.

What's going on here? It's not just that people like the look of that democracy on the other side of that fence over there. Just as important, they are rapidly losing faith in the local autocrat's

---

*The creation of the wooden mills in Manchester meant that more sheep and fewer people were needed in Scotland—hence the Highlands Clearance policy, which brought the Stevensons to America.

hitherto-unquestioned ability to predict and shape the future. For years, the Soviet Union and the Eastern bloc maintained control over their peoples by depicting life in the West as violent, decadent, and trashy. But, as soon as those subject peoples got access to Western television (admittedly violent, decadent, and trashy), they saw that their own emperors had no clothes. "If that's what an American supermarket looks like," they said, "then violence, decadence, and trash look OK to us!" Suddenly, the Supreme Soviet was simply irrelevant. It had no power of prediction.

The fax machine was widely credited with sparking and sustaining the Tiananmen Square revolt in 1989. When the crackdown came, therefore, the Chinese leaders went after technology as well as individuals.[12] Even today, the religious autocracy in Iran is trying desperately to control the flow of information into and out of that country, in part by tightly restricting the number of long-distance phone lines available for Internet links. Vietnam, too, is trying to put all Internet access through a single pipeline. And Singapore puts all its noncommercial Net users through a government-controlled server that limits access to "improper" Web sites. What these autocrats are trying to do is limit access to alternative visions of the future, thereby buttressing their own monopoly on the power of prediction. It won't work, and the Iranians should know this better than most: the Ayatollah Khomeini ran his revolution from Paris using hand-held tape recorders. Eventually, the message gets through, and the troops refuse to fire on their own people.

■ Democracy, Choice, and Business

Democracies work not because they are morally superior. They work because the rules are clear, because people have more or less agreed to play by the rules, because the rules for *changing* the rules are clear, and because people can make independent decisions about their individual futures within an agreed-upon set of constraints.

There's always room for cynicism on this point of free choice, especially when it comes to voting. For example, I heard the U.S. presidential election in November 1996 jokingly referred to as a choice between "the evil of two lessers." The candidates don't present a real choice, we make it tough for certain people to register and vote, most people aren't sufficiently motivated to vote anyway, and so on and so on. But, on balance, democracies serve their citizens pretty well. The checks and balances within them tend to smooth out the bumps and make transitions relatively smooth.

In addition, the process of democratic debate helps citizens look into the future and decide which vision of that future most appeals to them. As things now stand in my home state of Massachusetts, almost every significant expenditure that is proposed on the local level has to go before the townspeople for an up-or-down vote. Do we want a new town library? Well, which future do we want—the one that includes the current, inexpensive (but antiquated) facility, or the one that includes a significantly upgraded (but expensive) building?[13]

Democracies also work because they are the context within which a wide range of corporations, of many shapes and sizes, is most likely to flourish.* Contrast this with the experience of nineteenth-century Germany, for example, where the Krupps flourished because they got to talk to Bismarck, but the shopkeeper and entrepreneur had no such access and suffered for it. This was the Kaiserian equivalent of insider trading: big guys in the deal stream, little guys out in the cold. From the little

---

*Theoretically, this is also possible in the Albanian National Widget Works, but my recent travels in Eastern Europe suggest otherwise. An enterprise without enterprise can't be healthy.

guys' perspective, this was a bad game, because the rules that were knowable were unfair, and there were lots of rules that weren't knowable by the common person.

The *zaibatsu* economic system that characterized prewar Japan had some of the same characteristics. It was rigged in favor of a small handful of huge economic players. But remember the law of requisite variety, discussed in Chapter 4? The monopolies and oligopolies created under the *zaibatsu* system stifled variety and innovation. "The world has never seen so abnormal an economic system," concluded General Douglas MacArthur, whose job it became, in the second half of 1945, to reconstruct the devastated Japanese social and economic infrastructure. One of the major postwar success stories was the Osaka-based Matsushita Electric Industrial Company, which had limped along since its founding in 1918 largely outside the *zaibatsu* system. Beginning in the 1930s, Matsushita had manufactured home appliances—a grubby field with which the powerful *zaibatsu* companies wanted nothing to do. When the Japanese economy was forcibly democratized by the Occupation forces, Matsushita and similar companies jumped to the fore and helped set the stage for the "Japanese miracle" of the 1970s and 1980s.

The links aren't perfectly causal, but the overlaps are strikingly consistent. Democracies tend to grow out of market economies (or vice versa). Market economies tend to be stronger, more varied, and more competitive than their state-controlled counterparts. Good ideas bubble to the surface and get exploited. Surpluses tend to pile up, controlled either by individuals or by corporations. People controlling those surpluses seek ways to protect the golden goose—and also the system and the specific enterprises that spawned her. Hey, we *like* what we've got going here; what do we have to do to keep it going?

Some people who ask this question go into politics. A small number get confused and join business school faculties. But many, many more go into business. And, in that business context, they seek to organize things in such a way that they can exploit the power of predictability. They create organizations that will help them shape their futures.

Or so they hope. What they often find, though, is that it's very difficult to make a good prediction. And this is the subject of the next chapter.

chapter six

How Hard Is Prediction?

It's tough to predict—
especially about the future.
Sam Goldwyn

The increasing complexity of everyday life in the late twentieth century adds fuel to our desire to enhance our predictability. Even if we set out to maintain only a basic level of certainty—say, that enjoyed by our grandparents—this is an increasingly elusive goal. As bigger and scarier strands begin to unravel out of the social fabric, and as things we once took for granted become risky, unstable, and undependable, we seek to compensate for all this unwelcome and mounting uncertainty. Most of us do so without using words like *projectability*, but we are nevertheless compelled to take small steps out onto the ice of prediction. What's coming next? How will you and I feel about it when we get there? Can we pick a better place to go? How can we get there?

There's the rub, as captured in Sam Goldwyn's classic nostrum. Prediction is extremely difficult. Why do one-third to one-half of the marriages in the United States end in divorce? I would argue that it's because our predictive powers are mediocre, at best. Why do four-fifths of all new businesses fail? Same problem. If you knew that your impending marriage or your incipient business were doomed to failure, would you enter into those commitments? Of course not.

I've presented some version of these ideas to dozens of audiences, and in almost every audience, a large number of people seem surprised to learn that prediction is tough. Their surprise arises, I think, because we get so many convincing messages to the contrary. We're surrounded on all sides by experts (many of whom have books, seminars, or software packages to sell). For example, many corporations invest astonishing levels of resources in long-range planning, and the individuals involved in that function talk confidently of scenario building, fulfilling the strategic plan, technology forecasting, country analysis, and similar techniques. And such planning is not infrequently a case of self-fulfilling prophecy. The prediction is made, and then the higher-ups pointedly tell their subordinates that "good managers *actualize* their plans"—a veiled threat that isn't often missed!

At the same time, we hear from economists both in academia and in the business world, who promise to predict the level of industry sales of personal computers in a given year or which way the stock market is headed.* The trouble is that, like the late fortune-teller Jeanne Dixon, few of these prognosticators are ever held to their predictions. Try this scenario on for size. Hypothetical stock market forecaster Joe Janus sends out 200,000 letters. (As they say in the movies, any resemblance to anyone who works on Wall Street is entirely coincidental.) Half of Joe's letters are bearish, and half are bullish. The market then goes south in a big way. Joe then sends letters to the 100,000 people who previously got the right "prediction," and again he tells half of

---

*Think how much is spent each year on stock market forecasts—even after the Nobel committee gave a prize to an economist who demonstrated that most such forecasts amounted to a "random walk down Wall Street"!

them one thing and half exactly the opposite. Well, if he does this seven times, each time throwing overboard the people who got the wrong message, he builds a constituency of true believers: 3,150 people who hang on his every word. In fact, most of the people in this group think that Joe walks on water. How many other people have been right seven times in a row?

"Futurists" have developed into a thriving cottage industry, thanks in part to politicians' fascination with Herman Kahn, the Tofflers, and other futurists. Think tanks weigh in constantly with seemingly definitive, seemingly hard-nosed projections: *Here's what's coming!* Meanwhile, of course, computer aficionados are telling us that their favored machines (or the software that runs them) can help us build our own preferred destinies. The Internet and the World Wide Web will help us "take control of our future," in part by stripping away unnecessary intermediaries and giving us direct access to vital information.*

Sorry, but this turns out to be more or less nonsense. Nobody you will encounter on TV, in the boardroom, on the Internet, or in the lecture hall possesses anything like the predictive "truth." What they *do* possess is a system of guesses, more or less based on some kind of model of the way the world works. The worst of these models have absolutely no data behind them. But even those based on some kind of data are fatally flawed, in part because they take for granted what they need to prove. As you'll see later in this chapter, you can't use your model to determine which data are relevant—and then build your model exclusively on the data that make the cut. This is the logical equivalent of saying, "Only Hungarians record good music. Therefore, when I hear good music on the radio, I can safely assume it was recorded by Hungarians."

---

*To be fair, this tide of experts is of our own making. Our hunger for certitude—and our media's predilection for the sound bite—combine to create all sorts of "authorities."

In short, everyone is selling some concept of the future, beginning with those late-night TV advertisers ("for entertainment purposes only") and working on up the ladder to Newt Gingrich's favorite crystal-ballers. And the more persuasive the presentation, the higher the price tag. But it should all be swept off the table. Except for its entertainment value, if any, there's nothing there.

■ Degrees of Complexity

Prediction is not impossible—just tough, as Goldwyn put it. To be good predictors, we have to ask the right questions, identify the key variables, choose the right measures, obtain enough (but not too much!) timely data at the right level of resolution, with the right power of magnification, and then calculate skillfully.

Asking the right question might seem like the easiest of these challenges, but it is not. In fact, it's usually the hardest. The trick is to ask a question that is small enough to be answerable, but big enough to be important. For example, as you approach an intersection in your car, the light turns red. You could put on your predictor's cap and ask yourself: *What color will the light turn next?*

Well, assuming the light isn't broken, your most likely prediction *(Green light next)* is a pretty good one. In fact, you've foreseen the future perfectly. But you haven't asked a big enough question, and you're not really any better off for having asked and answered it.

What's a better question? How about: *What are my chances of making it through this intersection alive after the light changes?* Depending on how dangerous the intersection is, this may be a really important prediction to get right—right up there with "do lunch/be lunch."

So, if this is the right question, what are the key variables? One is the time of day. Is it morning rush hour, meaning that the sun is up (good) but the traffic is heavy (bad)? Or is it three o'clock on New Year's morning, when the lighting is poor (bad), the traffic is light (good), and a large percentage of the drivers out there are weaving their way home from all-night parties (bad!)? And, as you wait in line at the light, are you the first car or the third car? Statistics show that you're much better off being the third car through the light, because the two cars ahead of you have probably had to deal with any cheaters who have chosen to blast through the intersection from the cross street.

Somewhere in here, of course, you make an unfortunate transition from being a savvy inquirer to a compulsive data gatherer and number cruncher. There is an *infinite* number of questions that could conceivably come to bear on this calculation about the intersection. What kind of car are you driving? Does it have an airbag? Is your seat belt on? What kind of car might be likely to hit you, in the worst case? Do they allow tractor trailers on that cross street? Are you more likely to get hit from the left or the right? How secure is that power line up there? Will an airplane fall out of the sky? But remember that a basic premise of this book is that we humans have to *act*. Aside from the fact that the guy behind us is now standing on his horn, we simply don't have enough time in our short lives to make a bullet-proof prediction about this intersection. It's time to act. Look both ways, step on the gas, and don't stop looking left and right (especially in Massachusetts).

The point is to pick and choose among the possible variables that might be studied. In this picking and choosing, you're in good company. I think that if non-scientists knew how most scientific research is actually done, they would have dramatically less confidence in that process. That's because scientific research involves the systematic *elimination* of variables, in order to focus on the variables that the researcher suspects to

101

be critical. The researcher says, in effect, "Let's just suppose we don't have to worry about that, in this case." And, over time, as the experiment is replicated successfully, the scientist gains confidence that this particular variable can be eliminated without consequence. There are many kinds of physics experiments, for example, in which the physicist simply ignores the effects of gravity. It's not that gravity has no effect; it's just that, in the context of this particular experiment, the effects of gravity can safely be ignored (or so the researcher hopes). Similarly in the study of chemical reactions, the temperature of the surroundings may or may not be important, depending on what the researcher is testing for.

Simplification of the experiment is the whole ball of wax. It can be done with great subtlety and artistry, or with thorough-going incompetence. The great scientist is generally the one who thinks in a new way about which variable is important under which circumstances—in effect squinting sideways at a problem and seeing that problem in a new way—or which discredited variable to add back into the mix. Albert Einstein was able to prove his theories about gravity by exploring an angle of deflection that became significant only in the fourth decimal place. But too many of us aren't Einsteins. As we simplify, we dumb down. Take the case of the humble egg. In my lifetime, the egg has gone from perfect food to pariah and now seems to be well on its way to rehabilitation. Part of the problem has been that we've been looking at eggs in isolation. We've linked a single variable (eggs) to blood cholesterol, and we've evidently made far too much of the results.

Let's go back out on the street. You've made it through that troublesome intersection alive. This and other evidence suggests that you must be a good driver. You're watchful, tuned in, defensive, alert. But wait a minute. Aren't you a good driver because you're *ignoring* all sorts of things? You're not decoding the license plates on the parked cars you're passing. Except incidentally, you're not looking at the paint schemes on the houses. You're not checking to see if the town has adequate numbers of fire hydrants. You're not on the lookout for exotic birds to add to your life list. In fact, you're systematically screening out the vast majority of the inputs that are available to you—far more than you're allowing in—so that you can get yourself safely from here to there.*

So we constantly make decisions about the level of resolution and the power of magnification that we're going to use to make a specific prediction. Day to day, we push toward simplification, toward the lowest functional power of magnification, in order to get from here to there. This strategy works well enough for coping with routine maintenance in our lives. But it falls down badly when it tackles more complicated tasks—and especially when we look toward the future.

Trouble on the Coast of Maine—and Elsewhere

Let's raise the stakes a little bit. The intersection analogy doesn't force us to make a key decision—that is, the choice of an appropriate measure—and this is something that we predictors can't afford to overlook. So let's tackle a different kind of question. Suppose that, for some obscure competitive reason, your boss asks you to predict how long it will take him to traverse the coast of Maine, from Kittery in the south to Eastport up north. How do you make *this* prediction?

Well, you might be tempted just to draw a straight line from Eastport to Kittery, declare it to be about 220 miles, calculate that he trots at about 6 miles per hour, and inform him that his journey will take him at least 36 hours. But you have a suspicion

---

*The cell phone—adding inputs—creates new kinds of problems for would-be good drivers.

that he won't be pleased if he finds out how you've made this prediction. (He may point out that he can't trot on water.) So you decide to get the best aerial photographs you can get hold of and begin recalculating the length of the coastline to reflect some of the bigger islands, bays, and inlets. You ask yourself some tough questions, such as: *What span of water is he allowed to step over? At high tide or low tide? How far up the Penobscot River should I make him walk? Are we talking August or April?* As a result of all this complication, the coast of Maine is expanding by leaps and bounds—300 miles, 400 miles, or whatever. Your boss's 36-hour march is now up to something like 67 hours.

Taking it to an illogical extreme, now suppose you flew up to Maine yourself, put on your hip boots, and actually *measured* the coast with a one-foot ruler, foot by foot by foot. Now, the Maine coastline is *really* growing fast, like something out of *Alice in Wonderland*. Depending on how conscientious you are with that little ruler, you might discover yourself a 10,000-mile coastline. Instead of 67 hours, your boss had better plan on 69 straight *days* of walking.

Well, this seems sort of extreme. Should you split the difference? Should you assume that your own walk up the coast (less the time spent on wielding that one-foot ruler) is a good approximation of how much time he'll have to spend? Why should you assume *that*? Based on what data?

My point is that, in this case, the *measure* itself is a key variable. It's very easy to make a bad prediction by pulling the wrong measure out of your toolkit. For both manager and plebe, getting the level of detail needed for action right is critical to getting the answer right. We admire managers like Bill Gates, whose actions proclaim loudly, "I'm willing to go into *great* detail, if that helps me to get it right."

OK, assume we've asked good questions, settled on key variables, and gotten good data. Now it's time to crunch numbers and make our predictions, right?

Well, yes and no. There's a problem, which I'll illustrate with a personal example. For quite a few years now, I've had this secret ambition to develop a comprehensive model of organizations in their respective environments (nothing grandiose—just all human organizations in all conceivable contexts). My academic colleagues tend to humor me when they hear me admit that my goal in life is to knock off old Chester Barnard, the vice president of New Jersey Bell in the 1930s who wrote a brilliant (if mostly impenetrable) analysis of organizations. I still admit to this lofty ambition, but I now admit that I have a problem. All the math works against me.

Let's say I want to put on a tie in the morning, and my choice of a tie depends on the opinions of ten people besides myself— eleven in all. (Let's say I live in an investment bankers' commune.) But let's also assume that each person's opinion depends on his or her perception of the other ten people's opinions, and we have to sort all this out before I can choose my tie. Fortunately, my commune has its own Cray supercomputer, and we type in the data and fire it up. How long before I get my answer? Believe it or not, about 11,000 years.*

Of course, we don't select our ties that way. But let's push a little harder on this notion of developing an all-embracing, dependably predictive model of reality—one that tells it not only like it was, but also like it will be.[1] (This would be a good thing. Assuming that you have a good intellectual properties lawyer, you'd be in a position to retire early.) Let's suppose, too, that you decide to consult a logician—that is, an expert in logic—to get the project off on the right foot. What you're likely to hear from the logician is that your model will be useless unless it is internally consistent. In other words, if your model is going to stand up

---

*Actually, this assumes that the algorithms of choice are linear functions and can be solved by evaluating an eleventh-order tensor matrix. But we're among friends.

under the heavy burdens you're going to place on it—comprehending and predicting reality—its basic building blocks can't conflict with each other. You'd better not be able to derive both "*A*" and "not *A*" from the same model.*

OK. You've finished with the logician. Now you go out into the desert and slave away for however long it takes, and finally you come dragging back in with a really high-flying model of the universe ("How It Works," or something catchy like that). It consists of exactly 100 basic premises, which are complex (but not hopelessly so) and internally consistent. Because you're market oriented, you've been clever enough to generate these premises both as prose statements and as mathematical equations, so that all sorts of people can benefit from your work.

Your model goes out in the world and begins to receive widespread acclaim as a work of true genius. Software companies and financial services types start tracking you down at your desert retreat. But soon one little hitch arises. The consensus from your admiring public is that you're only about 90 percent of the way there. A delegation arrives at your doorstep with a simple request. If you'll integrate just 10 more premises into your model and make *that* work, then all of humanity will acknowledge your greatness.

Well, we're back to the same hitch I mentioned above. I've resolved not to bury my readers in the mathematics that underlie my arguments in this book, and I'll stick to that resolve. But the fact is, to cross-check each of the 10 new premises with each other and with the existing 100 (individually and collectively) would be a task of almost incalculable enormity. Are you sitting down? It would require all the computational power of my commune's supercomputer—running continuously

---

* Bertrand Russell enjoyed demonstrating that you could prove almost anything using a non-self-consistent model. For example, he proposed the following premise: $1 + 1 = 1$. He then posed a challenge: Prove I am the pope. Easy: I am 1, the pope is 1, but $1 + 1 = 1$, so I am the pope.

since the Big Bang, through the present, and way on up to some uncertain date in the distant future.*

Perhaps you've already backed up one step and said, "Hey—if just adding 10 to an existing 100 is a hopeless task, then developing the first 100 is probably equally hopeless." Correct. The point is, perfect and all-encompassing systems are, for all practical purposes, an impossibility. The work of Hilbert, Gödel, and others—as well as more recent discoveries in chaos theory and nonlinear mathematics—demonstrates convincingly that a comprehensive, self-consistent theory of how things work cannot be developed.[2] Let me say that again: Mathematically and logically speaking, there's simply no such thing. Even if a fairly good model of reality *could* exist, it would be so complicated that it would be virtually useless. You couldn't run the necessary calculations.

Remember the general's map that we considered in Chapter 4? The only way for the general's map (on which the private's fate partially depends) to be absolutely reliable is for it to have a one-to-one relationship to reality. In other words, it has to be as big as the great outdoors—and therefore not very helpful. There are way too many data, calculation becomes impossible, and the map isn't even portable. And if you can't use your tool, it's not a tool.

■ Still More Trouble

Other factors make prediction tough, too. For example, the issue of *separability* comes into play in almost every realistic projection into the future. Ask me if I like butter. Umm, well, yes and no. I enjoy a little butter on my toast in the

---

*Honest. Think of it as $2^M - 1$, in which M equals the number of already existing axioms.

morning, yes. In fact, that's a real treat, and one that I've been denying myself since the early days of the cholesterol controversies. (Eggs, butter, and bacon: all old and disgraced friends.) But if you plunk down a big slab of butter on a hot plate and offer me a knife, a fork, and a straw, I'm going to be less enthusiastic. It turns out that my taste for butter is nonseparable from the contexts in which I find the butter, so my answer to the question "Do you like butter?" is necessarily contingent. And, in most cases of meaningful projection into the future, there are many, many such contingencies.[3]

Yet another complicating factor is *commensurability;* in other words, seeking apples-to-apples equivalencies. Ask me which I like best: Brahms, the Beatles, or swordfish. Again, I have to stop and think about it. What's the basis for such a choice? How do I say, "This one is better than that one," and under what circumstances? I can't. They're noncommensurate. OK, I like Brahms better than the Beatles, and swordfish better than hamburgers. But, to tell the truth, there's nothing I like better than eating a big burger with *Rubber Soul* playing in the background. Pure bliss! But what logical conclusion did I just reach? I can choose Brahms over the Beatles, the Beatles over swordfish, and swordfish over Brahms—maybe because I would consider it gauche to choose the Beatles over Brahms, but I don't impute any symbolic meaning to choosing swordfish over Brahms.

Those economists I made fun of earlier in this chapter would argue that most things can and should be assessed along a single measure of utility. In other words, like the scientists also described above, they want to build a relatively simple model and use only one standard to assess the usefulness or desirability of a certain outcome. Utility *über alles!* But what about Brahms, the Beatles, and swordfish? If I'm starving, to hell with the music—I'll take the swordfish (broiled in butter, please). But, if I've just eaten grandly and now want to settle back and enjoy feeling satiated, it will probably be Brahms. If I want to drive down the coast highway with the top down, pretending to be young again, it will probably be the Beatles.

Again, as I will say continually in this book, the point is that we need to *act*. These rather homely examples are intended to demonstrate how difficult it is to make the choices that precede action, when we can have only partial knowledge of the future consequences of our actions. To paraphrase what Sam Goldwyn said, making reasonable assessments of likely future consequences is *tough*.

What's the likely effect of a "little pollution"? For that matter, what's the effect of a megadose of toxic chemicals? Love Canal was considered a death zone for years, and now houses are again being built on the site. (*I'm* not buying one, by the way.) How confident are we in our current predictions about life on the canal, 20, 30, or 80 years down the road? I recall the definitive predictions made in 1983 about the number of PCs that would exist by 1986—a modest three-year leap into the future. The prediction? 6 million. The reality, by 1986? 2 million. In other words, off by more than a little. And when the turf gets bigger, the prediction can get outlandishly far off.

Let's get down to the personal level again. Think about making a commitment to a specific job and workplace. How in the world do you make *that* decision? How do you get a bead on what life will really be like, in this more or less unknown setting? What will the job be like in 20 years, and what will you think of it at that point? Suppose you get fired from this job, whatever it turns out to be 20 years from now? How will other prospective employers value your experience? Now think again about all those failed marriages and businesses. And yet you still have to decide. *Act!*

■ Town Meeting and Beyond

I live in New England, where we practice one of the purest forms of democracy in the world: the town meeting.* As I've become more interested in notions of predictability and projectability, town meeting has become a more and more fascinating phenomenon. Can we predict the outcome of a town meeting?

The answer, again, is "Not very well. Wish we could, but most of the time we can't." Prediction is very difficult, especially when people are involved. If you ever *did* perfect "How It Works"—the model of the universe described above—town meeting would be an excellent venue for field-testing that model. Most likely, your debugging phase would begin almost immediately.

There are good town meetings and bad town meetings. I suspect that, on the whole, they've gotten worse over the past two centuries, for reasons that should become clear in a moment. A bad town meeting (like many today) is transactionally oriented. It consists of hundreds of people coming together with more or less self-defined and isolated agendas, trusting each other only minimally, if at all. It's a little like an Arabian bazaar without the fine craftsmanship. Coalitions rise and fall. Causes (even noneconomic causes) tend to be judged along straight economic lines. People vote their pocketbooks. Each new town meeting represents a new start and a clean slate.

But town meeting was invented in a very different cultural context. Back then, the colonists of Massachusetts needed to

*Town meeting—the process whereby New Englanders get together and do the town's official business—was an annual affair until Massachusetts's finances became unpredictable in the 1980s; now town meeting sometimes has to be called two or more times a year.

watch each other's backs. They needed their neighbors for barn raisings, for the creation of shared resources, and for contending with a regular diet of emergencies. They needed their neighbors' kids to marry their own kids, and ultimately they needed a neighbor (if not a kid) to bury them. Town meeting, in that long-ago era, was essentially a validation of the interconnectedness of things. It was a certification of mutual dependence. The Golden Rule prevailed, in part because everyone knew that whoever they *didn't* treat as well as they treated themselves would be around for another 10 or 20 years to get even. Life was hard, winters were long, and King George was erratic—but life was *predictable*. Your neighbors stuck around and did what they were expected to do. So did you.

Suppose you were able to take a straw poll at one of those eighteenth-century town meetings. Imagine that you asked the membership to rank the following three concepts in order of importance: freedom, justice, order. Which is most important, and which is likely to lead to which? Chances are they'd rank them in that sequence—freedom, justice, order—on the assumption that out of freedom comes justice, and out of justice grows order.

Now, take the same straw poll outside a mosque in Qum, Iran. Think you'll get the same sequence? Not likely. The collective frames of reference are utterly different, and unless you know the cultural context, you'd better not hang out a shingle as a predictor.

You can run the same experiment in a business context. What's most important: customer satisfaction, quality of work life, or shareholder wealth? Will a factory worker put shareholder wealth at the top of his list? Will an uninvolved shareholder worry much about the quality of work life? Again, not likely. And, without consensus, the business may be in real trouble. As you'll see in later chapters, this is the central job of the manager: to create deep agreement on priorities and to build consensus that the predicted future *here* is better than alternative futures elsewhere.*

So—you might well ask—after lots of meandering, this is where this chapter intends to wind up? At a town meeting in Massachusetts in the 1760s? in Qum?

Not quite. Let me stop at a fine French restaurant first. I'm new to this *monde rafiné*. I'm here mainly because I want to impress my date. I sit down, take one look at the menu, and realize that I'm in deep trouble. My high school French deserts me. (The fact that the prices are out of sight adds a little more pressure.) I don't want to make an absurd choice, and I don't want to end up ordering sweetbreads by accident. The waiter, who seems more sympathetic than many guys in places like this, politely suggests that we try the "chef's menu," which, he explains, is a preselected sequence of dishes from soup to nuts. "Good idea, Pierre," I say smoothly, reading off his name tag. "I generally agree with the chef's choices on Thursdays." Face is saved.

Now, let's admit that, at least from one perspective, I've just chickened out in a big way. It would have been much more exciting to order blind and see what arrived on the table. On the other hand, the chef has taken the time to design a progression of tastes, smells, and sights that work together extremely well. There is almost no chance that we could have eaten better by throwing darts at the menu or depending on my childlike French to pull us through.

Organizations are like chef's menus. We join organizations so that we don't have to make a whole bunch of tiny, mundane, and uninteresting decisions, every single day of our lives, frequently in someone else's language. And, at the same time, organizations tell us what we *should* like. They give us values. They

---

*Some managers unwisely delegate this responsibility for consensus building to consultants. I heard an interesting description recently about the role that a McKinseyite plays in the corporate setting: "changing how 50-year-old white men see the world."

serve as a vehicle for refining or distilling tastes, especially in cases where corporate culture is vigorous. They enhance our predictive powers and minimize the atomistic elements of our lives.

And good organizations are like good town meetings. We join organizations to engage in coordinated actions, to move society forward, and to make our predicted futures come true. We build on a collective sense of what's important in order to invest in the future.

Prediction is extremely difficult, especially when it counts. But in the next and subsequent chapters, I suggest ways we can enhance our predictive powers—individually and collectively.

chapter seven

Acting to Make the Future Happen

*Let us be such as help the
life of the future.*
Zoroaster

So what have we learned so far? We've learned that prediction
is at least two things: important and hard.

Why important? Because we have to *act*. Uh oh! That gnarly
looking horned rhino is tossing its head and pawing the ground,
looking straight at me! Quick: either *run* or *charge*!

Why hard? All kinds of reasons, starting within each of us,
looking out of our own windows on life. What future do I want,
and what's the best way to get there?

Even before we crawl out of our individual windows, projectability rears its ugly head. How will I feel about this future,
if and when I get it? This raises issues like separability and commensurability—butter and the Beatles, respectively, as explained in
the last chapter.

Then we get other people involved, with all of their dark
currents and their *own* projectability issues, and the mind starts
to boggle. So let's see now. How am I going to feel about how
you're going to feel about how I'm going to feel—and how should
that affect my actions in the present?

But let's back up one step, before all those other oddballs enter the picture. In most cases, we as individuals need to pick, structure, and sequence our actions in order to (1) make good predictions and (2) make our predicted futures come about. That's what this chapter is about.

Of course, there are specialized circumstances in which almost any systematic course of action is as good as the next. When you're totally lost in the forest, for example, it's not a bad idea to keep walking in a straight line—toward the sunrise, a distant mountain range, or whatever. Primitive hunters used to throw bones on the campfire to pick a path for the next day's hunt. The Plains Indians followed the smoke from their campfires to locate the buffalo. In the language of the contemporary discipline of operations research, these hunting techniques were randomized search strategies. And, because they were aimed at predicting the random wanderings of animals, *systematic* randomness was the best tool available for the task at hand.

But most of the time we need better tools than straight lines and systematic randomness. In this chapter, we'll revisit three of the activities we've already introduced in previous chapters and start to think of them in a new way. These three activities are *observation*, *calculation*, and *action*. This time, though, we'll be asking some specific, important questions: How can we best look into the future? How can we make a predicted future come about—capitalizing on the inevitable, while avoiding the unacceptable? How can we *act*?

We'll also look at the specific tools that can be used in each predictive phase (observation, calculation, and action). The three tools that we call upon most often in the prediction game are *simplification*, *categorization*, and *generalization*. We'll look at each of these three tools as we go through the sequenced activities of prediction.

Beginning on the level of the individual, we'll begin to turn predictive liabilities (such as the need to calculate lots of stuff in a hurry) into predictive assets. This will set us up, in later chapters, to tease out prediction in the context of human organizations and the critical predictive opportunities and responsibilities of the manager.

■ Observation for Prediction

In order to make better predictions, we first observe. In other words, we try to figure out what's going *on* out there.[1] Real-time observation can be scary and dangerous—horned rhino!—but assuming you survive it, you've got some nice data to draw upon (sometimes called "experience") as you take the next steps toward effective prediction. Good observation at the right power of magnification is the first key prerequisite to the art of prediction. And, within the broader activity of observation, we use the three tools just introduced: simplification, categorization, and generalization.

Simplification.   The point here is to examine the key variables, identify those that are most relevant to the future, and begin the kinds of measurements that would help inform the observation process. Take the basic decisions that you have to make in setting up a personal investment program. Will you invest in stocks, bonds, or both? Are you going to stick with domestic issues or go global? Will you invest only in listed securities, or will you do private issues? The answers limit or expand your need for observation.

Categorization.   Here we have to start putting things in the right boxes. First, in the case of a charging beast, what are we observing—a rhino or a rabbit?[2] (Cuddly? Horns?) Second, how fine a distinction do we have to make in this particular case? If I'm going to play tennis on Saturday, for example, I put a certain level of care into choosing my partner. But, if I'm going to get married on Saturday, it's a different story. I apply a higher standard of care and make lots more distinctions. Let's say my dining room has splendid red walls, and I've decided that I want all the accessories in my life to match that red. I buy my new red shoes without even consulting the paint swatch that I carry around in my wallet. But I slow down quite a bit when it comes to buying that crimson 12-by-14 oriental rug.

My grandfather used to tell a story about a farmer who signed on a hired hand named Jake. The farmer told Jake to plow the north forty, roughly calculating that this task would take at least a day. But, before lunch, Jake turned up barely winded, looking for his next job. The farmer then told Jake to muck out the barn—a half-day job that Jake completed in an hour. For the next two days, it was the same story: everything that Jake took on, he completed in record time. Then the farmer told Jake to go down into the root cellar and separate the good potatoes from the rotten ones.

The farmer figured that a normal person could finish the job in an hour, and that the thoroughly amazing Jake would be done in ten minutes. But, lo and behold, four hours went by, and Jake was still down in the cellar. The farmer went down to investigate. He found Jake sitting on the floor, staring at a potato in his hand, with a forlorn look on his face.

"What's the matter with you, Jake?" the farmer asked. "You all worked out?"

"No, sir," Jake replied sadly. "I love working. Hell, I could work all night. It's these damned *decisions* I hate!"[3]

Business is nothing *but* decisions. Being in business means we have to *act*—which means that we want to minimize the amount of time we spend categorizing things. At the same time, we don't want to settle on an easy categorization today that will limit our options tomorrow. Question: Is company Z, huddled along-side us in the supply chain, a competitor or an ally?[4] Similarly, is that longtime contractor of ours—the one we think we'd like to build into our future plans—an insider or an outsider?

Generalization. Simplification leads to categorization, which leads in turn to generalization: *When I'm in this kind of situation, what do I look for? What are the telltale signs?*[5]

The next time you're in a car dealership, adopt your best fly-on-the-wall stance and watch how the salesforce handles the incoming prospects. A good salesperson knows instinctively who's a looker and who's a buyer. But this "instinct" is, in fact, evidence of years of training in simplification and categorization, which eventually leads to highly effective generalizations.

Managers develop their own kinds of generalizations. For example, when considering a job applicant, what we're really asking is, "Is this person one of *our kind*? Will she 'fit' on our team?"

There's a story about a former OSS agent who went looking for a job in the private sector. He settled on a likely company and obtained a job application. The first tough question on the application read as follows: "What skills did you gain in your previous place of employment?" The former spook didn't know what to write, so he simply told the truth: "I learned to lie, cheat, steal, and kill."

The agent got the job and began making his way up the corporate ladder. Two decades later, he finally was named CEO. This meant that he gained access to all employee records. One day, he peeked into his own file. There, on his original application for work, he saw his "lie, cheat, steal, and kill" answer circled in red, with the handwritten notation "Hire! One of us!"

Over time, we learn which sources of data are reasonably accurate, and we build that wisdom into our generalizations. If and when we're proven wrong—for example, when we spend a lot of time on the showroom floor with a hot prospect who turns out to be a looker—we need to recalibrate our observational lenses. We need to go back over our simplifications and categorizations, search out our error, and fix our generalizations.[6]

■ Calculation for Prediction

First we observe; then, based on that observation, we calculate. The calculation phase involves the same three tools that we've just examined: simplification, categorization, and generalization. We'll look at these tools again in a minute, but first some general observations about calculation.

First, what is *calculation*? One sense of the word is "to arrive at a solution through mathematical processes." This is good employment for those of us who are mathematicians, but it rarely pertains to real-life problems. It's the other sense of the word we're interested in here: "to reckon by exercise of practical judgment," as Webster puts it.

Why is calculation important? Well, for one thing, it helps us test our observations. Let's face it. We humans are inclined to make sweeping generalizations that are breathtakingly dumb. "If someone has a firm handshake and looks me in the eye," we say, "boy, I can *trust* that guy!" This is a guiding principle that serves until the first charlatan overhears us talking about it and decides to use it against us. Calculation protects us from ourselves—and, by extension, from charlatans.

But calculation serves another purpose that is critical to prediction: it pushes us into the future. Once we know what we're looking at—or at least once we *think* we know—we have to ask and answer the two key prediction questions: (1) what's going to happen? and (2) if I do something, what can I *make* happen?

A third observation about calculation, included especially for the benefit of those math-phobic readers who might otherwise be inclined to zip right by this section. Maybe the concepts of "comfort" and "calculation" will never go together for anyone other than us math geeks. Maybe for normal people, contemplating the act of calculation never quite feels warm and cuddly. But it should—because you already do it all the time.

Think about it. No matter who you are, if you're human, you're an amazing calculator. Humans calculate with a relaxed, out-of-my-back-pocket kind of genius that computer designers can only lust after.[7] How does the left fielder know to break for the warning track directly behind him a millisecond after the ball has made contact with the bat? How does he combine some newly derived data—instantaneous interpretation of the speed of the swing with the sound of the ball hitting the bat—with the stuff he already had in his head before the first inning, like this particular batter's stats, the wind speed, the wetness of the air, the proclivities of this pitcher, the friendliness of this park to left-field home runs, and so on? Scientists tell us that this is an inconceivably complicated calculation.

And it's only an extreme and speeded-up example of the kinds of things that you and I do every day. We gather and simplify data. We analyze our data and make calculations based on them. Then we make our predictions and *act*—all in one or two blinks of an eye. Calculation problem: *Should I take an umbrella to work? Well, what did the Weather Channel say last night? What does the barometer tell me? How bad do those clouds look? Will I care if these clothes get wet?* If you listen carefully, you can almost hear the snap, crackle, pop of those synapses firing.

Or, to take a real-life calculation problem that presented itself quite a few times during a recent northeastern winter: *If there really is a blizzard coming at rush hour, should I leave early? Well, my pal Joe over in the next cubicle seems to be a clever guy, and I know he's got a 40-mile commute into the teeth of the alleged storm; what's he planning to do? How bad do those clouds look? What's that meteorologist on Channel 4 saying?* (He's pretty good.) *And how good is my car in the snow? Uh oh. Did I ever get those snow tires mounted? If everybody bolts from the city at 4:00 P.M., am I better off waiting until 7:00? If I bet wrong and get stuck in the city, what will the good and bad consequences be? Can I get a hotel room? How bad do those clouds look* now?

This is what you and I do when we make decisions like these, right? But we don't usually wrap our conscious minds around it, except maybe intermittently. Like the magical left fielder, we do it in a flash, or maybe in a couple of flashes. We get a "gut instinct" or "go with our hunch"—*Go home now!* That's not what's really happening, though. What's really happening is that we're gathering, sifting, analyzing, and—yes—*calculating*, all toward the goal of making the right decision. Just because we'd have a hard time pointing to the moment of calculation (and recalculation) doesn't mean that it wasn't there in the mix, playing an important role. Back to our three tools: simplification, categorization, and generalization.

Simplification.   In earlier chapters, I tried to convey how quickly things can spin out of control when you start calculating with multiple variables. I used the example of choosing a necktie. The remedy for this problem is obvious: take variables away. I have a separate rack of ties in my closet that holds all the ties that I can't even *consider* wearing on a business occasion.[8]

Suppose you want to build yourself an elaborate, sprawling mansion. One way to do so would be to design and build it all at once, which would require an immense amount of calcula- tion up front. How will all these various stresses interact? If we change this particular roofline, how will that seemingly simple change reverberate through the whole structure? The other ap- proach would be to start out by designing and building a small piece at the heart of your personal San Simeon, and then growing outward, organically, over time. Your architect would die a thousand deaths using this approach, but you'd sure simplify the calculation process. Almost immediately, you'd be looking at a particular beam and asking, "How much load will *this* guy have to support?" Everything would have to be overbuilt, absent a plan for the future.

"Staging" (or phasing) the problem, in other words, helps make it manageable, if costly. The analogous situations in business are obvious. It's the rare company that has to spring into existence full-blown overnight.* Most businesses have the luxury of building incrementally (and therefore calculating on a manageable scale). You want to conquer the world, but you start by making your first sale. You calculate individual steps intensively, but you don't calculate all consequences of all steps out into eternity.[9]

Categorization. In the calculation phase, as in the observation phase, there's a great advantage in categorizing things effectively. The question to ask yourself is: *What's the* type *of problem I'm dealing with here?* The answer to this question allows you, in turn, to figure out which rules of thumb apply in this particular calculation problem.[10]

For example, is this a people problem, a strategy problem, or a marketing problem? Is this a debt problem or an equity problem? It helps to push problems into specific boxes, in order to make the right calculation at the right level of specificity.[11] Muscles and computers are binary (that is, either on or off) for good reasons— you can pile up a lot of complexities and accomplish highly sophisticated tasks provided you use simple enough building blocks.

Again, as in observation, we calculate to a useful depth, but no farther. Careful refinements may be needed in the case of close calls, but not otherwise. You're almost always better off turning a so-so calculation into a great one (through *action*, as described

---

*Federal Express was one such exception—half a system isn't much better than no system—and this created large challenges of calculation for all the involved players in that startup. Many rounds of venture financing later, FedEx is a success—but the only winners among the investors were those who stayed to the end.

below) than arriving at a brilliant calculation a few years too late.

Generalization.   Calculation is much aided by effective generalization. We generalize in several ways. First, of course, we draw on our own experience. *Should I close the skylights in the attic before I go out for the day?* Calculation: *Well, past experience tells me that, whenever the air gets this thick and still and oppressive early on a summer morning, something weathery is going to happen.*

The second way we generalize is from other people's experience. This is where rules of thumb (or, in the business world, standard operating procedures) come into the picture. They are really the accumulated folk wisdom of the ages, distilled into more or less useful little nuggets: *When ice is as thick as your thumb, you can walk on it.* It's not just my personal experience that I draw upon as I decide whether or not to venture out onto the pond; this is something that my grandmother told me as I sat at her knee.

In many cases, rules of thumb are barely distinguishable from folklore. As such, they aren't always dependable or even comprehensible. I mean, which dimension of my thumb am I talking about—sideways or lengthwise? And what if the ice is as thick as your skinny thumb, but not my fat thumb? How come I fell through and you didn't?

It's questions like these that ultimately lead to science, which is the third way we generalize. Scientists generalize, either brilliantly or not so brilliantly, as they observe and calculate. They hazard the guess that this particular variable isn't so important, under these specific circumstances; then they test the guess. If it turns out that their guess was right, science moves forward. If not, they regroup.

Science quickly gets too opaque for practical use by us commoners. But we're nothing if not resourceful, us commoners. As soon as the relevant science gets too complicated for us to *act* upon, we again invent shortcuts for decision making—a kind of rule of scientific thumb. Visualize one of those satellite pictures on the evening news that helps us understand the weather coming at us. (You see that huge mass of clouds sliding up the coast? Take the umbrella!) Or picture those radar images showing a storm's relative intensity across a region. When that bright orange patch heads toward my house, I think about putting the car in the garage.

We should take a few minutes at this point to wrestle with some antique terminology. *Deduction* and *induction* are the two kinds of logical toolkits that we humans normally strap on. They help us select what we're going to observe and how we're going to categorize our observations.

Deductive reasoning (as you may recall from your high school logic class) starts with a few basic principles and builds out toward reality. Euclid's theorems are a case in point: parallel lines never converge except at infinity, the angles of a triangle always add up to 180 degrees, and so on.

So here's how a deductionist's mind works: *Parallel lines never converge except at infinity. I'm standing between two railroad tracks. They are parallel. Therefore, these railroad tracks will not converge.*

This is the foundation for much of mathematics and science. Take the chemistry model, for example. Chemistry is a set of principles from which the chemist can deduce probable results from proposed actions: if this, then that. According to classical chemical theory, each element has a certain number of protons and neutrons in set configurations, with electrons whizzing around them in stable orbits like those mechanical rabbits out at the dog track. Now, it turns out that absolutely none of this is true.* But so what? For the past half-century or more, we've been able to do some really great stuff with chemistry, because

---

*Ask a molecular physicist to explain, in English, Schrödinger's explanation of electrons as "probability waves."

we've been able to observe, simplify, and predict with confidence how things would combine, which elements would be active and inactive, how the active ones would interact, and so on. It's "simple repeatable": when you do X in Y particular way, Z happens every time. What could be better!

There are some deductively based systems outside of the realm of science and mathematics. Religion is one. FASB (the Financial Accounting Standards Board) is another. The army is a third: when you run across a guy with more stripes on his shoulder than you have on yours, you salute. Period. And, like chemistry and FASB, it works as long as it works—and then it doesn't.

The great, huge problem arises when we try to dress up Deduction—an elegant but essentially mechanical creature—and take her to the ball. What do I mean? Pick up any ten management books written in the last two decades, and what you will find in all of them (unless one is Max DePree's inductive little book about leadership) is deduction run amok. I distill this phenomenon in a bogus book title: *In Search of the One-Minute Megatrend.* "If you treat people as type Y, they will be good," these books proclaim, "whereas if you treat them as type X, they will be bad." Or "All the world is divided into five forces. Therefore, . . ."

Therefore, *nothing.* Decision rules that cut short the processes of observation, calculation, and action lead the manager down the garden path—and give him or her great comfort all the while. What's worse, they make *productive* calculation much more time consuming. If you ever run into a neodeductionist, put him to the sword. Ask him to lay out a deductive system that would enable the average Joe to distinguish between a fully clothed man and a fully clothed woman.

For most of us, in other words, life isn't a whole lot like chemistry or the army. Life usually involves a blend of both deductive and inductive reasoning.

Inductive reasoning is what your doctor does when he's trying to figure out what's ailing you. It's what your mechanic does when he keeps swapping out one expensive part after another to cure your car of that annoying habit of stalling unexpectedly. It's what we all do: we experience things, we develop a rough model based on that experience, we *act*, and we revise accordingly—in other words, action on the fly, in real time, under the gun.

Of course, relying exclusively on inductive reasoning harbors its own pitfalls—particularly if you haven't built in the necessary time to accommodate revision. Look, for example, to Bertrand Russell's inductionist turkey: every morning he happily rushes out of the tall grass when he sees the farmer, because he knows that means food. That inductive reasoning works very well for him, until one fateful Thursday morning in late November.

Sherlock Holmes, celebrated logician, was a class act because he was highly skilled at both induction *and* deduction. "Dogs bark at intruders," he told the always-obtuse Watson, "unless the intruder is a friend." An inductive generalization. "This dog didn't bark. Therefore, the intruder was a friend." Elementary deduction. Meanwhile, of course, Holmes was scrambling to turn up all the clues he could to make his dazzling leaps of logic—an ongoing inductive hunt, to make possible future deductive brilliance.*

Most of the examples you and I could cite from our own experience have both inductive and deductive elements. It's useful to think of our worlds as inductive seas punctuated by deductive islands—a logical crazy quilt. Obviously, we don't begin every day by running inductive experiments on how to get the catfood can open. (Deductive logic sequence at 5:34 A.M.: *All catfood cans are openable by means of a can opener. Therefore, this catfood can is openable by means of a can opener.*) We don't reinvent the physics or mechanics of the laws of driving. (Deduc-

---

*Logically, you *can* say, "All dogs are animals; this is a dog; therefore, this is an animal." But there's no logical basis for saying, "It has rained for 1,000 days straight; therefore, it will rain tomorrow." But hey—bring your umbrella anyway.

tive logic sequence at 6:34 A.M.: *Cars can move forward when the light turns green. That light has just turned green. Therefore, I can go.*) We more or less consciously create little subzones of our worlds in which deduction is a functional tool for prediction. Meanwhile, we're "inducing" like crazy—*Cat still alive? Traffic lights working? Wipers needed to see the traffic lights?*

We observe, and then we calculate. Based on the phenomena we're seeing out there, how can we think correctly about them? Can we get away with tossing this particular one into a deductive subzone? Or do we have to start from scratch? If we're starting from scratch, what does this odd new thing most remind us of?

Even though you're already a great calculator, I would be remiss if I didn't tip my hat to some of the calculation tools that have been invented over the centuries. Ben Franklin had an interesting habit when it came time to make a decision of any consequence. He used to draw up gigantic lists of all the pros and cons inherent in a given problem, and then go with whichever list was longer. I don't advocate this approach for everyday life as we head into the twenty-first century—it's too slow, for one thing, and I suspect that, the farther you got down one of Ben's lists, the more you'd start to see Ben's preexisting biases.

Were it not for the advent of computers, we could safely ignore the contributions of George Boole, a long-dead English mathematician and logician. In his *Analysis of the Laws of Thought* (1858), Professor Boole argued that judgments are equations—a notion that whole squadrons of deep thinkers elaborated on in the early part of this century and that underlies a wide variety of tools that purport to help managers make decisions.*

---

*Boole is also in the ascendant because his eponymous "Boolean logic" underpins the search engines employed by the World Wide Web and other high-tech applications.

There's the notorious "decision tree," for one, which has in-
duced shudders in legions of undergraduate business majors.
This is a device for mapping all the possible eventualities that
lie ahead and assigning probabilities (and often values) to the
various branches on the tree. By the time you climb all the way
out on a given limb, you supposedly know what that endpoint is,
how likely it is to happen (predictability), and how you'll *value*
it (projectability).

The problem is, nobody actually *uses* this stuff. And I think
the reason is because it's almost impossible to construct a
decision tree without building in your own biases. It feels a bit
illicit—or at least phony. It's like Ben Franklin's unequal lists, but
sneakier. It's like the question my wife asked me back when she
was still my fiancée: "Do you want to get married in that ugly,
dark brown chapel down the street, or do you want to go someplace *nice*?" How well do you think the Dark Brown Chapel
Endpoint would have fared on her decision tree?*

Lots of other tools have come into being with the advent of
the computer, ranging from linear programming to dynamic
simulations. These can be useful for understanding the relative
importance of different variables under different circumstances.
Negotiators sometimes use simulations to get a better sense of
the other side's bargaining position. But again, the real-life
constraints on these tools tend to relegate them to the sidelines.
When decision makers render judgment on them, they tend
to say things like, "Well, not bad. Not bad at *all*—for a computer."

We human calculators have to get better reviews than that—
which means we have to earn them. This involves understanding
(as best we can) where our data have come from. It involves a
loose-but-tight, provisionally deductive approach to categorization: "I'll assume that Albanian software tools for navigating the

---

*Or, as my colleague Mihnea Moldoveanu asks pointedly, "Can you ask
yourself a fair question?"

World Wide Web are terminally uncompetitive—but only until one of them sets the world on fire." And it involves calculating in as precise and relevant a way as we can hit upon. What are the data that we can bring to bear on this question, without stretching too far? If we're absolutely buried in data, where can we cut off the stream of inputs with a reasonable degree of confidence and conclude that "enough's enough"? How can we surface the hidden biases that we might be bringing to this calculation? Who or what might be a good antidote to those biases?[12]

■ Action for Prediction

It may seem odd to include an action phase in our prediction-making process. Don't we predict first, and then act?

Well, yes and no. Action certainly follows prediction, since we've already agreed that effective prediction involves making things come out the right way (as opposed to crystal-ball gazing), and to do this, you've got to act. But action also precedes prediction, because it's the only way to test the models you've derived through observation and calculation. The results of action, when put through a succession of inductive and deductive screens, create better models for prediction.[13] And action brings about a different world, which then must be factored into the predictive process.

One of the great unwritten books of all time is *The History of Model Testing*, subtitled *Putting Your Money Where Your Mouth Is*. (I hereby place this idea in the public domain and hope that one of my readers will follow up on it.) In ancient Rome, when the construction crew finished up one of the arches over which the centurions' carts would rumble, the authorities routinely ordered the architect to stand underneath the arch when the bracing and scaffolding were being removed. A couple of millennia later, the U.S. Army adopted a policy of asking each of its parachute packers to take a random jump every now and then, using a chute that he personally had packed. And Howard Hughes didn't really cement his legend until he took his gigantic "Spruce Goose"—which gleeful skeptics had said couldn't possibly get off the ground—out for a spin, skimming along the wavetops near Long Beach. In each of these three cases, someone was expressing a large measure of confidence in his model of the world. In fact, he was predicting his *survival*—or at least his financial well-being—based on that model.

Lesser heroes in this pantheon are those who played what I call "You Bet Your Son." These include, for example, William Tell, who allegedly used Bill Junior as an apple stand in a crossbow exhibition; and Edward Jenner, who infected his son with swinepox to demonstrate the efficacy of vaccination.

Again, in the action phase, we pick up our same three tools: simplification, categorization, and calculation.

Simplification. How do we simplify our actions? Lots of ways. First, we push for "severability"—meaning that we cut all the unnecessary connections between our proposed action and the rest of the universe. For example, we limit the number of people who have to act in concert. We "localize" the action. We set limits on the steps inherent in the action. (Complex actions go wrong more often than simple ones.)[14]

We also speed up the time frame of the action. The longer you sit in the middle of an intersection, the more likely you are to get hit. So get out of that intersection sooner, rather than later.

Categorization. Simply put, we choose to act in some categories, and we choose not to act in others. I know my own skill set, and therefore I rarely volunteer to sing with the local opera or dance with the Boston Ballet.

As in the previous phases, of course, every action we take is subject to review. Even the action categories themselves are open to constant revision. Sometimes, we discover, formerly functional links between the observed and the categorized get unstuck, forcing us to scurry off in search of new categories.

Generalization.   Earlier, we talked about rules of thumb in service to calculation. They are even more important in the action phase. Raising a kid? *Spare the rod and spoil the child.* Hungry? *Eat breakfast like a king, lunch like a commoner, and dinner like a pauper.* Planning an outing? *Red sky at night, sailor's delight. Red sky in the morning, sailors take warning.*

We also talked earlier about classical chemistry, which combines a number of axioms into a systematic representation of something—in short, a *model.* And there's nothing we actor-predictors like better than a good model that allows us to take action.

Thanks to chemistry, you can, with great confidence, build a very expensive factory and chop up complex hydrocarbons into methane, butane, and all sorts of other smelly component parts, because the model is (as my academic colleagues would say) "robust" enough. It *works.*

On the other hand, no model fits every situation. Sometimes we make false analogies and set up big problems for ourselves in the process. Did you know that, when the first generation of applied nuclear scientists went to work at the Argonne National Labs at the University of Chicago in the 1930s, they placed a large bucket of sand next to their primitive reactor? It's true. And do you know why? What they were planning to do, if the chain reaction got out of control, was *dump the sand on the pile and put out the fire.* Just like you or me, putting out a grease fire in the kitchen. Except that the kitchen would have been a good piece of Chicago, and the sand wouldn't have worked.

But, hey, that's just a bigger goof than most of us make. You and I have done similarly odd things on a smaller scale, right? In human culture, for example, firm handshakes and unwavering looks in the eye are good things. In Dog Culture, firm handshakes may be OK, but an unwavering look in the eye may well be taken as an act of aggression, meaning *Bite me*.

Sometimes it's no one's fault when a model comes up short. Sometimes the world gangs up on one of our favorite models, such as Newtonian physics, exposing its weaknesses for all to see. This century's vast improvement in measurement tools has created all kinds of problems for model builders—and especially for scientists. Indescribably small errors in otherwise-elegant models became mountainous embarrassments. Science, wringing its hands, began to tell us that we could *never* develop an axiomatic system that was both complete and consistent.

Well, OK, but practically speaking, we've still got to build chemical plants. We still simplify, categorize, and generalize in the name of *action*, because we have no other choice.

■ Ode to Uncle Lou

We observe and calculate, trying to figure out a chaotic world. But that's only an intermediate goal. Our real goal, as you've read more than once in these pages, is to bring about the world we want to inhabit in the future. (One thing is certain about today: by lunchtime, I'm going to be hungry. Where's the food going to come from?) So observation and calculation move us in the right direction, especially if we use the right tools. Then comes action.

Let's run through a real-life example. I need a watch. You've found out about this, and you've offered me a real good deal on your watch. Should I buy it? Or should I look elsewhere?

Well, how well do I know you? Aristotle (father of deductive reasoning) would posit that, if you're my blood brother, you probably won't stick it to me over a watch. So, fine: I buy. But life isn't usually so cut and dried. Suppose you're a more or less unknown quantity to me. Now I have to ask myself whether you'll fork over the watch when I give you my money. (Why are you so insistent on my coming along, bringing cash, and making the swap in a particular dark alley at midnight?) But I have a pretty good sense of how to sharpen my predictive powers: through observation. First, I check the wanted posters in the local post office. Then I keep an eye on you until someone *else* ventures down that alley, and see what happens to them. The body count either mounts or it doesn't.

But suppose I want to enhance my observational powers further. The post office is closed for the long weekend, you don't sell your watch very often, and I can't wait around forever. At this point, maybe I should consider alternatives for which observation and calculation come more easily.

For example, do I really have to buy *your* watch? Why couldn't I just go downtown, find that guy with the pushcart full of watches, and keep an eye on him? He talks fast, but he sells lots of watches. And, if I remember right, he has some sort of license from the city. I might not get as good a deal from him, but—assuming he doesn't fail the test of my covert scrutiny—I'll certainly wind up with a watch of some sort. And if the watch quits working after three days, maybe I can complain to the city about peddler number 348 and get some sort of adjustment.

And then, of course, there's always my friend's Uncle Lou, who owns the fusty little jewelry store in one of those pricey suburbs west of Boston. He caters to the carriage trade, and his store may be the only place in the world where you actually have to pay full freight for a Rolex. You can almost feel your predictive powers bursting into full flower when you walk in his door. (In fact, absent an armed robbery or a typhoon, you could script the whole transaction in advance.) You will pay too much, but the watch will be genuine and will work as advertised, and he'll change your battery free of charge forever.

Identifying these three different alternatives—dark alleys, pushcarts, and Uncle Lou—forces me to clarify my own perspective on the proposed deal. What, exactly, am I looking for? Where can I get the most observationally derived experience for decision making? Which standard operating procedure (categorization) will give me enough data points to calculate with some confidence? Conversely, how much uncertainty can I stand in the name of a bargain? How will I feel about each outcome, and why? What am I *really* looking for?

This, of course, is only the individual perspective. This is only one middle-aged guy buying a watch. Prediction gets much more complicated when more than one person is involved—a topic I'll deal with in more depth in the later chapters of this book. For the time being, though, let's just recognize that, as soon as *you* get involved in the prediction game (rather than just me alone), we have to engage in a joint definition of terms. This means making sure that there's enough common ground (of terminology, skills, abilities, and perspectives) to permit such a process. It doesn't make a whole lot of sense to tell a color-blind person to stop at the red light—unless, of course, they've already learned the convention that red is always on top and that, when you say "red," you mean "top." (By the way, stay out of those intersections with the horizontally mounted lights, since they're a little less predictable.) In order to have effective prediction, in other words, you have to have a good handle on the conventions whereby antecedent, action, and consequence can be represented and understood by all parties. But more on this later.

■ Taking Action—and Surviving It

So what?

This is what a real-world predictor (such as yourself) always asks, sooner or later. "Sure sounds good to me, Howard, but we can't spend all our time observing and calculating."

Exactly. Taking action is where it's at. We take all the steps outlined above in order to take *effective* action. Acting effectively (an outgrowth of observing and calculating effectively) is the only reason to wrestle with this book. Suppose you observed the migration patterns of every animal in the world and used that information to calculate where a tasty one was likely to be found at a given point in time. Meanwhile, you were becoming the foremost authority on the physics of spear throwing.

All good and useful preparation for lunch. But, if you don't ever get around to actually chucking the spear, you go hungry. So what we want to do is minimize the amount of time that we spend on pre-action steps and maximize the time for action. The sooner we start trying to impale lunch, the greater our chances of getting lucky. And we might even have time to change our tactics, choice of weapon, or hunting habits, based on what we learn out there in the field.

More than that, if we play the game right, taking action is *fun*. You don't develop predictive expertise just to put it all up on the shelf. You observe, simplify, analyze, and calculate in order to get really good at something—and then to *do* it. This is how we steer toward our chosen futures. And, if you weren't somehow drawn to the drama of business and the marketplace—making something, selling something—you probably wouldn't be reading this book.

Taking effective action means playing to your strengths. It means picking, practicing, specializing in, and playing your own game.

Part of this is knowing the overall odds for and against breaking into the game you're interested in. The movie *Hoop Dreams*—which was denied the Oscar for Best Documentary on a technicality—tracked the high school and college careers of two black kids from Chicago, both of whom firmly believed that, if they honed their skills, they could someday join the ranks of the National Basketball Association. No one in their universe had any incentive to tell them the truth—that only a handful of young players breaks into the NBA each year, and that very few of these ever achieve stardom.

Another part is knowing *your* odds. If you're five foot nine and fat, should you be aiming for the NBA or an MBA?

Another piece of it is understanding how the game is changing. I have a friend who spent years becoming an ophthalmologist, specializing in laser-based microsurgery—only to find that ophthalmology and most of medicine's other "ologies" are increasingly unwelcome in the pinched landscape of the HMO and managed care.

Another piece is knowing when to take action by leaping in with both feet, and thereby getting in the game first. As they say, it's a whole lot easier to roll things down the hill than to throw them up the hill.

And a final piece of taking action is knowing when *not* to take action. The people who are most likely to get hurt by forays into the stock market are the innocent lambs who plunge in as buyers when the Dow Jones average hits at a record high for the sixteenth day in a row (or whatever). The train's leaving the station! Time to get on board! In fact, the market is a game for smart, nervy people who can devote a whole lot of time to it and can afford to be wrong almost as often as they're right. If you're making good money buying and selling Lionel trains in the train-buff market, think about hiring a proxy with steel teeth to do your Wall Street trades for you.

What's the common theme in all of these observations about action? It is that business competence (and other kinds of competence) grows directly out of predictive expertise. Take action as boldly and as forcefully as you can—but only after you've laid the proper predictive foundation. Arthur Perdue, the father of chicken magnate Frank Perdue, once phrased it neatly: "I never put my foot down that I didn't know where I was going to be standing."

Another key point is that, in a world of rapid change, you can't assume permanence in your predictions. You take your best shot, and you stay committed to a constant cycle of observation, calculation, prediction, and action. Over the long run, prediction is a process of perpetual recalibration—albeit with deep roots.

I don't know if you've had dinner recently with a nuclear engineer, but I did recently, and I don't recommend it. I mean, here's a whole subspecies, deeply invested in its advanced degrees, that committed itself to the wrong future. In the late 1950s and early 1960s, resource-poor New England fell in love with the prospect of cheap, unlimited nuclear power. ("We'll show those smug, oil-rich Texans!") Legions of young guys with pocket protectors went through MIT and CalTech in hopes of joining this booming industry. Then they spent years in the salt mines, honing their nuclear skills. Then came Three Mile Island, Chernobyl, and Seabrook. *(Whoops! I've got to become a specialist in decommissioning.)*

"Oh, well," said the more resilient among these nuclear engineers and technicians, "there's always the Cold War." Wrong!

In fact, I don't think we can blame these talented nerds for putting down a bad bet 35 years ago. This is a clear illustration of the limits of predictability. Who could have predicted the implosion of the Soviet Union even in 1985, let alone 1955? But I do think the facts argued strongly for a rolling recalibration, along the way. They should have been asking themselves: *What do all those odd people chaining themselves to the fences out at the reactor site mean? How will my MIT degree hold up if they get what they want?*

The facts also argued for a clear definition of terms along the prediction trail. What do we mean by "energy security"? Be *clear-eyed*, now. Do we mean the same thing today as we meant yesterday? Will a mounting pile of high-level radioactive waste undermine that sense of security, over time? And what did and does "national security" mean? To me, it was telling to observe what happened when both sides in the Cold War introduced MIRVs (multiple independently targeted reentry vehicles, if my memory serves me) and cruise missiles. Almost as soon as these ugly things crawled out from under their rocks, people—even military people—started labeling them as "destabilizing." In other words, in the name of making life more predictable, they made life *less* predictable.*

In hindsight, these were terribly expensive mistakes, in terms of both national treasure and human resources. These costs could have been minimized for all parties through a regular revisiting of reality (through observation, categorization, and calculation). For example, do we top-military-brass types, Russian or American, want to live in a world populated by MIRVs and cruise missiles? Ugh! Sounds bad! Well, can we think of a better future to live in? Only if we try together. Which brings us back to our old friend, projectability.

■ Getting to Projectability

You've noticed that projectability (figuring out how you're going to feel about that future when you get there) has

---

*Ironically, because MIRVs made the total destruction of society—that is, unpredictability—more likely, they therefore helped hasten the end of the arms race.

been peeking out from behind all of the examples on the preceding pages. Part of the umbrella/no umbrella choice involves working backwards from the likely outcomes. If I gamble and don't take the umbrella and it rains, how will I feel about my full-leather suit getting soaked? (It's my only one, after all.)

One way to get to effective projectability is by being careful about the *frame* that we put around a given choice.[15] As in the watch example, what's important is to whittle away at the question on the table until we get to its real kernel. Maybe we can't anticipate fully how we're going to feel about something 20 years hence. But, if we aren't crystal clear about where we're starting from, we've got no chance of reward or satisfaction down the road. It's a bit like a moon shot. It's tough enough getting there if you blast off at exactly the right moment, pointed in exactly the right direction. If you're a little fuzzy on takeoff, that fuzziness gets more and more exaggerated over time.

Fuzziness in recent American history: when Jimmy Carter ran for president in 1976, he promised the American people that he would never lie to them. He was elected, served four more or less unhappy years, and was put out to pasture by the voters in 1980. At that point, Carter was saying, "Hey—I *delivered* on my promise [read "my prediction"]. I didn't lie to you!" And we were saying, sheepishly, "Yeah, well, Jimmy, what we were *really* looking for was leadership. Sorry."

Unfortunately, we can't rerun history and pluck a different Democrat out of the pack for 1976. But the example illustrates the perils of putting the wrong frame around the question. Bad frame: How will I feel about a President Carter, who promises that he won't lie like that other guy? Good frame: Deep down, what I'm really looking for is *leadership*. Does Carter have what it takes?

The point is to project yourself into the right future universe—through the processes of observation, calculation, and action—and *then* explore how it feels.

Another way to get to effective projectability is to act on what's most meaningful to you, which in turn involves understanding and invoking your core values. At the end of the day, if I'm a devout Buddhist, I'm going to be worrying about my karma and my chances for getting successfully out of this tedious reincarnation loop. Well, assuming I stay devout, that's likely to be true at the end of a day 20 years out, too; so I'd better measure my schemes—all my alternative futures in *this* life—against that very important touchstone.

There's another piece of this, as implied in the preceding paragraph. It's a really good idea to reinforce those core values, once you've projected yourself into a particular future and picked it. This sounds a little circular, but (as the Buddhists would tell us) that's life. So by all means attend that revival meeting. Do what it takes to secure that peg on which you've hung so much. The magic, knowledge, and expertise of your particular tribe is reinforced through this process, and all but the most compelling contradictory evidence is weeded out.

If taken to extremes, of course, this can put your tribe at risk. But it can also be a tribal advantage. When you sail into the waters of another tribe that's taken its magic too far, they can actually help you spot and stay out of certain kinds of traps. "Well, we don't give a damn *what* those nuts say," you can all say to yourselves as you weigh anchor, "that emperor back there is buck naked, plain and simple." And as they wave good-bye to you, of course, they're happily going back to celebrating their sartorially splendid emperor and making their chosen future come to pass.

So, to some extent, we build our futures on the strength of our belief structures—and we try to structure them in such a way that allows us to simultaneously reinforce our values, and keep an ear tuned to the wisdom of the clear-eyed among us. Sometimes, hope and grit make our predictions come true.

■ The Advantages of Thinking Tribally

Notice the progression within this chapter. We start out thinking in isolation about umbrellas and blizzards, and wind up sailing to strange waters with members of our tribe.

This reflects an important reality. Even if you're the world's best observer, simplifier, analyzer, calculator, actor, and projector, you can't do it all for yourself. You can't read a million books a year. You can't play three instruments at once. If you live in Massachusetts, you can't grow your own cotton; if you live in Louisiana, you can't grow your own apples. If you want both cotton shirts and candied apples, you've got to put yourself in a bigger picture. In fact, most of the evidence suggests that, if you're human, you can't even be particularly *happy* by yourself.

I've argued that core beliefs play a vital role in making projectability possible. Very few such beliefs spring full-blown from our own foreheads. They are instilled in us by our families, our coreligionists, and our cultures. Beyond the instinctual level, there aren't many convictions that we carry around with us that someone else didn't think of first—and probably a long time ago.

And, finally, our tribes *reinforce* those convictions, thereby improving our predictive powers. In the next chapter, therefore, we'll explore in greater depth the importance of thinking and acting tribally.

chapter eight

You, Me, and Agreement

Can two walk together,
except they be agreed?
Amos 3:3

There is a small sect of Tibetan monks who, over the centuries, have developed an amazing ability. Each individual in the sect can somehow subdivide his vocal cords and sing two or more notes *at once*, with layers of rich overtones and undertones.

The problem is, you and I aren't in that sect. So how are we going to get multiple notes going concurrently?

One more time: by working with other people, with the ultimate goal of bringing about a desired future. This is a complex and demanding task. Perhaps the best evidence for the complexity of working with other people can be found in the business section of your local bookstore. The next time you go there, look at the astounding number of titles that purport to help managers lead, retool, reengineer, restructure, or reinvent a human organization (preferably a *learning* organization).

But hold on a minute. As the second half of this tour of complexity, pick up a couple of these books and read their dust jacket copy. I can just about guarantee that the authors (or at least their publishers) will promise you great things if you and your company will only agree to subscribe to a relatively simple notion or two. Got an unmotivated or unempowered work-force? Easy: "Culture is the answer!" Worried about your inability to introduce new products, streamline the production process, break into new markets, or reorient the control system? Easy: "Leadership is the answer!"

Easy to *say*, that is, but not so easy in practice. In this chapter, I introduce some basic principles about agreement. What is it, and where does it come from? Knowing the answers to these questions is an important prerequisite to future building. Only after we understand what makes an agreement can you and I begin to pick up and use the kinds of tools that we find lying around in bookstores.

■   ## The Predictive Perspective

Let me introduce you to a framework that I'll call the "predictive perspective" and run through a number of examples that will help make my larger point about predictability in a group context.

As long as Adam was the only human on earth, there wasn't much need for fences, and nobody was worrying about property rights. Everything was pretty much Adam's for the taking, and nobody was likely to take Adam to court for wretched excess. But the arrival of Eve ushered in the age of the human group. This had both pluses and minuses. Other people have taken the credit, but it was probably Eve—confronted with the problem of keeping Adam in line—who first said things like "Your freedom ends where mine begins" and "You can't shout, 'Fire!' in a crowded theater."

Like individuals, humans in groups crave predictability *over time*. (This is part of what we've been talking about in the last seven chapters.) But they also demand predictability *in space*. Robert Frost was being gently ironic when he observed that good fences make good neighbors, but think how often this line is quoted as the unvarnished truth.

In Exhibit 1, I plot a variety of human activities in terms of their unpredictability in time and space.[1] What you'll see, as we work our way through an exercise like this—in this case, involving property rights—is that Frost's fences have an appeal in both domains.

Simply put, we don't worry much about an isolated act with minimal future implications in time and space. You want to pound a nail into that two-by-four, out behind your shed? Pound

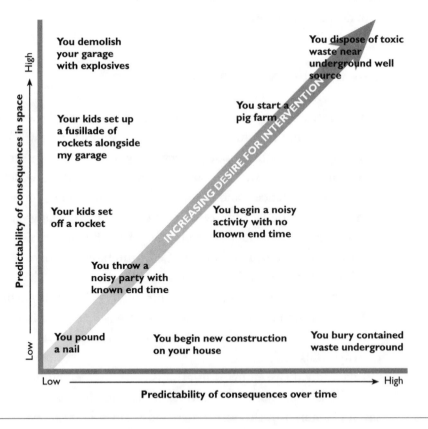

Exhibit 1   **Predictability and Property Rights**

away. But, following the horizontal axis out to the right, when I notice that you're engaged in some serious new construction on your property, I begin to worry about unpredictability over time. This thing, whatever it turns out to be, looks like it might have an impact on the neighborhood for years. Better call the town building department and see if you've pulled a permit. Similarly, I don't care if you cut your short grass, or turn over your garden, or put in a worm bed. But, when you propose to cut down that magnificent 200-year-old sugar maple just on your side of our shared property line, I take notice. And, still further out this same axis, if I spot you using a backhoe in your yard at midnight to bury some dinged-up oil drums with death's-heads and other cryptic markings on them, I'm *really* going to think about the implications of your actions over time.

Some activities present more unpredictability in space than in time. It's the Fourth of July, and your kids decide to start firing off those two-foot-long bottle rockets they picked up on their visit to Grandpa in Florida. Well, it hasn't rained in six weeks, and when that first fiery rocket returns to earth on your property and sets a pile of leaves on fire, I take notice. When a *second* rocket lands directly on my garage roof, I dial 911.

Suppose I decide to destroy my collapsing masonry garage. Pulling it down piece by piece will take far too long. I decide that demolishing it with a pile of explosives will do the trick very efficiently. On Saturday morning, you come outside to sort the recycling and spy me, suited in goggles and industrial earplugs, digging holes and depositing charges along the edge of my garage (which, coincidentally, borders the fence to your yard). You decide pretty quickly that you don't like this measure of uncertainty I'm injecting into your life. In other words, your carefully tended Japanese rock garden was occupying a far more predictable space—not to mention your septic system and the gas main—before I introduced an impending crater and shower of fallout.

And, of course, most activities have an impact in both time and space. If I call you up and warn you that my teenagers are planning a party next Saturday night, and that I'll make sure the noise ends by midnight, you'll probably be fairly tolerant of this intrusion. But, if my kids wait until I leave town one night and throw an impromptu beer bash—which keeps growing into the wee hours—you're very likely to call the cops.

Farther out on this diagonal of unacceptability, we encounter a pig farm (which generates strong odors and heavy runoff, and probably attracts rodents, too) and, finally, the disposal of toxic wastes near an underground well source. This is one of the worst cases imaginable, for no one can say with any certainty where its impacts will be felt (space) or how long they will last (time).

The smarter we get about things like waste disposal, the more clearly we perceive the limits of our knowledge. Our growing sense of the underlying *connectedness* of things makes us a little more humble—and it's a good thing, too! In the 1950s, it was common practice to stick noxious stuff in the ground (or, if you had a seaworthy barge or a nice long outfall pipe, to throw it in the ocean). Today, we no longer bury gasoline tanks; we leave them above ground where we can keep an eye on them. It's not that we like looking at the ugly things particularly; but we're willing to sacrifice aesthetics in order to enhance our predictability in time and space.

Let's look at Exhibit 2 in this series, this time plotting the distress we feel as a society over the death of an individual within our human group. The vertical axis indicates how much influence the deceased individual could have been expected to have on society—in a sense, how much impact he or she would have had in "space." The horizontal axis shows the time frame within which that impact could have been expected to be felt.

In the lower left-hand corner we find the assisted suicide, with the family present and reconciled to the death—perhaps even helping. Going up the vertical axis, we find, first, the old and

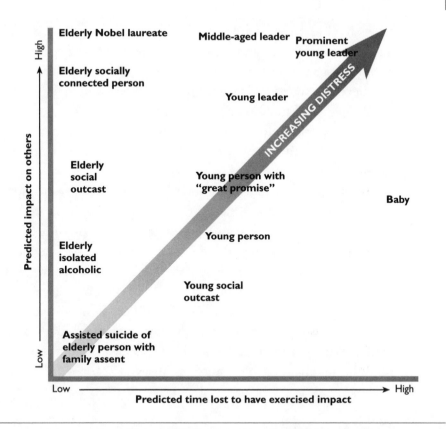

Exhibit 2   A Predictive Perspective on Distress over Death

isolated alcoholic, who has neither much time left nor much potential for social impact; the elderly social outcast, who is functional but out of what we perceive to be the mainstream; and, at the peak, the elderly Nobel laureate, whose significant potential for impact on society is bounded mainly by old age. Even at the very top of this ladder, in other words, our grief is still bounded.

Let's look out along the horizontal axis. Most of us are reluctant to label any young person as being absolutely without potential to have a positive impact on society. (These kinds of labels tend to be self-fulfilling.) But most of us would agree that a sociopathic young gang member whose gang has declared war on middle-class society would have a largely negative impact. The young social outcast falls somewhere on this lower edge of the graph: plenty of time to have an influence, but by force of circumstance unlikely to do so. A baby, by contrast, has more time and, given the benefit of the doubt, probably has more potential for impact than the social outcast.

But the interesting neighborhood on this graph is, again, along the diagonal that we can ascend from lower left to upper right. Halfway up, we find the young person with "great promise"—the high school valedictorian, the boy standing on the burning deck. And up in the upper right-hand corner we find the prominent young leader, whose early demise causes us the most distress of all. For many of us over the age of 50, John F. Kennedy's assassination certainly fell somewhere in this quadrant. Kennedy presumably had many more years of service to society ahead of him, both during and after his tenure in the White House.

Getting to Agreement

These two exhibits help make two points. First, the members of a given human group (in this case, turn-of-the-twenty-first-century American society) share a large number of collective beliefs. And, second, many of these beliefs can be interpreted through the lens of predictability.[2] We like things that go "according to Hoyle," that follow a predictable set of rules, especially when we share a common objective. In fact, we require agreement in order to act together, and we tend to fight or derail things that break the rules. (They're "not cricket.")

This is a good news/bad news situation. The good news is that, on the macro level—for example, mobilizing for action against Saddam Hussein's Iraq in 1990, or funding the Head

Start program, or finding a liver for Baby Jessica—we have fairly deep reservoirs of consensus to draw upon. (Plus, these are easy to agree on, because when you get right down to it, only a few people will actually have to cooperate and do the work.) The bad news comes in two flavors. First, societal consensus is a fragile commodity, and one that is easily dissipated. And, second, most bargains aren't struck and most tasks aren't performed on the macro level. Think of life in the business context. It's agreement down in the trenches that we need if we're going to take coordinated action to arrive at a desired future—and that kind of agreement can be very, very hard to come by.

Let's wrestle briefly with what constitutes an "agreement." I think that depending on the particular circumstances in which we find ourselves, we have to agree on either

- **What we want**
- **How the world works**
- **Both**

Obvious? Less so than meets the eye.[3] "What we want" means the benefits we're seeking and the kinds of tradeoffs we'll make in order to secure those benefits. Even where no tradeoffs are possible or necessary, there are usually minimum conditions that have to be met to permit agreement, or maximums that can't be exceeded, or both.

Suppose you're the student and I'm Professor Stevenson, and you and I agree that what you really want is a course in salesmanship. As the teacher, I may be tempted to force-feed you salesmanship for 24, 48, or even 72 hours—just as much as it takes to teach you how to reach all kinds of recalcitrant customers, and not a minute less! But, at the same time, I had better acknowledge that you have some bare-minimum needs that you must satisfy in order to subject yourself to me in the first place: sleeping, eating, finding a bathroom at appropriate intervals, and so forth.

There are also maximum thresholds inherent in most agreements. You and I may agree that tunafish sandwiches are a good, healthy solution to the recurring challenge of the midday meal. We smile and shake on it. But this "agreement" may mean very different things to the two of us. You may be a covert member of the highly secretive Cult of the Tuna Worshippers, who have taken a blood oath to eat tuna today, tuna tomorrow, and tuna forever. Meanwhile, my loyalty to tuna begins to waver the first time I get downwind of a backyard barbeque.

So *clarity* is critical when we're deciding on what we want. The question "Exactly what are we agreeing to, anyway?" always has to be asked.

Another important axis of agreement is "how the world works." This may sound obvious, but it's not always all that straightforward. Entering into an agreement, you and I have to agree on cause-and-effect relationships. If X happens, then Y is likely to follow. Assuming that our agreement will keep us in touch with each other after the deal is done, we also have to agree on how we're going to communicate and coordinate with each other. And, if we achieve our shared goal, we'll surely have to put some distribution rules in place to divide up the spoils.

Note that, in the list of bulleted points above, I was careful to say it was an "either, or, both" situation. In Exhibit 3, you can see different kinds of agreements falling in very different parts of the agreement universe, depending on how much coordinated action is needed on the part of the agreeing parties.

The vertical axis shows increasing agreement on what we want, going from bottom to top. The horizontal axis, moving from left to right, indicates increasing agreement on how the world works. The lower left-hand corner indicates the zone of "No common ground." Down in this disputatious neighborhood, you and I disagree on what we want, we disagree on how the world

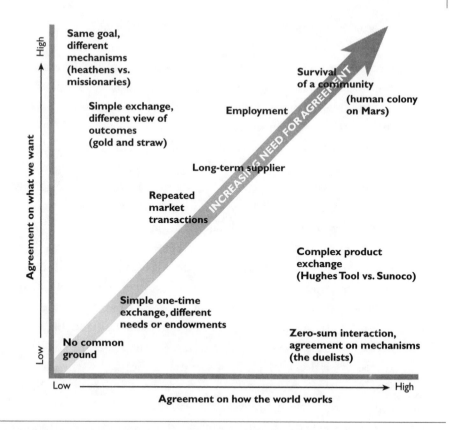

High

Agreement on what we want

Low

Same goal, different mechanisms (heathens vs. missionaries)

Simple exchange, different view of outcomes (gold and straw)

Survival of a community

(human colony on Mars)

Employment

Long-term supplier

INCREASING NEED FOR AGREEMENT

Repeated market transactions

Complex product exchange (Hughes Tool vs. Sunoco)

Simple one-time exchange, different needs or endowments

Zero-sum interaction, agreement on mechanisms (the duelists)

No common ground

Low ⟶ High

Agreement on how the world works

Exhibit 3   **Necessity of Agreement for Coordinated Action**

works, and we probably don't like each other's hairstyles, either. Not a promising locale for consensus building and working together!

Look up at the top of the vertical axis, where it says, "Same goal, different mechanisms." This is a case where you and I agree substantially on our goals but disagree fundamentally on how the world works. Say, for example, we both want to go to heaven: same goal. But you believe that the way to get there is by converting heathens, and I believe that the way to get there is by boiling missionaries. Again, we have a major impediment to agreement and coordinated action.

Now look out at the right-hand side of the horizontal axis, where I've located "Zero-sum interaction, agreement on mechanisms." Imagine that you and I are pointing pistols at each other's heads at point-blank range. We have complete agreement on how the world works, but we have total disagreement on our desired outcomes.

These are the two extremes, and as usual, most of the interesting stuff goes on in the grey areas in the middle. Look back up at the upper left-hand quadrant where it says, "Simple exchange, different view of outcomes." This is a case where the need for coordinated action is minimal, but agreement is possible because we view and value things differently. Suppose you and I both love gold, that soft shiny stuff that so tempts us humans. One day, you discover a way to turn straw into gold (or so you believe), and you come up the road to my farm and casually offer to buy the big pile of straw that's stacked up behind my barn. Do I sell? You bet I do. I don't care all that much about how you think the world works. You want to buy, I want to sell, and we both see a way to wind up with the gold.

Back down toward the lower right-hand side of the graph, we have what I call a "complex product exchange." I'm Hughes Tool, and you're Sunoco. You want to drill a deep well offshore, and I'm responsible for providing you with a drill bit that can chew its way down four miles into the earth's crust and never be seen again. In this case, we have to spend a great deal of time reaching agreement on how the world works. Exactly how durable does this bit have to be? How stable will your drilling platform be, and how much torsional twist is the drill likely to be exposed to? Am I right in assuming that my liability stops when you accept delivery of the bit?

Now let's work our way up the diagonal, from lower left to upper right. Imagine that you and I are members of two warring tribes. I'm from the coast, and my tribe has a hammerlock on the salt supply. Your tribe is from the inland forests, and you therefore control the fresh meat supply. Well, once a year, we see the need to get together and make a trade. It's a simple transaction—in the "what you see is what you get" vein—but it's also one that has to recur over time. We have enough agreement both on what we want and on how the world works to overcome our substantial differences and meet on the Great Flat Rock under the Big Tide Moon. Then we can go back to killing each other off (and rubbing salt in each other's wounds).

What goes into a repeated contact in the marketplace? Obviously, much more coordination, and therefore much more agreement. Suppose I'm selling you a microprocessor for use in your new line of portable computers. Obviously, my chip has to work as part of a larger system. It has to work under a variety of circumstances, over a relatively long period of time. For these good things to happen, we have to agree on a variety of cause-and-effect relationships.[4] If the product is used like this, then the following will happen. We also have to agree on what will happen in the event of certain kinds of failures.

A long-term supplier relationship carries this relationship a few important steps further. If you're supplying the transaxles for my high-end sedans, you have to be pretty intimately involved in my design processes. We have to agree not only on present-day circumstances, but we also have to signal each other very carefully about what our future is going to look like. If I'm planning a shift to front-wheel drive five years from now, you need to know that ASAP. If tighter fuel-economy standards mean that I have to lose an average of another 200 pounds across the cars in my fleet, you might be able to make a key contribution.[5]

In the upper right-hand corner of our graph is "Survival of a community." In this case, I'm thinking of one of the earliest European settlements on the North American continent or, looking forward, of the first human colony on Mars. All members of the community absolutely have to agree on what they want and how the world works. Everybody has to pull his or her weight. Everybody has to understand and buy into the possible scenarios that lie ahead of the community—even to the point of agreeing on whom to sacrifice first if the community begins to run out of food. As Spock, model citizen of an isolated band, said toward the end of *Star Trek II*, by way of explaining his decision to sacrifice himself, "The needs of the many . . . *[gasp]* . . . outweigh the needs of the few."

■ Getting Agreement Right: A Matter of Degrees

Here's a key point to take away from the preceding discussion: in many cases, we really don't need complete agreement to get to a reasonable level of mutual predictability. It may be enough simply to agree along one axis (you want to buy the straw; I'm happy to sell it) and not worry a whole lot about the other axis. We have to agree on what to agree on *now*, and leave the rest to the future.

In some cases, of course, too much agreement can be a bad thing. In business, the KISS (keep it simple, stupid) principle applies more often than it does not. Struggling to reach agreement on what we want out of life makes perfect sense if we're the marooned colony out on Rigal IV in the Delta Quadrant. It makes almost no sense if I'm Hughes Tool and you're Sunoco. At the end of the day, we need to *act*, and action is much easier when we understand clearly how deep our agreement needs to be.

In the next chapter, I focus on ways to modify behavior to bring about agreement—and by extension, predictability—and we'll pick up some of those tools that are still waiting for us back in the business section of the bookstore.

chapter nine

The Technology of Agreement

If the future were known,
every intelligent man would
kill himself at once,
and the Republic would be
peopled wholly by morons.
H. L. Mencken

When a prediction turns out to be accurate, it usually means that one of two things is happening. Either you're making very good assessments of the future—using the tools and attitudes outlined in Chapter 7—or you're making your predicted and hoped-for future come about.

Even though we're sociable (and sometimes even altruistic) animals, we basically tend to seek predictability for ourselves and our loved ones, on our own terms—and maybe then we worry about the other guy. When we can get to our goals by ourselves, we usually do. Life is short, and I don't want to spend a lot of time persuading you mulelike characters out there to subscribe to the farsighted and compelling Stevenson Agenda.

But, in most cases, as it turns out, making a desired future become real requires coordinated action: you and I working together. This is another of the many paradoxes associated with predictability. "If you want something done right," the old saying goes, "do it yourself." Sounds good to me, because nobody is more predictable to me than me.[1] But we find that, for the really important stuff, we have to trade away some of our personal predictability in order to achieve a mutual predictability.

This, in turn, requires some level of *agreement*. As discussed in the previous chapter, agreements are based either on what we want, on how we think the world works, or on both. The examples in Chapter 8 demonstrated that these two dimensions of agreement have very different impacts on the process of future building. You might be able to get it wrong about why you agree and still be able to move forward.* But, if you've got it wrong as to why you *disagree*, you'll almost certainly do the wrong thing when it comes time to take action. Your actions are likely to exacerbate the problem.

For all shared tasks there is a required level of agreement. But this level varies widely from task to task, and the trick is to figure out how much agreement is needed for the task at hand. If you and I are on the hook to put together the new swingset in the schoolyard, that's a small challenge to our ability to forge an agreement. If we agree to write a book together, we're raising the agreement hurdle dramatically.[2] If we decide to get married, we're going off the chart.

Deliberate change is hard and slow, both because of and despite the fact that we're compelled to work in groups. Building a future takes a continuing investment of time and energy. And it's pretty clear that, as a society, we're less willing today to sacrifice for the common good than we were in the past. Imagine trying to build the interstate highway system today, for example. Would enough people accept the relocation, the dirt and noise, or even the inconvenience associated with such a project? Not likely!

Consensus is hard to forge and hard to sustain. If we seek to change too much too fast, we risk breaking down whatever fragile consensus exists. An unwelcome action reverberates across our

---

*As my colleague Charles J. Christenson says, "We don't have to agree on the whereas's, as long as we agree on the be-it-resolveds."

delicate coalitions in subtle and unpredictable ways. When traffic grinds to a halt alongside that new highway construction site, immobilized drivers see the ghost town of houses claimed by eminent domain—and the group of construction workers enjoying their well-earned but ill-timed coffee break—and they fume about meddling, muddling government. Even the individuals who *don't* lose their homes to the highway start thinking about opting out of the group consensus: *Hey—if the highway department can tuck it to that guy, I could be next!*

And just to complicate things still further, the grounds of agreement often need major adjustment and renegotiation over time. Things change, and complicated things change in complicated ways. Think of the obstacles to real peace in the Middle East, for example. The nations and would-be nations of the region continue to wrestle over important and seemingly intractable issues like the ultimate fate of Jerusalem and Jewish settlements on the West Bank. But as soon as there is a sustained drought in the region, another underlying source of conflict— water rights—will inevitably shoulder its way to the front of the debate.

So, even after we recognize that we need agreement, we still have to acknowledge that we're unable to move the grounds of agreement very far or very fast, and that we may have trouble retooling our agreement to keep up with changing circumstances. There are exceptions, such as wartime, when deciding what to do next tends to come easily. And no wonder. The arrival of the barbarian horde outside the walls of the city persuades people inside the walls to close ranks on how the world works *(barbarians bad!)* and what they want out of life *(survive the barbarians!)*. But, absent an invasion by Romulans or Klingons, we turn-of-the-century humans aren't likely to achieve an overall consensus that is overwhelming and durable.[3]

Let's not give up hope just yet, though. I coined the "Technology of Agreement" title for this chapter to emphasize the *tool-*

wielding aspect of agreement. You'll recall our visit to the book-store at the outset of the last chapter, where I made the point that there are many tools for present retooling and future building out there today. Many of the tools being promoted as panaceas for managers, however, have their impacts along only one of the two key dimensions of agreement: what we want and how the world works. This means that the manager has to be sure he or she is using an appropriate tool to solve a given problem. The best tool, when misapplied, becomes a bad tool. Which tools in which circumstances: that is the theme of this chapter.

■ The Modes of Exchange

Agreement usually entails some sort of exchange: money for goods or services, barter, or whatever. Let's bring back our old friend, the two-axis chart, from Chapter 8 (agreement on what we want, agreement on how the world works) to graph how and where exchanges usually take place.

Exhibit 4 captures the kinds of situations described in the last chapter and lumps them together into a couple of large groups. These are what I'll call the "modes of exchange," within which we humans either do or don't interact effectively. We've already commented on the lower left-hand corner (where, as you'll recall, even our hairstyles clash). If we can't agree on *anything*, the mode of exchange is nonexistent. Stay separate! I'll have my general call your general; their footsoldiers will fight it out.

Out at the other end of the implied diagonal is the "clans" mode of exchange, which—at least in isolation, and in a static world—is internally cohesive and functional for its environment. I stress the usefulness of isolation here, because things can and do go wrong when two or more highly functional clans come into contact with each other, or things start to change

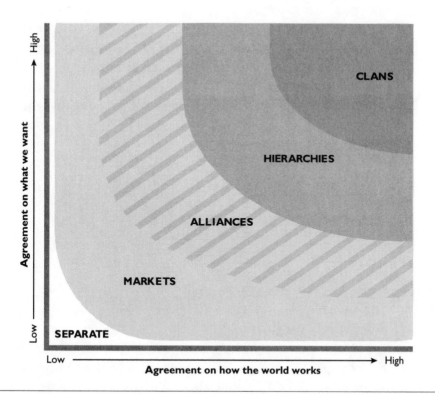

Exhibit 4   Normal Modes of Exchange

fast for other reasons. Think Lebanon, or Somalia—or recall my example in an earlier chapter of the Big Ships coming over the horizon for the first time. In such cases, new kinds of agreements (or UN-policed buffer zones) become necessary.

Between separate worlds and clans are the areas where there is at least some agreement on how the world works, and on what we want. These modes I'll call "markets," "alliances," and "hierarchies." Markets are the arena in which some transactions go from being impossible (*hate* that hairstyle!) to being possible. In the purest conception of markets, these are venues in which only a bare minimum needs to be agreed upon. I set up my crude little rack in the bazaar, hang a Bokhara rug over my cross-pole, and put a price on it. You either buy it or you don't. You don't necessarily like my mustache, and you don't necessarily count on finding me here tomorrow. Even if you do, I don't necessarily admit that I've ever seen you before. For narrative purposes, let's call this a "low market." Imagine a banner hanging over the entrance to the (low-market) bazaar: "What you see is what you get!"

In fact, most markets work, not despite the fact that I'm from out of town, but specifically *because* of it. They satisfy that desire we all have for diversity and novelty. (My steady lunchtime diet of tunafish sandwiches is perfectly adequate but boring! Every once in a while, I *must* have a hot dog off that cart on the corner.) And, more important, markets create channels through which to merge our different endowments and needs. You and your six brothers need introductions to my seven marriageable daughters.

Markets can be still more complicated than this, of course. For example, they can involve repeat transactions over many years. As our earlier example illustrated, when you coastal folks have all the salt and we on the plains have all the meat, it's in both of our best interests to meet somewhere in the middle each autumn and to trade. Think of the New York Stock Exchange, whose members have been sitting down together and buying and selling many of the same stocks forever. But think, too, of long-term suppliers, many of whom engage in major exchanges of technology with their key customers over time.

These are markets in which what you see is *not* necessarily what you get, and in which trust and shared experience begin to play a part. Let's call these high markets (obviously, with the NYSE as my lead example, I'm not intending a value judgment here) "alliances." A stock certificate is always a stock certificate, right? Well, yeah, except when it isn't, so you'd better be sure you're trading in the right market. I sell you a pill that I claim will cure your illness; or I sell you key components for use on the disassembly line in your poultry processing plant that you intend to run round the clock, three shifts a day, for months at a time. Buying the rug in the bazaar is an easy transaction; these are not.

You'll note that Exhibit 4 shows distinct areas for these relationships. These boundaries are merely an academic construct to facilitate discussion. In fact, there are no discrete separations among the modes of exchange. For example, parties move from low to high market all the time, for all kinds of reasons. After filling out that multipart form one too many times, I call FedEx and set up an account, and the forms come preprinted. Or a group of corn farmers and grain merchants, after meeting several times a year for a decade, decides to ally themselves by establishing a commodities exchange. Similarly, a complex exchange in the marketplace can lead the two involved parties to "rezone" themselves into a hierarchical relationship, and members of a hierarchy can opt for the clan.

Hierarchies mean much more agreement between participants on what they want and/or on how the world works than do markets. They are the zone in which collaborations, joint ventures, employees and bosses, soldiers and generals, priests and popes are found—in fact, all kinds of teammates. This is the mode of exchange within which our goals are congruent, our relationship is necessarily longer term, our technologies are either running in parallel or converging, and there tend to be substantial legal entanglements.[4]

By now, some of this may be sounding a little familiar to you. That's because I made a similar point in Chapter 8 using slightly different language. Watch what happens when you superimpose this chart on one from Chapter 8 (see Exhibit 5).

For example, it's clear that only certain kinds of transactions fall within the zone that I've set aside for "Markets." As a culture, we're still suffering through a sustained (and I would say misplaced) infatuation with markets.[5] We like to put on our Market

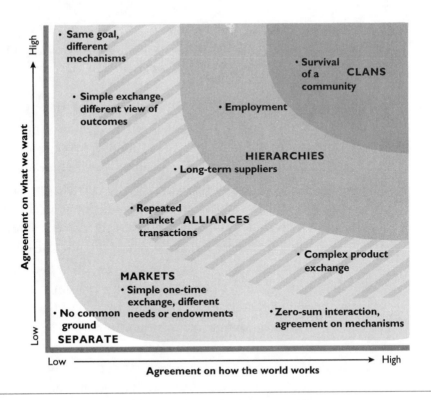

Exhibit 5 Necessity of Agreement for Coordinated Action

Glasses and apply the Market Test to whatever poor beast happens to slink into our field of vision. (Once again, "If all you have is a hammer," as the old saying goes, "everything looks like a nail.") Take the employment relationship, for example. You and I would be crazy to let market forces dictate our company's personnel manual. If we're going to reach basic agreement about the nature of employment that you offer and I accept (or vice versa), then we'd better make sure that we're organized in an appropriate *hierarchical* way.[6]

Other inferences aren't quite so cut and dried, but they still give us food for thought. What's the difference between engaging in repeated market transactions and being a long-term supplier (both of which fall in the markets zone)? As I've said, it's in part a matter of degree. Long-term suppliers can be located on the northeastern end of the alliances zone, or—depending on the specifics of the relationship—they can land in the southwest neighborhood of the hierarchies zone.[7] For example, say I manufacture engines, and you've long been my independent turbocharger source. What happens to our relationship when I supply millions to fund your basic research, and your findings revolutionize turbo technology? Well, it gets complicated.

Companies make a mistake when they misassign their key vendors to the wrong category. This is common (and very dangerous!) in cases of technological development. IBM, for example, treated Microsoft like any other vendor in the marketplace, even while it was investing heavily in Microsoft's technology base. The lesson? "Hey, guys—If you're going to give away the family jewels, better to do so within the family" (that is, within the hierarchy).

Locating ourselves on this kind of spectrum is also a matter of momentum. Which way is this relationship headed: northeast, into full-fledged partnership? Or southwest, into a relationship driven exclusively by market forces? Some changes along one of the two axes of agreement can push us upward, whereas other kinds of changes—which may arise concurrently!—push us downward. More on this in a moment.

Again, there's no single right way to get our arms around these issues. But, as we attempt to engage in coordinated action to achieve mutual predictability, it's important to figure out

- **Where our relationship is today (the level and nature of our agreement)**
- **Where it may be headed**

- What factors, changing in which ways, might push our relationship into a more productive (or less productive) corner

■ The Big Mo: Toward or Away from Agreement?

Where is the relationship today, where is it heading, and what contextual factors might affect it drastically tomorrow? The effecct of such changing circumstances is what politicians used to call the "big Mo": momentum. Consider Exhibit 6.

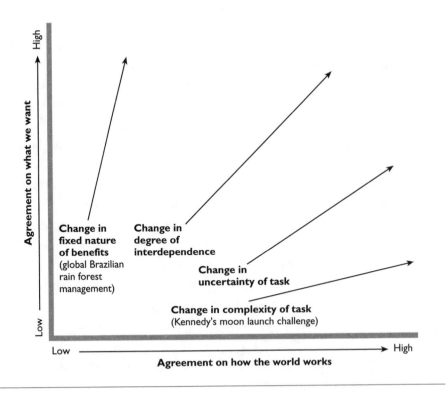

Exhibit 6 **Changing Circumstances: Changing How We Need to Agree**

Sometimes momentum, fueled by the pressure of external circumstances, calls for a heightened degree of mutual predictability, along either or both of the two axes of agreement. Think again of the moon landing. That goal, on which President Kennedy very visibly hung the nation's technical and scientific honor, required an extraordinary consensus on how the world worked. No matter that the scientists, the politicians, and the astronauts all wanted different things out of the project; Kennedy's intervention (and the nature of the challenge) created an overwhelming degree of momentum toward agreement.

Often we are shoved into each other's arms in more subtle ways, as a consensus builds around us. The environmental movement is a good case in point. Once upon a time, before the closing of the frontier, people didn't worry too much about the carrying capacity of the land, the coexistence of species, and so on. You clear-cut the land, used up the soil, and moved on. In the Age of Separate, we didn't meet often, and we didn't stay in touch. But today, when the Brazilian farmer tries to do the same thing, he finds himself coming under pressure from graduate students in Massachusetts, who feel they have a stake in his decision. The Brazilian farmer is increasingly being pushed into a high-market (or even a hierarchical) relationship with people he's never met and most likely never will meet. And if the task is highly uncertain or depends on a high degree of coordinated effort—like starting a new company, for example—we need to agree on many more things. On many dimensions, we have to move our level of agreement toward the northeast.

We can also track the impact of changes on existing agreements. Exhibit 7 shows where and how different kinds of change have their respective impacts. When any change of consequence occurs, it puts more or less pressure on all kinds of existing agreements.

Social change, for example, usually means a decreased level of agreement on what we want. Think of the dramatic social

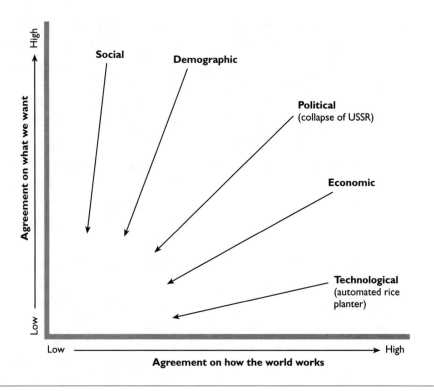

Exhibit 7 **Changing Circumstances:**
Impacts on Existing Agreements

changes that occurred in the United States and elsewhere between 1950 and 1970. Lots of people abandoned (or put significantly less stock in) traditional notions of home and hearth,
electing instead to "do their own thing." Religious leaders condemned much of what was going on as sinful, while intellectuals
applauded the ferment as liberation. Men were initially affected in more or less modest ways by these sweeping changes;
women and children were affected in dramatic ways, many of them
not anticipated. The societal fabric, which basically is woven
out of consensus and trust, began to get a bit tattered.

Meanwhile, the impact of these changes was being magnified by political, economic, and technological changes, which greatly reduced our national consensus on how the world worked. People (particularly young people of draft age) began to question the underlying premises of the Cold War and wound up informing the government that they had no intention of dying in the jungles of Southeast Asia. It wasn't just that Lyndon Johnson, and then Richard Nixon, were perceived by a number of their countrymen to be either misguided or malevolent. It was that more and more people—soldiers, hardhats, hippies, Mormons, stockbrokers, and pop stars alike—perceived these leaders to be terminally out of touch with how they saw the world working.

To make the same point in a simplified context: what happens when our clan encounters massive social change? Referring back to our old-standby exhibit, our clan is driven substantially down the vertical axis (agreement on what we want) and slightly backwards along the horizontal axis (agreement on how the world works).

But when our clan is confronted by a major technological improvement in agricultural methods—an automated rice planter—we have a very different kind of problem. Suddenly, we no longer have to stoop down to plant the rice by hand, one plant at a time, and this is a good thing! On the other hand, this technological change creates massive unemployment even as it is pushing the productivity of our agricultural sector through the roof. Many traditional roles will change, and the social and economic hierarchy will be turned upside down. As a result, we'll have to scramble to rethink our position on how the world works—and, shortly thereafter, we may have to revisit the question of what we want (productivity or guaranteed employment).

Russia experienced these two phenomena in reverse order. First came a crunching collapse of consensus on how the world worked. Almost overnight, terminal out-of-touchness struck the

USSR—and suddenly there *was* no USSR. It had been swept away by a tide of information about how the world (especially the Western world) really worked. But then came an almost inevitable fragmentation of consensus along the other axis: what we want. I say "inevitable" because the collapse of the old order almost always creates economic dislocation, which in turn creates financial distress for individuals, families, and communities—and people break for cover.* Boris Yeltsin's narrow reelection victory in July 1996 shouldn't obscure the fact that, although something like half of Russians favored further progress toward democracy, another 40 percent favored a return to some sort of communism.

Technological change tends to create opportunities for some while it destroys established markets for others, and the social and legal brakes that have been put in place over the centuries can't always keep up. There are already several "virtual wine brokers" doing business on the Internet, for example. They provide a high-service approach to supplying you with exactly the right kinds of wine for your particular needs, which turns out to be a service that lots of people feel they need. (Some of us will confess to being a little intimidated by the wine-buying process.) It turns out, though, that this wonderful service violates the laws in something like 41 states, because it bypasses the liquor distributors who hold the exclusive franchise to sell wine in those states (and thereby to raise taxes for the state).

The same kinds of problems can arise within the confines of a single company. Companies are hierarchies, which means that there's some degree of agreement on what the individuals within them want and how the world works. But not *total* agreement. Different companies shade toward more agreement along one axis than along the other, as do groups within individual companies.

---

*The collapse of totalitarianism permits people for the first time to openly ask themselves *What do I want?* and for the first time, there is more than one acceptable answer.

The manufacturers and marketers of the Brass Tacks Fasteners Company, for example, all agree that they want Brass Tacks to succeed. And, in stable times, they can tacitly emphasize their general agreement on what they want and minimize their disagreements on how the world works. But watch what happens when Brass Tacks—which, let's say, has been performing very well in the United States—now decides that it has to jump with both feet into the international arena in order to stay competitive. At this point, the marketing group says, "Hey—this is a new ballgame. We've gotta adapt our products to reflect the particular tastes and needs of these new environments we're entering." The manufacturing group, hearing this new line of reasoning, is horrified. "Wait just a minute there," they respond. "We've gotten where we are today by simplifying our production process, minimizing unnecessary variety in our product line, and getting our customers to conform to *our* standards. Give 'em any color paper clip they want, as long as it's silver."

Or let's suppose we're contemplating jumping into an important new relationship—let's say a new joint venture—which will immediately face a shared challenge of great complexity and uncertainty. Imagine it's a cable company teaming up with a long-distance carrier teaming up with a content owner, trying to nail down tomorrow's single-pipeline network. With this kind of immense task complexity, we absolutely *have* to agree on how the world works. Standards will mean everything. It's very possible, even likely, that a market-defined relationship will let us down. An extended duration-of-contact should push us toward greater agreement along both axes; that is, toward a hierarchical relationship.*

---

*Now run the same scenario (bad enough as a hypothetical!) with real people and real companies plugged in. Try plugging in, for example, tough guys like Rupert Murdoch and his News Corp., teaming up with John Malone's TCI, and MCI controlled by the British utility giant British Telecom. *That* sounds complicated.

Again, things can also go in the other direction (or should). Look at Apple's experience. For years, Apple was about as clannish as they come. As long as there was no serious competition in the PC realm, that approach served it fairly well. But because Clan Apple insisted on controlling its operating system and standards, it stiff-armed all the legions of software and hardware developers who otherwise would have walked on hot coals to work in a close relationship with Apple. Because very few people knew Apple's standards or how the Apple "box" worked, almost nobody could act as an independent developer for the Macintosh.

Meanwhile, farther up the coast, Microsoft was going in the other direction. "You want to write an application based on our operating system? Cool. Let's talk license." You can walk through computer superstores today and see the consequences—dire for Apple, happy for Microsoft.

Many authors in recent years have written about "core competencies," "the learning organization," and so on. What I'm doing in this series of exhibits is proposing a new slant on what's critical to keep inside your organization and what's critical to let go. IBM (in the example cited several pages back) erred in one direction; Apple erred in exactly the opposite.* IBM should have pushed its agreements *out* of the zone of the marketplace and up into the zone of hierarchies, and Apple should have come in out of its clannish isolation and struck up some nice alliance-based agreements with some independent geeks.

■ Tools and Domains

To recap the logical yarn I'm spinning here: we want predictability; we therefore have to work together; we therefore need

---

*In both cases, Bill Gates was the beneficiary, which explains why he is the richest man in the universe.

agreement on what we want, on how the world works, or on both. We've seen that changing circumstances can create the need for new agreements, pushing groups into more cooperative relationships with each other—even if they're innately suspicious of such changes. (Clan Apple is now trying to shove itself southwest along the hierarchical diagonal, through licensing agreements and joint ventures, in a desperate effort to stay in the game. They've even licensed producers to clone their boxes.) We've also seen that changing circumstances can put intense pressure on existing agreements and force a clan, a company, or a country to rethink its most basic assumptions. Going from an informal business alliance to a formal partnership is one example. So is a corporate repositioning in the marketplace—the Brass Tacks example—the deregulation of an industry, or a moon landing.

People, companies, and countries confronted by significant change have to ask themselves a fundamental question: *Is where we are where we'll need to be?* The answer is usually "no." And, when this is the case, there are only three possible responses: bail out, reduce the necessity for agreement in the first place, or seek agreement more broadly and deeply.

Bailing out is sometimes the smart choice. Prince Charles and Princess Di might have avoided an unpleasant decade with a sensible bailout strategy. But bailing out brings its own forms of unpredictability, because you start over with no agreements. (I suspect the singles scene is daunting even for Diana.)

Reducing the necessity for agreement (or, more precisely, reducing the grounds on which we have to reach agreement) is another sensible approach. The point is not to say, "We want to be in a clan! How do we get there?" A smarter strategy is to say, "Let's figure out which things we really need to agree on, and which we can ignore." Even if you and I can't agree on terms for a formal partnership, maybe we can still agree to collaborate on a job-by-job basis. We'll return to this approach later in the chapter, when we talk about something called "disaggregation."

The third choice is to seek agreements that are broader and deeper. *Is where we are where we'll need to be?* To most readers of this book, this won't come across as a startling new question. In fact, it's the question that good managers ask themselves a hundred times a day. And, when they conclude that the answer to their own question is "no," what do they do? They do the same thing you and I do: they reach for a tool.

New chart, same axes. Exhibit 8 shows different kinds of tools for creating different kinds of agreement, or for moving our level of agreement along either one or two dimensions.

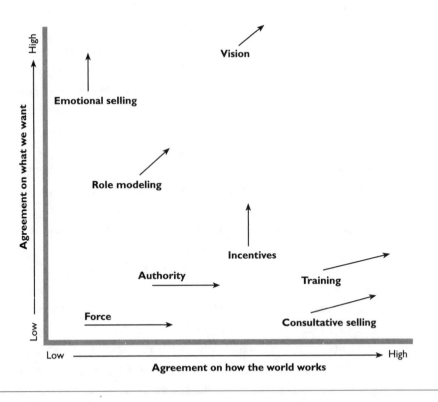

Exhibit 8 **Tools That Increase Agreement**

Let me take a moment to emphasize the importance of placement on this graph. The locations of these tools are not random, nor is the direction of each arrow. They have been placed in the "geographic" location that corresponds to the particular levels of agreement in which they meet with the most success. Your choice of tool depends integrally on the level of agreement you share at the outset and along which axis you want to move. Let's pick up a tool—say, for example, force. When do I use force, and what's it good for?

Force is the tool that Generalissimo Stevenson uses when three conditions obtain:

- **There's little or no existing basis for agreement.**
- **I want to get you to accept my view of how the world works.**
- **I don't give a damn about whether you and I want the same thing. In fact, I assume we don't.**

If my use of force goes according to plan, two good things happen: you accept my worldview, and I get what I want.[8]

How about salesmanship, or "emotional selling"? I put on my emotional salesman's hat when two preconditions exist: when there's already a lot of overlap between what you and I want (but not necessarily much overlap in our views of how the world works), and when I want even more agreement about what we want (meaning "I want you to want more of what I want more of"). You might argue that a second kind of salesman operates along the horizontal axis. I assert that what I call "consultative selling"— that is, getting you to want my newest high-tech toy by showing you lots of charts and graphs that convince you that it fits the way the world works—is effectively a kind of training. More on that later in the chapter.

Incentives, to cite another commonly wielded tool, presuppose a certain amount of agreement about how the world works. They do nothing much to *increase* consensus along that axis, but they're very good at forging consensus about what you and I want. I'm paying you to want what I want. Go get it for us. If your problem with me is specifically that we don't agree enough on how the world works, and I try to coax you with incentives, it will very likely backfire on me and push us even farther away from agreement on one or both axes. For example, offering you big piles of money to work Saturdays will be persuasive if you're worried about your looming mortgage; but offering you big piles of money to work Saturdays performing drug tests on mice will not endear me to you if you're a vigilant animal rights advocate.

Where's vision in this universe of tools? As you can see, it's well up into the upper right-hand quadrant of our graph. This means that it presupposes substantial agreement along both axes and that (if applied successfully) it will generate more agreement on how the world works *and* what we want out of life.

Stay with me here, because we're closing in on two key points. The first is that certain tools work really well to accomplish certain agreement-forging tasks. But the second is that you'd better not pick up those tools unless you already have the necessary level of agreement behind them. Generalissimo Stevenson— hated and feared by his countrymen—is well advised to resort to force; he'd be a fool to lean on the "vision thing" too heavily, because he hasn't put himself in the right corner of the world to use that tool.

Some tools work to reduce the necessity for agreement, as indicated in Exhibit 9. Standard operating procedures, for example, are far removed from discussions of what we want out of life. What they're really good for is minimizing arguments over how the world works. Every time we plow the back forty, we turn up a zillion boulders that have to be removed before we can plant the field. Standard operating procedure: I'll bring the tractor and the stone boat, you bring five local guys with strong backs

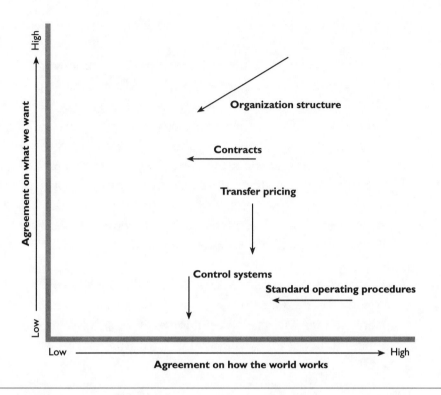

Exhibit 9   Tools That Reduce the Necessity for Agreement

and weak minds, and starting at 7:00 A.M. sharp we'll move the damn rocks.

Standard operating procedures work particularly well if the specific details of the procedure fall into what Chester Barnard called the "zone of indifference": you might be slightly more efficient after your midmorning coffee break, and the guy next to you might love the throaty roar of a tractor engine between midnight and dawn. But we all understand both that somebody has to make a few (more or less arbitrary) rules—such as when we're all going to show up—and that we all have to follow those rules if this job is going to get done. If you don't have a personal stake in the rule-making agenda and you're happy with the arrangement whereby I pay you to do it my way, I can lay down the law.

Control systems presuppose some agreement on how the world works, but they drive down the need for agreement on what we want. "I don't care what you want," says the effective control system. "You're going to do so-and-so, and by tracking certain kinds of numbers, I'm going to reinforce that behavior."

Contracts start at about the same place in terms of preexisting consensus, but push things in a very different direction by reducing the necessity to agree on how the world works. "We don't have to agree on all that interpretation-of-the-universe stuff," says the good contract. "We simply agree on the following deliverables."[9]

Organization structure presupposes still more agreement along both axes. Once the structure is put in place, it allows people to say, "We share a common goal. Now, you do your thing, I'll do my thing, and we'll get it." More on this later.

OK. So let's assume that we agree that choosing the right tool for a given job depends fundamentally on how much we agree and on how much we need to agree, in each case. Now I want to argue that there are really only four basic ways by which humans in groups create agreement. They are

- **Power**
- **Culture**
- **Management**
- **Leadership**

These four domains map directly on our trusty old "what we want/how the world works" grid, as in Exhibit 10. I draw these domains as ovals with overlapping but prescribed, finite edges (once again, the entrepreneur/businessman in me feels the need to qualify the academic boundary setter). In the real

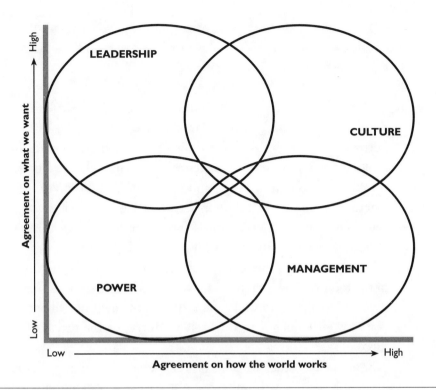

Exhibit 10   **Assessing and Building Agreement: Four Domains**

world, of course, there's no specific line where one domain
ends and the other begins. But these domains do correspond
roughly to an orientation along the two axes. Why are the
domains important? Because individual tools group together
logically within domains, and no domain contains all tools.
This becomes critical when you set out to take action. As we've
established in earlier chapters, two principles should guide
our actions: understand where and how we agree (and need to
agree) in a given situation, and pick the right tool to bring about
the desired consequence. Knowing which domain you fall into
will provide insight into which tools will work.

Let's look at each of these broad domains in turn, and think about the tools that are employed within each domain to create agreement among leaders and followers.

Power. Here we are in the bad-hairstyles, Generalissimo Stevenson domain again. Think of how Marshal Tito dealt with the Serbs, Croats, and Bosnians for all those years. He herded them all together into one more or less artificial nation, put a huge thumb down on all of them, and said, in effect, "I don't care whether you agree with me or with each other on what you want out of life. What I want is for you to look down this gun barrel and agree with me on how the world works."

Tito was an extreme case, of course, and he used only certain of the tools of power to forge consensus. But, as Exhibit 11 implies, if you're spending a lot of time in low-agreement neighborhoods, you're pretty much forced to rely on force, or the threat of force.

Some of the other tools of power include, for example, role modeling (people will imitate you if you seem to embody their own value system) and expertise (people will tend to heed someone who seems to understand how the world works). Sometimes when the world is very uncertain, a loud voice shouting "Follow me!" is all that's needed.

Is the exercise of power a "good" way to achieve consensus? This is a question that turns on both ethics and effectiveness. Let's agree that, though throwing your weight around may not be fair, it's undeniably effective. As in Yugoslavia, the exercise of power tends to make life very predictable for at least one, and often (in some senses) for both parties. As I've argued repeatedly in earlier chapters, it's the lack of *mutual* predictability that leads to conflict. If the predictability imposed by force is one-sided, so one party can't know what it needs to do next, it's not likely to last very long. Mutual predictability, when power is constrained by accepted rules, may well prove durable.

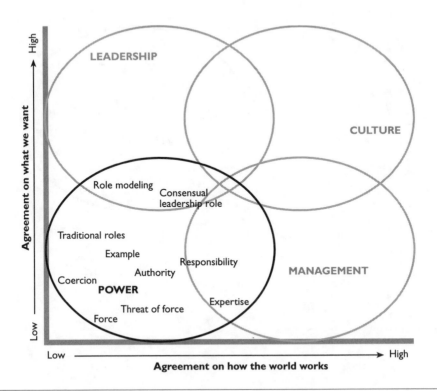

Exhibit 11   **Assessing and Building Agreement: The Tools of Power**

Culture.   Back out on the other end of the spectrum, where Apple and the various Lebanese and Somali clans dwell, we find a range of cultural tools for modifying agreement (Exhibit 12). Religion is one of the most important of these. Religion says, in effect, "This is how our group will organize itself for human interaction, and here is how we will measure success." Only a shade different is a constitution, which focuses a bit less on what we want and a bit more on how the world works.

Apprenticeship is possible in part because all the participating parties share at least some common ideas about what they want, but—more important—because the members of the clan

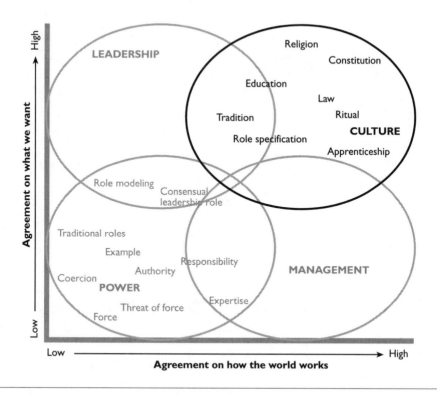

Exhibit 12   **Assessing and Building Agreement:
The Tools of Culture**

absolutely agree on how the world works. (To make a Stradivarius, you use this kind of wood, you season it for this long and in this way, you bend it and shape it in these special ways, and so on.) And in comparing this exhibit with the one before it, notice how the tools of power tend to be personal, or at least personified, whereas the tools of culture (law, ritual, education, and others) tend to be grounded more in shared values.

The ethics and effectiveness of culture as an agreement generator? Well, as we've seen, this is an interesting neighborhood. Agreements forged here are mutually acknowledged and tend to encompass very broadly a wide range of goals and means. They

180

are effective, in that they require very little coordination. (Think of a school of tropical fish turning on a dime.) On the other hand—as with Clan Apple—they can be dangerously unresponsive to change and intolerant of diversity.

Management.   Due south of culture on my graph is management. My readers in the business community will recognize in Exhibit 13 most of the tools that I've listed for modifying agreement in this domain.

Note that standard operating procedures and training are very low on the "what we want" scale. Recall the rock-picking

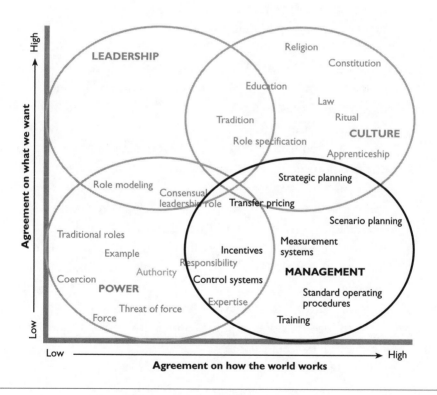

Exhibit 13   **Assessing and Building Agreement: The Tools of Management**

exercise we went through earlier. When you call me up and tell me that henceforth all operating group meetings will be held on Mondays at 8:00 A.M., I'm not likely to have any strong opinions on the subject (unless I like to sleep late after a tough weekend). I know that this particular meeting could happen at almost any time of day, on almost any day of the week, without causing the company any particular problems. But hey—*somebody* has to make the call. And, because you're signing the checks around here, I'm happy to defer to you. I'll be there at eight o'clock sharp.

Management tools span a good chunk of the "what we want" axis. Look, for example, at the difference between strategic planning (which requires some substantial agreement on both axes) and training (which demands far less buy-in on "what we want")—but they don't work terribly well unless we *do* agree on how the world works. In other words, the fact that everyone in the operating group takes it for granted that they need to meet once a week really boosts attendance at that eight o'clock Monday meeting.

Given a requisite initial level of agreement, management tools can promote agreement in ways that are both ethical and efficient. For example, they can improve competence, thereby making action effective in the real world. By increasing agreement on how the world works, they may eliminate the need to hit upon the "best possible solution." I'm thinking, for example, of the Chevy Lumina—truly a dreadful car, but one that seems to represent some kind of consensus at General Motors—and Microsoft Word, which at last count required 13 disks to load on my computer and has the look and feel of an armored personnel carrier.

On the other hand, management tools can serve to highlight differences between you and me, which in turn tends to decrease our efficiency. And, although most management tools don't hurt the potential for coordination, neither do they

necessarily increase it. In some cases, such as poorly designed
incentives, "close enough" just ain't good enough.

Leadership. In the upper left-hand corner of Exhibit 14, spookily far
away from some of the management tools we've just been
talking about, are the leadership tools necessary for modifying
agreement.

As in our other domains, leadership calls upon a spectrum of
tools for modifying agreement. Charisma, for example, depends on a preexisting consensus about "what we want," whereas
vision—the topic of so many leadership tomes in recent

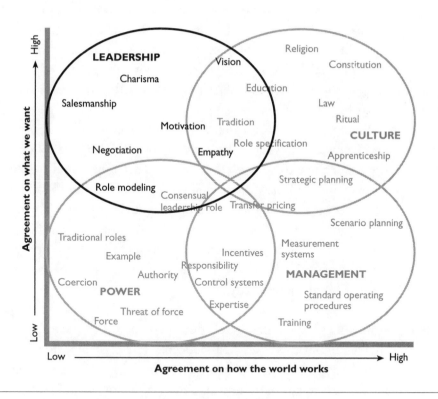

Exhibit 14   **Assessing and Building Agreement:**
The Tools of Leadership

years—has to grow out of high agreement on both what we want and how the world works. Negotiation (as you'd expect) becomes a more useful tool when there is less-than-universal agreement on what we want or how the world works.

Below that we find salesmanship, the "emotional selling" I mentioned earlier. What I'm referring to here is sales-by-association: if you buy my product, you'll be getting more of what you want. ("Drink Glotz beer and hot bodies will follow you down the beach.") As Charles Revson used to say, "I sell *hope*." As foreshadowed earlier in this chapter, the other kind of salesmanship, "consultative selling"—more appropriately located in the management domain—attempts to change your understanding of how the world works. Picture almost any ad that depends on diagrams of your intestinal tract or that invokes vehicle safety statistics. ("You thought dual airbags up front was good enough? Ha! Volvo introduces *sidewall* airbags.") And, of course, some of the best sales people do both—and know why and when each is appropriate.

Again picking up our ethics-and-effectiveness sunglasses: you and I can probably agree that it's a good thing to give followers the free choice to follow. (We'd rather have a beer and a cigar with a Churchill than with a Stalin, for example.) But the flip side of this coin is that leaders have only limited scope to change what people want. The continued effectiveness of our leader, moreover, depends on our shared understanding of the consequences of a given action—and, as we've seen, societal consensus is a fragile commodity.

Disaggregation. I apologize for throwing a new term in so late in the game, but this is a useful concept. The preceding four tool domains (power, culture, management, and leadership) are all about leading and following. They are about broadening and deepening the areas of agreement between people or groups.

But, as we discussed earlier, there are times when it's better to *reduce* the grounds on which we're trying to reach consensus.

This may sound heretical in a book that's about enhancing predictability. In fact, it's not. Predictability comes from understanding where you and the other guy *are* in the world. The world is a place where existing agreements are sure to come under pressure and are likely to come unglued. In most realms of importance, and also in many trivial realms, it takes a tremendous amount of energy to move people from square 1 to square 1.5. It takes a huge commitment of time and other scarce resources to change an organizational structure in response to external change.

Again, if we don't *have* to be in a clan, let's not kill ourselves getting there. Let's disaggregate (or separate out into component parts) certain issues in order to reach agreements in specialized kinds of circumstances. And let's agree to systematically ignore the things that we don't agree on, when that disagreement doesn't affect our capacity to work together: "I don't have to like your cats, and you don't have to play on my softball team, for us to successfully pull the rocks from that field." This is the "getting to yes" realm, in which you and I trade things that we value differently in order to achieve mutual gain (Exhibit 15).

At the heart of this domain, obviously, is the contractual relationship. This is the neighborhood within which markets are well organized, and unions and guilds tend to be equally well organized. The professions and their members tend to fall in the southeast end of this domain—not necessarily agreeing on what they want, but definitely subscribing to a shared vision of how the world works. The building trades are actually an excellent metaphor for disaggregation. Hey, you carpenters frame the place out, and call my electrician friend Joe when you're ready for him. And, when all of you are done with your stuff, me and my fellow plasterers will pick up your keys and get to work.

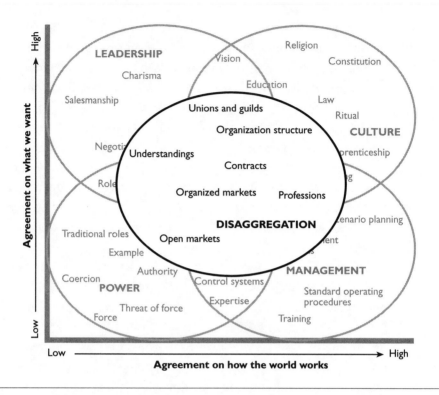

Exhibit 15   Disaggregation: Negotiating the Terms of Agreement

In business, most people are willing to let the marketing and accounting departments go about their business in a mainly disaggregated way. But people used to say the same thing about marketing and engineering, too, and look what happened. Some bright business school types realized that outside forces were demanding more teamwork from these two functional areas in the realm of new product development. In this key area at least, disaggregation became *less* effective, and people began looking elsewhere for appropriate tools with which to forge a broader and deeper agreement.

Seen through the ethics and efficiency lenses, disaggregation can be a good thing, because it allows for the necessary degree of coordination without subjugation (ethics) and minimizes the number of required agreements (efficiency). But, on the down side, as in the new product development example just cited, disaggregation makes coordinated change with other groups difficult. It may also generate unnecessarily high transaction costs, as you and I struggle to define and distribute the value that we have just created together.

■ **Mopping Up**

This chapter has been about how we act together to create a future we desire, in a dynamic context. Mutual predictability is at the heart of this process. The systems that worked for us yesterday (and the ones that will work for us tomorrow) worked because they made our behaviors mutually predictable. And, as I asserted at the outset of this chapter, you're better off making predictions come true—based on agreement and implemented with the right tools—rather than simply hoping to know the future by relying on good guesses.

We need agreement in order to enhance our mutual predictability and thereby to build the future. There are five domains within which we tend to find ways of working together: power, culture, management, leadership, and disaggregation. Within each of these domains of consensus building, there are different tools that can be used to change the degree and necessity for agreement along one or both of our two axes: what we want and how the world works. No toolkit is inherently "better" (more effective, more ethical) than any other. Power is useful when there's little chance of anything else working. Culture is useful when we mostly agree with each other along both axes. But it's *not* so useful in the absence of such agreement (which is why I cringe when I hear management gurus calling for "More corporate culture!" as the universal fix-it).

Leadership is where I go if I need a toolkit for modifying agreement on what we want. Management is where I go if I need a toolkit for modifying our level of agreement on how the world works.

But, at the end of the day, the day doesn't end. This is a very dynamic arena. Agreements we thought we had yesterday may not exist today. Agreements that allowed us to work together on yesterday's tasks may not be sufficient to tomorrow's tasks. The tool that worked yesterday to accomplish a given task may not work tomorrow. And new markets may let us increase our efficiency by agreeing not to agree on as much. The ground shifts.

People in leadership positions therefore have to engage in constant reassessment. Do our agreements of yesterday still stand? Will our agreements of yesterday still work tomorrow? If not, how will we work together to forge agreements to allow us to work together? Or should we *reduce* our zones of overlap and minimize the need to reach agreement in the first place? If so, let's disaggregate.

Obviously, these are concerns of leaders and followers in all walks of life. In the next chapter, we'll look more closely at how predictability is honored (and dishonored!) in the broader society.

chapter ten

Society and Unpredictability

*I hold that man is in
the right
who is most closely in
league with the future.*
Henrik Ibsen*

Question: How do you get a roomful of Harvard Business School alumni to growl in unison?

Answer: Ask them what they think of the U.S. tax code.

But the next logical question—"So why are you all growling like that?"—would get you to a more interesting point. Off the top of their heads, some surely would answer that tax rates are cruel and confiscatory. One or two might volunteer that there hasn't been a good president since William Howard Taft. But, if you probed a little deeper, you'd find out something interesting. What most smart people with control over significant financial resources *really* object to is the variability of the tax code; in other words, its unpredictability.

What was the most prosperous era in recent American history? Most of us would agree that it was the period from about

---

*Ibsen wrote this in a letter to a friend in 1882. President Eisenhower appropriated the sentence verbatim for his 1956 speech accepting his party's nomination for president. Being closely in league with the future is evidently appealing to both Danes and Republicans.

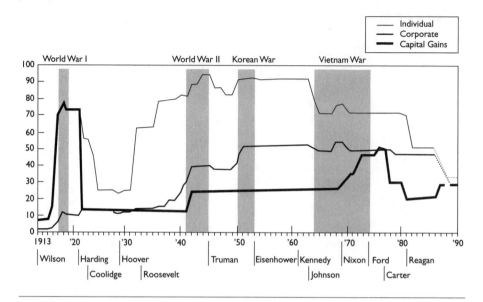

Exhibit 16   **Federal Taxes on Income: In Search of Predictability**

Source: "Ups and Downs of Federal Taxes on Income," *Wall Street Journal*, 18 August 1986.

1950 to about 1965, give or take a half decade or so on either end. Now look at Exhibit 16. What was the only period in the income tax era (which began in 1913) during which the top rates for individual, corporate, and capital gains remained almost perfectly constant?

No surprise: there's an almost-exact overlap. And note that, despite what the Taft crowd might tell you, prosperity and high income taxes are not mutually exclusive.* Now, it's certainly true that other factors made more important contributions to the prosperity of the postwar decades. It's also true that the stability

---

*Nor are Republicans and tax increases, it seems. Note that Presidents Kennedy and Reagan share the honors for presiding over the deepest cuts in the top individual rates, and President Nixon pushed the capital gains tax through the ceiling.

190

of the top tax rates in this period is a little deceptive. (The regulations governing the *application* of these rates grew from one trim book to seven fat ones between 1950 and the present.) But I think you could get almost any room full of capitalists to say that stability in the tax rates is better than instability—that they are more likely to invest and make long-term bets when they have some confidence that the rules of the game won't get changed on them.

We don't have that confidence today. "Whatever the rates are now," as my colleague Hank Reiling writes, "you can confidently bet that you and your company will experience different ones if you both enjoy a normal life expectancy. It may be both realistic and prudent to build into your long-range tax planning this factor of frequent change."[1]

Well, yes, Hank; that's the only way to stay in the game as it's currently played. But the hidden problem here is that, faced with unacceptable levels of unpredictability, many people with resources to invest either hedge their bets or opt out of the game altogether. And an economy that people are unwilling to bet on with confidence and enthusiasm is a hobbled economy.

Learn to Love Your Lawyer?

Where else does unpredictability hurt us on a societal scale? How about in the application of justice?

Those of us happily outside the legal profession like to think of the law as permanent, unchanging, and God-given— something that Somebody Important with a raggedy beard dragged down from a mountaintop, long ago. But this comes from the area of the brain that is responsible for creating and sustaining happy delusions, such as: *I still look great in a bathing suit.*

Part of the problem is inherent in the very nature of the legal system, which is tormented by the dilemma posed in earlier chapters: the need for change battling with the need for stability. In a 1949 lecture to the Association of the Bar of the City of New York, William O. Douglas reflected on the doctrine of *stare decisis*, lawyer's Latin for the general inclination of judges and lawyers to look to precedents for guidance.* Why, Douglas wondered aloud, did so many more lawyers want to *find*, rather than *create*, precedents? One answer, Douglas acknowledged, is that precedent is a good rock on which to anchor a client's case. But he went on to cite what he saw as another, perhaps more fundamental reason for this attachment to precedent: "The lawyer himself shares the yearning for security that is common to all people everywhere."

So lawyers, too, are human and seek predictability like the rest of us.** (So much for the lawyers-as-aliens theory.) But—as Douglas went on to explain—that can't be the whole story. The law *has* to evolve, or it becomes dead and irrelevant. This is particularly true in the field of constitutional law. Judges are sworn to support and defend an over-200-year-old document, but not necessarily the decisions that have been handed down in the interim. So, in practical terms, if the membership of the Supreme Court turns over rapidly, there may well be a rapid evolution in constitutional law. Similarly, technological, political, and economic shifts require us to reexamine assumptions in the

---

*The expression in its entirety reads, *stare decisis, et non movere quieta*, or "to stand by decisions, and not disturb things that are settled." In other words, don't rock the boat. This is how lawyers make their world predictable.

** Jonathan Swift was less charitable. "It is a maxim among lawyers," he wrote in *Gulliver's Travels*, "that whatever hath been done before may legally be done again; and therefore they take special care to record all the decisions formerly made against common justice and the general reason of mankind. These, under the name of precedents, they produce as authorities, to justify the most iniquitous opinions; and the judges never fail of directing accordingly."

law. For example, breakthroughs in medical technology have brought about the need to define privacy in new ways. Think of the earlier example in which U.S. Army soldiers refused to make DNA information available, or consider how the introduction of new life support machinery has called into question people's definitions of life, ownership, and autonomy. As in earthquake zones, things that we thought were solid turn out to have this unpleasant *plastic* quality.

Well, at the very least, this tends to create some anxiety for us commoners. Judicial activism—whereby a judge makes "new" law through his or her novel interpretation of an old one—has great potential to blindside us and undercut our future-building efforts. One more time, so I can be sure I've got it right: gerrymandering to achieve a specific racial mix in a congressional district was a bad thing, and then it was a good thing, and now it's a bad thing again? And, similarly, affirmative action in hiring was, for decades, something my business could get sued for not doing. Now it's something my business can get sued for doing?

And this is only the "*good*" type of unpredictability that's built into the legal system—the type that has the potential to right old wrongs. What about the bad types? In the post-*Miranda* age, many law-abiding citizens have become convinced that the law is erratic at best, and may even be hostile to their interests. Evidence that would almost certainly send an accused individual up the river is excluded for procedural reasons. At least to those of us with our noses pressed up against the legal glass, it seems as if the guilty go free, the incarcerated get furloughed, and paroled felons become grist for the political mills. Politicians make hay (although not much law) out of the notion of "victims' rights." Even the jury system—long considered one of the most compelling arguments for democracy—has been under a cloud ever since the Simpson cases and similar decisions. How predictable is a system in which this group or that group is reluctant to convict "their own kind," even in the face of overwhelming evidence? How predictable is a system (ask others) when government officials fabricate evidence?

Equally troubling is the reality (or at least the semblance) of a court system that is paralyzed by both the number and the complexity of the cases on its docket. Cases take years to come to trial, during which time the alleged offender (assuming deep enough pockets and a less-than-heinous crime) is very likely to be on the streets. Or the savvy offender finds ways to wriggle around the spirit of the law by observing its letter. I have a friend in North Carolina, for example, who isn't a very good driver by legal standards. In fact, he's terrible at obeying speed limits. In the Tarheel State, you lose your license after you're caught speeding three times—period. No ifs, ands, or buts. Except that my friend has discovered that, if you get your offense upgraded from "speeding" to "reckless driving," you'll pay a whopping fine, but you'll almost *never* lose your license.

We also recognize that cause-and-effect relationships are damnably difficult to establish on this strange legal turf. We want fewer criminals on the streets, so we establish mandatory sentences. This does indeed prevent those soft-hearted judges from coddling criminals—but it pushes the local district attorney away from filing certain kinds of charges, and it tends to fill up our prisons with the kinds of small-time marijuana peddlers who are inept enough to get caught.[2] Once the prisons get overcrowded, the time-to-trial gets longer, and the accused stays out on bail longer—or, worse, the charges against him or her are quietly dropped.* All of this adds up to randomness, and unpredictability, in the eyes of the casual observer.

---

*Several states, including my home state of Massachusetts, have gone into the prisoner-export business. Or, more accurately, the state of Texas, proprietor of a truly huge prison system, has gone into the prisoner-import business. The unpredictability factor, of course, is that a non-Texan sent to a Texas prison is likely to sue on the grounds of cruel and unusual punishment. This has already started to happen.

Many of the proposed "fixes" to our legal system have the same double-edged quality. They are presented as predictability enhancers and often wind up instead giving us that *bad feeling* in our stomachs. *(Uh oh! What's going to happen next???)* Take alternative dispute resolution (ADR), for example. Sometimes referred to as "private justice"—a phrase that I'm adding to my personal list of oxymorons—ADR serves a useful purpose in unclogging the courts and keeping legal costs down. "ADR has become so appealing," says Frank E. A. Sander, one of my Harvard colleagues over at the Law School, "because the judicial system has failed so many people."[3] (I know that one friend of mine would concur. He was involved in a nine-year lawsuit, which generated 180,000 documents. When the case was finally resolved, fully *two-thirds* of the multimillion-dollar settlement went directly to the lawyers.)

Some in business feel the same way. "The issues are timeliness, predictability, and fairness," says an executive at Toro Company, which has jumped into ADR with both feet.[4]

Uh oh—expert testimony, from professors and business practitioners alike, that the standard legal processes are unacceptably unpredictable. But what about this ADR alternative?

Well, according to *Business Week*, both the rights of discovery and the process of presenting evidence are truncated in the arbitration and mediation processes (the two main tools of ADR). And throw old *stare decisis* out the window, too—in ADR, judges can ignore the accumulated weight of case precedent in reaching their decisions. The decisions of arbitrators are essentially unappealable and are not bounded by the conventions that traditional judges tend to observe. Try this one on for size: early in 1996, the California Supreme Court ruled that the arbitrator in a dispute between Intel and Advanced Micro Devices could impose "unusual and even bizarre punishment," as long as that punishment had at least a tenuous link to the dispute at hand. My friends in the

California business community were a little unnerved by *that* turn of events. Manufacturers of jet skis and pressure cookers, ask yourselves this question: "Can the return of the dunking stool be far off?"

It's clear to me that our societal need for predictability argues for an increased reliance on the legislative branch of our governments and a decreased reliance on the judicial apparatus. Sure, Congress is subject to lobbying, logrolling, and all the other venal sins that have driven that body to the bottom of the list of Institutions Held in High Esteem by the General Public (just above "dog-track owners," as I recall). But at least the mechanisms of the legislative branch are reasonably open to scrutiny and therefore lend themselves to interpretation by us future builders.

Having said that, I'll also volunteer to our legislators that not every change is an improvement. Predictability means either continuing with something that we already know and understand, or moving comprehensibly and coherently toward something new.

■ The Erratic Reign of Technology

Technology is a little bit like the law. We expect it to provide solutions to our problems and to deliver projected improvements to our lives. As it turns out, these expectations are unrealistic—sometimes wildly so. This gets to be more of a problem as we depend more and more on those ubiquitous bits and bytes.

The summer of 1996, for example, was not a great season for technology. The $80 million computer network that IBM set up at the Olympic Games in Atlanta to provide instantaneous results to 13 news organizations was mainly a fizzle. Paper made a surprise comeback, as couriers toting laser prints and faxes to and fro across Atlanta filled in for the overwhelmed network.

IBM wound up sending a letter of apology to its customers. "All of us at IBM," wrote IBM's general manager of global services, "are as frustrated as you are."[5]

In August, the president of America Online (AOL) wrote a similar letter to his 6 million customers. "Wednesday was a bad day for me," Steve Case's electronic letter began, "and I know, for many of you." At 4:00 A.M. on August 7, AOL technicians attempting to upgrade the system's networking software wound up freezing and crashing the entire system—a blackout that lasted 18 hours.* "We have come a long way in terms of making AOL a part of everyday life," Case continued, "and now we need to raise the bar in terms of quality and reliability. Today's outage reminds us that despite the recent progress we've made in expanding our AOLnet network . . . we still have a long way to go to make AOL as reliable as must-have utilities such as electricity and the telephone."[6] A subsequent marketing success—an offer of unlimited usage for a flat fee, beginning in late 1996—overloaded AOL's circuits, and brought new kinds of unpredictability to the enterprise.

Part of the problem is that technology has become ubiquitous in the lives of many (even most) people. Think about the cell phone, the beeper, and the fax machine—they are either joined to our hips or lurking in dark corners of our homes or offices . . . just biding their time . . . just waiting for us to let our guards down. And over in that same corner is your PC, a wonderful innovation that has introduced five new kinds of unpredictability into your life for each efficiency it has made possible. I discovered this equation during my last few interactions with lawyers and publishers. An anonymous paralegal downtown runs a global search and replace on some live document (very efficient!) and

---

* Case should have taken note of the experience of Netcom Online Communications, which a few months earlier had delivered a 13-hour blackout to its 400,000 subscribers—for essentially the same reason.

winds up inadvertently changing the meaning of a key sentence. And then, of course, no one rereads the whole document to see if it still makes sense. Why bother? Computers don't make mistakes, right?

Well, not as often as the people running them do. Technology has the unique ability to take a small-scale human error and multiply its impact exponentially. The Chase Manhattan Bank learned this lesson recently. It intended to send a moderately aggressive letter ("Your account is currently in a default condition") to some 90 problem customers. Instead, due to a couple of typos, the letter went to 11,000 customers.

Technology also affords us the opportunity to broadcast mistakes and carry out vendettas on a grand scale. In 1994, Intel's Pentium chip was discovered to have a bug in its mathematical logic. This news flashed out over Webs and Nets unvarnished and unanalyzed, transforming the once-friendly and predictable Pentium microprocessor into a scary liability. (It took a while for Intel to make it clear that, for the vast majority of PC users, the glitch would have absolutely no significance.) Recently, the courts have decided that AOL doesn't have absolute rights over the kinds of messages that get broadcast to its member base by individual members. It's not hard to envision a scenario in which a disgruntled user of the Whatever software package sends out an all-points bulletin intended to scare the entire AOL subscriber base away from Whatever. But what if Whatever doesn't really deserve this treatment, except sort of, in some circumstances? Don't most of us earnest technoklunks walk away from this experience with a higher level of anxiety about our tools?

Another part of the problem is competitive pressures. Cliff Stoll makes this point in his recent book *Silicon Snake Oil*. Software manufacturers release Version 3.2 before it's really, truly ready, and we wind up wrestling the beast to the floor (usually with little or no documentation). "Am I asking too much," Stoll inquires rhetorically, "that commercial software be tested and bug-free upon shipping? Apparently so, because I've never received such a product."[7]

Here's where we hapless consumers fall back on some of those inductive rules of thumb described in Chapter 7. "Never buy a car made in Detroit on a Monday or a Friday," as the saying used to go. "Never buy a new software package," my colleague Jim McKenney advises, "until it's been out for nine months."

Technology also has the perverse tendency to recomplicate itself. In *Why Things Bite Back: Technology and the Revenge of Unintended Consequences*, Edward Tenner points to the simplification that resulted when "user-friendly" interfaces, full of adorable little icons, became the norm.[8] As long as Apple controlled the world of icons, things were great. Then a zillion other manufacturers started designing icons, and things got less great. And, as it turns out, some concepts ("undo") just don't sit down and pose for the icon artists.

Still another part of the technology problem is that technological "solutions" are imposed on us piecemeal, by people who have only partial control over part of the problem and who unwittingly create new problems as they go along. Where I work, we are currently in the mode of "continuous upgrades" to our various computer networks and systems. (Remember "continuous improvement" in Chapter 1?) Upgrades are nice—it's soothing to think that I have the latest armorclad version of Microsoft Word—but they're also chaotic. Little bugs and incompatibilities appear. Printers stop responding. The Net mysteriously becomes unavailable. And meanwhile, of course, every upgrade creates the real risk that my home equipment will no longer be powerful enough to keep up and that I'll have to spend another boatload of money on a new PC for home. Sometimes I shoot my mouth off: wouldn't it be better if we just froze everything solid for two years at a time—zero tolerance of changes—saved up our money, and then invited in all the propellerheads for two solid weeks of chaos?

The technological bottom line is that we simply don't know where our inventions are going to take us. I once read an interesting essay about how the steam engine that Thomas Newcomen and two of his cronies invented in 1712 to pump water in the little English town of Dudley led directly and inevitably to modern medicine. We conceive of jets as a faster way to move people around, and lethal viruses (featured later in the chapter!) thank us very much and consider us fools. We predict, correctly, that the Green Revolution will greatly reduce the incidence of famine around the world; but we don't quite anticipate the overpopulation and habitat trashing that also ensue. The truly wonderful scientists and engineers at Bell Labs invent the transistor and accidentally wipe out the domestic radio, TV, and audio amplifier industries.* Oops!

In the late eighteenth century, a young Englishman named Ned Ludd broke up a few machines that were used to produce stockings. Some 30 years later, a group of unemployed workmen, angry at the new weaving technologies that (in combination with a nasty recession) were putting many in their ranks out of work, banded together as "Luddites." They roamed the midland counties of England, smashing textile machinery in an effort to turn back the clock.

Of course, the Luddites failed. Technology continued to move forward inexorably, in part because it helped many more people than it hurt. (And let's talk turkey here. The Luddites weren't much interested in the fact that the new looms were making high-quality cloth available to the common man for the first time.) Communities that try to stop progress wind up as backwaters. But it's as dumb to say "technology can do no wrong"

---

*Oh, all right. Give management in those industries their due as well.

as it is to say "technology can do no right." We need to embrace technology, and then be prepared to mitigate some of the inevitable and unpredictable harm that ensues from that embrace.

Think of fire insurance and unemployment insurance. These are mechanisms designed to spread small-scale catastrophes over a huge base. We, the insured, give up a little money to gain a large degree of predictability (for either ourselves or our heirs). Shouldn't we think similarly about technology? Singapore imposes a 1 percent of payroll tax on all Singaporean employers, to be used for retraining of technologically outmoded employees. I'd vote for that!

■ Regulation: Now You See It . . .

Yet another factor weaves unpredictability into our larger social fabric: the on-again, off-again nature of government regulation.

For ten years, gas station owners were required by the Environmental Protection Agency (EPA) to let local fire departments know about any flammable materials they had on the premises. This meant filing an EPA-specified report—a tedious process, which one businessperson (the owner of 24 Arkansas gas stations) estimated cost him around $50,000 each year.[9]

Now, as a result of the Small Business Regulatory Enforcement Fairness Act of 1996, these reports don't have to be filed anymore. OK; that's a good thing. But what will happen if some future Congress sees political advantage in reregulating all those gas stations and fire departments? It's hard to draw up a meaningful ten-year strategic plan in the context of regulations that wander in and out of our business lives unpredictably. And the teeth of the law reside in the fact that small businesses can now sue federal agencies that appear to be placing undue regulatory burdens on them.* To me, the prospect of armies of small business proprietors taking the Feds to court (see above!) is not necessarily reassuring.[10]

One problem with regulation is that it depends so heavily on cost-benefit analyses. These are only one step removed from the predictions of those fortune-tellers on UHF stations whom we talked about in earlier chapters. Cost-benefit analyses are essentially a stack of judgments piled up on top of one another. A miscalculation at the bottom of the stack sends the whole thing off kilter, and there are usually miscalculations throughout the stack, compounding one another and leading to truly loony conclusions.

For example, what are the costs of implementing a proposed regulation? Or, less often, what are the costs of *not* implementing it? Most of the time, we don't have a clue. OSHA's 1987 plan to reduce foundry workers' exposure to formaldehyde—a laudable goal—was estimated to cost around $10 million, and the affected industries howled. As it turned out, the tighter standard turned out to cost almost nothing, because manufacturers realized they could change the formulas in their resins, thereby lowering formaldehyde levels with no noticeable impact on product quality. Similarly, in 1990, the collective wisdom of Washington had it that it would cost $1,000 per ton of coal to reduce sulfur dioxide in the atmosphere. A half-decade later, the real premium for keeping our northeastern lakes and forests alive turned out to be only about $140 per ton.[11]

Age, sex, and race discrimination; sexual harassment, wrongful termination, product liability—the realms in which regulation can inject unpredictability into our lives goes on and on. My point is *not* that regulation is a bad thing, in and of itself. (If you

---

* It's worth noting that the EPA is already one of the few federal agencies that can be sued by a private party for *failing* to enforce the law. I predict that regulatory law will continue to be a growth industry.

like hot dogs but don't like regulation, reread Upton Sinclair's *The Jungle*.) My point is that regulation should be shaped in ways that both permit progress and enhance predictability. Tell me how the game is going to be played—and then *keep* it that way, absent evidence of some horrible miscalculation.

The concept of "grandfathering"—letting a preexisting condition continue into a changed context—has a bit of an odor to it. I think this is true because most nonconforming land uses (such as pig farms in planned-unit developments) exist because they've been grandfathered into the unhappy neighborhood that has grown up around them. Odors notwithstanding, I like and advocate the concept of grandfathering in this troublesome realm of regulation, especially if it could be combined with a sensible approach to depreciation of assets. Under current (changeable) regulation, people don't run at the cleanest possible levels—they run *exactly* at standard and hold the rest in reserve for the next standard change. As an environmentalist, I'm appalled! But, as a businessman, I fully understand. Businesses have to be able to write off big investments in environmental controls (for example) over the depreciable life of a facility. Accordingly, the regulations that *necessitated* that investment in the first place should apply to that investment until it is fully depreciated. Again, tell me how the game is going to be played, and then let me play it that way.

I also think that there's a regulatory equivalent to the "technology insurance" I mentioned above. Let's say that 25 million people derive great benefit from a new measles vaccine, and then 4 people die from adverse reactions to that vaccine. Should the manufacturer of the vaccine get whacked with a $100 million judgment? Or should the community of 25 million beneficiaries help defray this cost?

I think that inventing a regulatory approach based on the latter would lead to a more rational, predictable society. It's a question of getting the incentives lined up right. If a normal house fire created the opportunity to sue somebody for $3 million, there'd be a hell of a lot more house fires. I can hear the plaintiff's attorney now: "Isn't it true, Mr. Weyerhauser Executive, that your company knowingly and recklessly allowed your highly flammable two-by-fours to be used in the construction of this family's house?"

The "lottery" aspect of the regulatory and legal systems creates unpredictability for all of us. We should work toward a restructuring of both systems so that it's perfectly clear that *actions* have *consequences*. (This is what prediction is all about.) People who shoot other people should not get fat book contracts. People who smoke cigarettes should not be eligible for $100 million settlements. (If that money goes anywhere, it should go to the society that actually pays most of the huge costs of respiratory and heart diseases.) Motorcyclists who don't wear helmets and drivers who don't wear seat belts should have credible consequences (higher insurance rates?) shoved in front of their noses. Cause and effect has both charm and power. *If* you engage in contributory negligence, *then* you will face the following consequences—and hiring an ambulance chaser won't do you a lick of good. And that's predictability.

■ Welcome to the Millennium's Front Porch

In 1977, Steven Spielberg gave us *Close Encounters of the Third Kind*, which featured cuddly, large-eyed, childlike creatures from outer space. Then, in 1982, we met E.T., the extraterrestrial—weirder looking, but still benign. (E.T., you'll recall, could rejuvenate dying house plants when his own batteries were at full charge.) But in 1996—four years from the beginning of the new millennium—we were introduced (in *Independence Day*) to a malevolent, foul-smelling race of invaders who were hell-bent on killing us all. In the process, they demonstrated their true heinousness by blowing up the White House and knocking over the Statue of Liberty.

It's no coincidence that, in the closing years of the century and the start of the millennium, we're also under cinematic attack by microbes. *Twelve Monkeys*, *Outbreak*, and *The Stand*—all featured hideous liquefying bugs of one sort or another, sweeping across the planet apocalyptically.

What's this all about?

Part of it is surely a nervous reaction to real-life scourges like AIDS and the *Ebola* virus.

Another part, I think, is that old instinct for requisite variety that we've talked about in earlier chapters. We're drawn to mysteries, excitement, the unknown—even the nasty stuff—in part because we know that variety is good for the gene pool.

But another contributing factor, and the one that I'm most interested in, is our aversion to the unpredictability of the terrain that lies ahead of us. With good reason, we feel that the links between actions and consequences are being clipped and nicked on all sides of us. Causes don't lead to the right effects. As a result, we can't turn our backs on the revenuers and regulators, the lawyers and judges, or the heavens and petri dishes.

Can we turn our backs on each other? That's the challenge we'll examine in the next chapter.

chapter eleven

Lone Wolves and Team Players

We are born for cooperation,
as are the feet, the hands,
the eyelids, and the upper and
lower jaws.
Marcus Aurelius Antonius

In a recent issue of the *Harvard Business Review,* two of my colleagues wrote the following: "Today's top managers recognize that the diversity of human skills and the unpredictability of the human spirit make possible initiative, creativity, and entrepreneurship."[1]

I hope you hung up, like I did, on that word "unpredictability."

As a longtime student of entrepreneurship, I have come to the conclusion that the most successful entrepreneurs are people who deal effectively with the future. They are people who push a new product into an established market or find a new market for an established product—but they almost never try to do both at once. In other words, they *limit* the degree of unpredictability in their ventures. In fact, they succeed only when they're able to make customers, suppliers, employees, and financiers share their vision of the future and the path to get there.

Perhaps in some cases the entrepreneurial instinct arises out of deep and mysterious pools of creativity, contrariness, and irrationality. Much more often, I'd suggest, entrepreneurship begins when someone says, "What rule is no longer working, and what's the alternative? Who *says* that we need a telephone monopoly? Who *says* that three TV stations are all that will ever be needed? Wouldn't we be better off if this changed?"

But let's imagine that the unpredictability of the human spirit in some way contributes to the birth of entrepreneurship. I'll still maintain that, once that spirited would-be entrepreneur starts to engage with the world, unpredictability becomes an unaffordable luxury.

Here are four fairly obvious rules for would-be entrepreneurs which I just made up to illustrate the point:

Rule 1: When the room is full of the venture capitalists you're depending on for backing, don't let your unpredictable human spirit take flight. Act like you're in it for the long haul. Don't make any sudden moves, or start speaking in tongues. As my colleague Myra Hart has documented, what gets you money is (1) knowing (about your business) and (2) being known. Both traits have to do with predictability.

Rule 2: When looking to lure top talent into this new venture, don't stress the scariness of life in a new venture, or the security that they'd be leaving behind if they signed up with you. Talk about stock options, 10-year plans, your policy of generous contributions to the company's gold-plated 401 (k), and similar reassuring things about how good the future will be in your shop. And it never hurts to drop a pointed reminder or two about the recent history of downsizing at their current place of employment.

Rule 3: When wooing your first customers, don't cite SBA statistics about how many businesses fail within their first five years. Instead, talk about your five-year plan for current-product upgrades and new product introductions. Talk with people who already know you and believe in you (who think of you as predictable). Get some sales reps with a little grey around the temples.

Rule 4: When building initial relationships with suppliers, don't talk about your personal plans to be financially independent before you hit 50. Talk about how your two companies should plan to invest in each other's technology bases, and how the two of you might eventually decide to push your very different information systems toward a point of mutually beneficial convergence.

You get the point. Successful entrepreneurs paint a picture of a believable future. (This is why entrepreneurship tends to flourish in troubled times, when people start looking for people with the Answer.) They make it clear, in all of their interactions with potential stakeholders, that they are more like the tortoise than the hare (although, of course, they're brimming over with brains, talent, and overwhelmingly compelling ideas). Or, to grant them a little more sex appeal, successful entrepreneurs are like those half-wild stallions that movie cowboys ride: they let their nostrils flare, but they don't spit out the bit. Spirited, yes; unpredictable, no.

Let's look a little more closely at this notion of individuals and their obligations.

■ Etiquette and Ethics Meet Prediction

In Chapter 7, we allowed ourselves the luxury of imagining a world in which we were the sole masters of our fates, envisioning and effecting our futures in splendid isolation. But I also sounded the theme of projectability and hinted that almost no future exists in isolation. In other words, even if we somehow pulled off a more or less unilateral future, our fellow tribe members would have opinions about what we had accomplished and would find ways to inform us of those opinions. And, because we're human, we would *care*.

Why is Ebenezer Scrooge such an interesting character? Because he seems both credible and unsustainable, all at once. What kind of monster, we ask, can resist the entreaties of hungry little children on crutches? We read *A Christmas Carol* for the millionth time in large part to experience the little rush of welcoming Scrooge back, once again, into the fold of humanity.

And, as implied above, it's not just emotional needs that prompt us to work in concert with our fellows. Life gets better when we specialize. You make the saws; that guy will make the hammers; those two guys will make the nails; and I'll get good at building houses—and we'll *all* live a lot better. Once we've made this deal, though, we're pretty much joined together at the hip, and we'd better not screw up. You'd better *keep* making those saws, and I'd better keep working at my own trade.[2]

In other words, it's not enough for me to predict the consequences of my own actions. I also have to be able to predict *your* actions to evaluate the consequences of my actions. And you have to be able to do the same vis-à-vis me.[3]

For most practical human purposes, predictability arises out of:

- **What I say to you (and you say to me)**
- **What I *do*, after making my commitments to you (and vice versa)**
- **What actually happens after all the bets have been placed (how good were our respective predictions?)**
- **The values that both you and I place on the outcomes we arrive at**

The middle two points above deserve a little extra air time. Suppose I'm the head of a vast but shaky conglomerate. You approach me about buying one of my divisions, and I agree. In fact, we shake on it. Then, one day at the breakfast table, you read in the *Wall Street Journal* that I've sold that very same division to one of your archrivals.

Hey, what can I tell you? Things change. I lied. But you have every right to be irritated with me. How are you supposed to conduct your affairs if you can't take people at their word?[4]

And it's not just my reputation that's at stake in circumstances like this. It's also your estimation of my predictive powers. And, finally, it's also *your* competence. After all, your entire organization counts on you to be right, at least a reasonable percentage of the time. Most likely you've been telling your middle managers that you've already landed my division and that they should definitely build it into all of their planning for next year. Suddenly my division is off the table. Your managers, standing around the water cooler, are likely to be saying, "Hey. This guy tells us X is going to happen, and we wind up with Y. How the hell are we supposed to do our jobs if the guy at the top can't do his?"

It has struck me in recent years that most of the rules of human interaction can be interpreted in terms of predictability. These rules range all the way from simple conventions and social etiquette to the highest-order ethical issues. For example:

Running a Red Light.   Easy. We've already been in this intersection. How am I supposed to proceed safely if I can't depend on you to obey the law? Most conventions of social behavior pull in this direction. It's just a lot easier if we don't have to negotiate these little things each time one of them comes up. Which hand do we extend in a handshake?* Which side of the road do we drive on?

---

*The presidential campaign of Bob Dole illustrated the point. Dole lost the use of his right arm in World War II and therefore shakes hands with his left hand. Dole's aides felt that by this late point in Dole's distinguished career, the populace must have been well aware of this fact and should automatically be extending their own left hands. Their regular failure to do so—although almost always innocent—was misinterpreted by Dole's handlers as an insult to the senator.

Lying. As above, you don't like it when I lie to you about selling you my division, because it makes the results of your actions unpredictable. In fact, we can deal more or less effectively with the people who tell us, straight out, that they're gunning for us. Like the schoolyard bully, they're nasty but predictable. We have lots more trouble with people who pretend to be our friends and then stick it to us. This is why in wartime we feed and house prisoners of war (the predictable enemy) and execute traitors (the unpredictable us).[5]

Stealing. Well, my property isn't of much use to me if it isn't there when I need it. Think of how differently you would feel about losing the use of your car under two different sets of circumstances. First scenario: after lots of ominous hints, the transmission on your classic 1961 VW microbus (27 windows and a sunroof) starts to go. You limp into your local garage at Thanksgiving, and your mechanic tells you he won't have it back on the road until after Christmas. Second scenario: your new Lexus is stolen, and—what with insurance claims and the like—it takes a full month to get a replacement car. Both cases involve a month without a car, but whereas the former case is irritating, the theft is infuriating. The difference is the *predictability* factor. Theft equals unpredictability equals bad.

Cheating. I only want to play a game that has a set of rules by which the outcome can be judged. If you cheat, it throws those rules into doubt, and it makes it harder for me to predict and achieve my desired outcome. The problem is accentuated in settings where there's a forced curve—meaning that, if you cheat successfully, it may result in my being thrown out of the game (or the school) entirely. Who would agree to play musical chairs with a bunch of cheaters?[6]

So, if you've dedicated yourself to a life of cheating, get ready to move around—but know from the outset that it's going to be difficult in today's world of instantaneous information. Remember the two rapscallions who briefly rode on Huck Finn's raft? The self-styled Duke and King duped town after town along the Mississippi—and their success depended on the fact that news took a long time to travel a few miles downriver.

Not so today. We contemporary cheaters face a much more sophisticated and rapid grapevine. Think of how often you've unexpectedly run into an old colleague or a college buddy in some faraway airport. Think how many times you've met someone at a party and discovered common acquaintances.* Well, the global business community is even smaller, and getting smaller all the time. If you can check people out through the network, then you can be checked out, too.

Alternatively, you may succeed, given some basic ground rules. Machiavelli offered a particularly salient bit of advice in *The Prince* for overthrowing a principality (which I would characterize as cheating on a grand scale). He proposed that, when moving in on a newly conquered area, you must either take it peacefully and in a spirit of cooperation (that is, create predictability), or you should *kill everyone*. In other words, should you resolve to cheat, cheat *thoroughly*, and win conclusively, for you may not get to play again.

Cheating is contagious, and—just like an infectious disease—it can inject massive unpredictability into an otherwise orderly system. Contrast the tax system in the United States, where it's assumed that most people don't cheat, to that in Italy, where it's assumed that most people do cheat. Think about how quickly a given intersection, or even a whole traffic system, can go from good to bad under the influence of a few cheaters.

---

*At a recent dinner party at our house in Vermont, the American wife of a close colleague discovered she was a former colleague—in Kenya—of the Norwegian father of a second guest.

Abuse of Power.   I had a young couple visit me in my office a few weeks ago, and the two of them told me about a serious problem that they were confronting. It seems that the young woman in this couple, who had recently gone back to work after a maternity leave, was informed by her boss that she would henceforth be expected to spend a lot more time on the road. So, for the past eight weeks, she had been required to leave town on Sunday night, not to return until late Thursday. Needless to say, my two young friends were getting a little frantic.

Their take on the situation—with which I agreed—was that this was an abuse of power. The work contract, implicit or explicit, is designed in part to restrict the boss's authority to certain limited domains. When your boss violates the terms of the contract, it imposes a high degree of unpredictability on you. (This is terrible, in and of itself; what's he going to try *next*?) It also forces you to become less predictable in the eyes of those around you. You can't serve out your term on the local planning board if your own life is plunged into chaos. You can't coach the girls' Peewee basketball team from out of town.[7]

Again, the offense is less in the *content* of a specific action than it is in the *context*. When the army reserves were called up in 1990 to provide extra bodies for the Gulf War, we heard very little grumbling from those whose lives were being disrupted so thoroughly. That's because, although a callup was thought to be unlikely, it was also acknowledged to be part of the bargain. Most young people in line to be called up had been in the habit of putting their own life decisions through the appropriate filter: *Well, what happens if we do get mustered? How will we cope?*

Murder.   Death delivers unpredictability in high doses. First, of course, the dying individual has the problem of not knowing what's on the other side of the Big Door. (No one has yet come back to tell us.) This is something most of us worry about at one time or another.* And second, a murder destroys the predictability of everyone in the vicinity.

But, even in death, there's a wide spectrum of predictability. If you're trying to build a future, the sudden heart attack is much worse than the long degenerative illness. Murder (especially a random murder) inflicts the most unpredictability of all. As far as I know, nobody I've met envisions a future that includes the random murder of a loved one. And, mercifully, not too many people try to bring such a future about.

Remember our handsome and compelling exhibits from Chapter 8? Let's use our predictive perspective to look at the ethics of weaponry in warfare, in Exhibit 17, and see where our sense of morality begins to get offended as more and more unpredictability gets injected.

First, we need to acknowledge that the morality of warfare has a major relativistic component. The rules change over time. In King Arthur's day, the act of killing was totally ritualized, and a self-respecting knight wouldn't have dreamed of attacking his opponent's horse. At least through the Dark Ages, it was considered immoral to attack at night. Well into the 1800s, generals (often those on the losing side) were outraged when their opponents attacked on more than one front at once. And the British troops charged with subduing the American rebels were shocked when the colonials refused to wear bright colors and fight out in the open, in straight lines. Things were so . . . *unpredictable*, when one side got to hide behind the trees and take potshots at the other! What if everybody behaved so poorly!**

---

*The Gnostics of the fourth century A.D. were an interesting exception to this rule. They believed so firmly in their concept of the Other Side that many committed suicide, just to make the crossing sooner. Needless to say, the sect is defunct.

** The fact that the armaments of the day—muzzle loaders and so on—were so inaccurate added a certain fatalistic spice to things, too. If you actually got *hit* by the iron thrown out by one of those things, it *must* have been God's will.

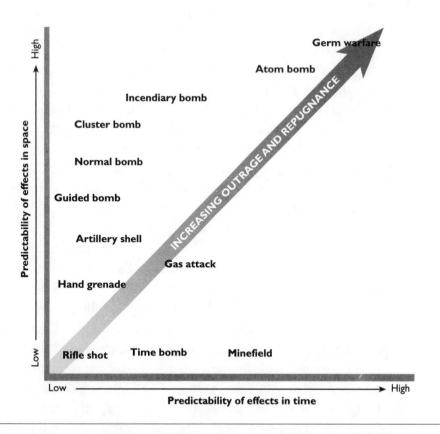

Exhibit 17 **A Predictive Perspective on the Ethics of Weaponry in Warfare**

Well, clearly the rules have continued to change. I think, though, that we can still locate today's weapons on a spectrum of "acceptable" to "unacceptable"—and the difference between an acceptable and an unacceptable weapon is its degree of predictability in time and space.

Again, we're looking at the unpredictability of the effects of certain actions in *time* along the horizontal axis, and in *space* along the vertical axis. Least objectionable of all—it seems to me, at least—is the single rifle shot that you direct at the guy who's

215

coming over the wall to kill you. Not a lot of time-and-space nuances *here*, by gum. It's kill or be killed.

But we're a little less certain about the grenade that we toss over the wall, in the general direction of the unfriendly fire. Climbing the ladder of effects in space, we can state that an artillery shell that lands within eyesight, or a so-called "smart bomb," is morally superior to the dumb alternative. (The buzz bombs launched by the Germans against London in the later stages of World War II are a good illustration of the latter.) Cluster bombs don't last long, but they wreak havoc indiscriminately over a large area, so they have a significant stigma attached to them.

Out along the horizontal axis, we see a time bomb, where the bomber knows when it will do its damage. Then comes a minefield: definitely limited in space (unless you lose the map, which the losing side almost always does), but almost unlimited in terms of time. Very recently, prominent military and civilian leaders around the world have begun a number of campaigns to ban land mines altogether. (An alternative that is also being proposed is to create mines that would turn themselves off after a specified period of time—perhaps months or years.) Why is this initiative receiving widespread attention? I think it's because we feel a profound repugnance when a small child is terribly wounded by a mine, long after the front has left a certain area, or even after the war is over. It's unpredictability over time, and we're repulsed by the consequences.

A gas attack may be more limited in its effects in time, but it's much more unpredictable in terms of space. (And a gas attack doesn't end all that cleanly, either, if you're its victim.) Watch what we encounter as we head up *this* diagonal: first, incendiary bombs, then atomic bombs. The conflagrations caused by firebombing are intended to be more or less unpredictable in terms of space, and they can burn for quite a while, too. Nuclear weapons produce not only physical devastation—widespread and indiscriminate—but also radioactive fallout (poison over time and space) and genetic problems (terror in both time and space).

Germ warfare, in the upper right-hand corner of our chart, is thought by most people to be the most repugnant offensive action of all. Well, why *is* that? I think it's because germ warfare is absolutely unpredictable in terms of its effects over time and in space. We haven't yet found germs that will kill only the other guy, and we haven't found germs that will last only a specified period of time. Note that the only two types of weapons on our chart that have been banned by international arms conventions are the two that fall directly on this diagonal: gas attacks and germ warfare.

The point, again, is that we perceive injustice, or even feel repulsion or outrage, when unpredictability is foisted on us. Every human interaction, including an activity as irrational as warfare, has its rules, and these rules are invariably designed to enhance predictability in time and space. When someone decides to break these rules, we are affronted. And, if we have the power to retaliate (whether to recreate the formerly predictable environment, or to "make an example" of the offending party), we almost always do so.

■ Lone Wolves, Cults, and Tribes

When the world is disorganized and unpredictable, a certain kind of critter emerges from the back of the cave: the lone wolf. The lone wolf looks at chaos and says, "Hey—there's *opportunity* out here! Why don't I just help myself to a little of this, and maybe a lot of that?" Chaos brings out bandits (sporting guns or briefcases).

One thing that should have become clear in the previous chapters is that people are pretty resourceful and generally find a way to get their needs met. As soon as the land becomes populated by lone wolves and other predators, the rest of us almost always decide that what we really need is *security*. That's when we either join a cult or sign up with a tribe.

Cults are reassuring in part because they are monolithic. Their members follow a few simple decision rules and tend to shoot any messengers who try to present contradictory evidence. The typical cult combines isolation (geographic and/or intellectual) with some sort of fervent passion. This is a heady brew, which often degenerates into dangerous paranoia, as with the Jonestown/Jim Jones tragedy in Guyana. *Why is that congressman flying all the way down here to visit us? Must be a trick! God commands us to kill him! God commands us to kill ourselves!*

We tend to think of cults as being religious phenomena, but in fact there are religious cults, political cults, and even business cults. What do you do when you (belatedly) discover that the Japanese have grabbed 25 percent of the American auto market? Start a cult of Japan worshippers—or, alternatively, start a cult of Japan bashers. Or set up a consulting firm that specializes in something like restructuring, and see how many corporate acolytes you attract. Or write *In Search of the One-Minute Megatrend*: the book I hope never to see on the bookshelves, but have a sneaking suspicion that I will.

I don't like cults, but I *do* like tribes. Tribes are groups related by blood or tradition whose members share a similar worldview, especially on key issues like security. Tribes aren't necessarily monolithic, but they know how to close ranks under pressure. They know how to set traps for predators. I have a plot outline for a western that will never get made, mainly because it's too boring. Billy the Kid slouches into the small Kansas town of Predictability, sporting his matching pearl-handled Smith & Wessons and just itching for a fight. He parks his dusty hide in the saloon, starts drinking whiskey, and gets increasingly belligerent.

The townsfolk (that is, the tribe) know exactly what to do. They send a group of 12 guys with shotguns over to the saloon to have a heart-to-heart with Billy. Billy hands over the Smith & Wessons—*"real slow-like"*—and skulks out of town. He tells this tale to every young gun he meets, and none of them ever visits Predictability. The end. Not exactly as gripping as *High Noon*!

The diamond-merchant community in New York City is a good example of a modern-day tribe. This is a tight-knit group whose members don't necessarily agree on much of anything outside their trade, but *within* the trade, predictability reigns. They pass immense value around town based solely on verbal agreements. They have their own language (a combination of Yiddish and trade jargon). Some surely pack guns. They look out for each other.

Becoming a Team Player

I've invented this little typology of lone wolves, cults, and tribes to make a point about future building. The point is, simply put, that we need each other.

Early in this book, we talked about the beast behind the rock: *Is it lunch, or am I lunch?* Let's imagine that you're walking through the jungle, and the beast turns out to be not a chicken, but a tiger. With really big teeth. You can hear its stomach growling.

If you're traveling with a lone wolf, you're in trouble. He looks at you and says, "Thank God I don't have to run faster than that tiger!"

You say, "You *don't*?!" (Sorry; you're the straight man in this scenario.)

And he says, "Nope. I only have to run faster than you."

Old joke. But you get the idea. Now imagine that you're a cult member. Same jungle, same tiger. You look to your leader, and he says, "Quick! Put this amulet on! This will save you!" (Uh oh!)

We've already run the tribe version of this scenario. The tiger pokes its head out of the underbrush, and from all around you comes the sound of cartridges sliding into shotguns. In Predictability, Kansas, in the New York diamond trade, and out here in the jungle, the tribe looks out for its own.

Most of us pass through stages in our lives of lone-wolfism, cultism, and tribalism. If we're lucky, we spend more time as a member of a tribe, and less time as wolves and cultists. Why "lucky"? Because we know that we can't know the future, and we know that we can't stop the future from coming. At the same time, we know we have to deal effectively with the future. In today's complex and accelerating world, dealing with the future is something we can accomplish only by marshaling the diverse resources of a tribe, communicating effectively within the tribe, and taking decisive, collective, and timely actions to steer toward our tribe's agreed-upon outcomes. And only in the context of the tribe can we truly mitigate the consequences of the unexpected and catastrophic.

It's not that anybody who's not in my tribe is a tiger. Far from it. My tribe and your tribe have to work out the intricate choreography of working together, peacefully, so that we can trade our diamonds for your oil. We don't have to agree on everything, but we have to agree on enough. And if bad-tempered aliens ever *do* land, we'd better start thinking more broadly about the definition of *tribes*.

I'll let that serve as the next-to-last message of this book.

chapter twelve

The Question

*The wise god covers with the
darkness of night
the issues of the future, and
laughs if a mortal
is anxious beyond what is right.*
Horace

When I was growing up in Utah, I was exposed almost daily to what my family used to call "momilies"—words of wisdom from Mom.

One momily went like this: Success is getting what you want, and happiness is wanting what you get. In retrospect, I credit Mom for being the mother of what I later came to call "projectability."

Here's another momily: Good decisions come from wisdom, wisdom comes from experience, and experience comes from bad decisions.

I always liked that one, but I was never exactly sure what it meant. Most momilies were either prescriptions for action or cautionary tales against taking rash steps. For a while when I was a kid, I thought that the good decision/bad decision momily was her version of the Icarus myth. Since you can't help yourself without having first hurt yourself, Mom seemed to be saying, lay low. Don't fly too close to the sun.

I'm smarter now about what Mom meant, I think. As suggested above, she was the inspiration for some of the ideas presented in Chapter 7, in which I described how an individual can sharpen his or her predictive skills. Venturing into the future? Figure out what's possible *(predict)*, pick a target you like *(project)*, take your best shot, see what happens (expect to get whacked upside the head sometimes!), learn your lessons carefully, and move forward into the future. Act as wisely as you can, and use that experience to act more wisely next time around.

Utah in the late 1940s was a relatively uncomplicated place, and my boyhood need to shape the future was modest. Unilateral action was still pretty productive. It was only after I got married, got on payrolls, and did other adult kinds of things that I began to worry about the kinds of ideas that show up here in Chapters 8 through 11. As it turned out, it wasn't enough to work on the future by myself. As soon as I began to set really complicated goals for myself, I needed to enlist other people in my future-building activities. This was when prediction met predictability and taught me the difference between prediction and projection. I discovered that not only did I have the extremely tough task of understanding the meaning of my future to me, but I also had to ensure that my fellow future builders and I would be mutually predictable if we were going to have any chance of succeeding at the difficult task we'd set for ourselves. To work together over the long run, our actions have to be mutually projectable. And, somewhere in there, I also learned the difference between success and significance.

Do Lunch or Be Lunch. When this tentative book title first began to float around my office, it ended with a question mark. Gradually, the question mark disappeared. I slowly decided that the title was a prescription—even an imperative. "Doing lunch" was not an option, but a necessity. If you and I are going to work together to keep the tigers at bay, we'd better know each other well enough to understand each other's moves. What are you (and I) doing, why now, and what does it mean to us both?

■ Clarity, Consistency, and Competence

Most management books eventually succumb to the magic formula disease: do these seven things and all will be well. I've already pointed out that things don't work that way in real life. In order to work together, we have to understand where we are on the axes of agreement—agreement on what we want and agreement on how the world works. We then have to understand how much agreement is needed to do what we want to do together. This sets us up to build futures together, for some period of time. Then things change, as they always do, and we have to be flexible enough to recalibrate.

But, despite my aversion to the kinds of grids and slogans that shortchange reality, I'd like to put into your mind three standards for words and deeds that I find necessary for building mutual predictability. They are *clarity*, *consistency*, and *competence*.

Clarity. Well, as suggested above, you and I have to make ourselves clear to each other.[1] Let's do lunch—or the thousand other small things that we humans do in the course of the day to build bridges, create a shared vocabulary, celebrate our history, and otherwise establish the deep reservoir of collective experience that allows us to work efficiently and effectively together.

Suppose you want to get a handle on whether or not your company can take on a project for which it has been prequalified, but which is orders of magnitude bigger than anything you've tried before. You turn to the colleague to your right and say, "OK, Pete, what do you think? Can we pull this off?" And

Pete says, "No prob." Well, if you've worked with Pete for ten years and you know Pete's got solid judgment, you're in good shape. But, if Pete's just been transferred from out of town or hired as a virtual team member, his judgment isn't calibrated, he may not be predictable, and therefore he can't enhance your powers of prediction.

So let's agree not seek or impose gratuitous transfers. Let's not set up incentives or career ladders that foster unproductive turnover—or, if that turns out to be necessary, let's agree to take compensatory steps to protect clarity. And when we venture out of our accustomed habits, let's make sure that our new partners get the chance to make themselves clear to us, and vice versa. Let's not assume that we mean the same thing just because we're using the same words. Let's work hard at building deep agreement about the value of being clear.

Consistency.   It's not enough for me to make myself clear to you once or twice. Predictability grows out of clarity over time—in other words, out of consistency.

Consistency is a tricky goal. I'm always amazed at how often Ralph Waldo Emerson gets misquoted on the subject of consistency. What he actually said was "A *foolish* consistency is the hobgoblin of a little mind," and that's exactly right. In an ever-changing environment, a foolish consistency is a short cut to oblivion. When the Japanese presented their price-and-quality challenge to Detroit in the 1970s, Detroit stayed true to its traditions (high prices, low quality) and got whomped.

What's needed is a consistent adherence to higher-order principles. By this I mean the values that are nonnegotiable, and by which you want to be known. It may be that "The most important thing we do is serve our customers," or "We obsolete our own products so others won't." When I'm faced with a tough choice, what's the highest-order tradeoff that I'll make?

What *won't* I do? Fill in your own blank: *I will never screw the customer. I will never hide a better technology.*

This isn't simple. It's easy to shoot too low or too high, or to lapse into either lofty generalities or humdrum specifics. What do I mean? Well, there's a huge difference between a Honda saying, "We strive to build a car that no repairman ever needs to touch," and a GM saying, "We want our mean time between failures to be 2,000 hours."

The former is an impossible goal that still keeps people focused and moving forward. The latter encourages compromises and corner-cutting: "Let's see. Am I close enough so I won't be caught? Is one-third of my output failing before 1,600 hours good enough?" The problem here is that tradeoffs come too quickly and easily.

Let's call it an "identity goal"—the thing you won't compromise, the thing you want to be known by, and the scorecard of your consistency. (It is clear to me that moment-to-moment stock price movements can't stand in for such a goal.) Stating your identity goal clearly and sticking to it does two excellent things. First, it makes you predictable to those around you—inside and outside of your own family, ball team, tribe, or high-tech startup. And, second, it almost always makes you better at what you do.

Competence. Becoming better at what you do is the last building block of mutual predictability. If your actions are based on a good model of how the world works, you have a much better shot at staying out of Chapter 11 bankruptcy. Barring a bolt-from-the-blue contextual change (such as the dinosaurs experienced), it keeps you nose to nose with or even ahead of the competition. It gives you the latitude to spend more time observing, calculating, and acting (and, within each of these, simplifying, categorizing, and generalizing). And, as Mom would say, you get enough time to cobble together a good decision after you've made a few bad ones.

Without competence, there is no predictability. The world *is* changing, and companies and individuals have to change if they're going to be able to compete in the real world. When I took physics at Stanford in 1963, there were only five basic particles. If I had wanted to keep doing physics, I would have had to keep learning and changing. And this is true in most fields. We have to use tools that weren't available yesterday. We have to invent new languages, agree on what they mean, and encourage ourselves and others to use them.

Competence requires smart investments in the right accounts. Can we know which account is the right one? No. There will always be uncertainty in our future. Those people who plan for only a single future (especially an unlikely one) are very likely to be disappointed. At the same time, we can't operate for *all* futures. Over time, to ensure our own competence, we have to give things up. We may have the raw talent to be both a professor and a middle linebacker, but there's almost no chance we can work hard enough at both to become competent at both.

Depressing, right? Not at all! Because getting *really good* at something is what starts to make change fun, and variety unthreatening. How does Tiger Woods feel as he looks out over the first fairway of a course he's never played before? Pretty good, I bet. Maybe even exhilarated. *Let me at 'em!*

■ The Question

Tiger may be a rare breed. He may actually be alone out there on the first tee, effectively setting up his future with no help from anyone else. But I doubt it. I bet he puts a good deal of time into building mutual predictability, one way or another.

I may look alone and heroic out there on the first tee, or up at that microphone, or wherever, but in reality—in all of life's complicated endeavors—I am not alone. I have to work with you. And, when I do, I must ask myself one question. When I'm faced with an important decision, with implications far into a future that I will necessarily share with others, I have to ask:

Am I making life more or less predictable for those who must depend on me, and on whom I must depend?

And, I think, so do you.

acknowledgments

Although acknowledgments are not often read carefully, I believe that anyone who wants to understand an author's intent should look there first. There are recorded the best clues about how and why the book was created, and whose energy and ideas (besides the author's) went into it.

As I set out to recognize all of the many people who contributed to this final product, I also recognize the impossibility of doing full justice to the task. Surely I've forgotten somebody. Most authors put their apologies at the end; I'll put mine up front. If you expected to see your name on these lists and are sorry it isn't there, I'm sorry. But call me—we'll do lunch.

There are three categories of contributors, with substantially overlapping membership. The first includes those who contributed directly to this book as it was being conceived and born. The second are the many courageous friends who read drafts and commented in ways that have improved the final product. The third category is more broad: the teachers, both formal and informal, who articulated so many of the challenges of predictability and provided so many of the examples that (I hope!) enliven this book.

Four people directly made this book possible. Without Jeff Cruikshank, this book would not exist. He took words on tape and on paper and wove them into this difficult linear medium while adding ideas and extracting clarity. For me, it was a partnership that created value beyond measure, and was fun besides!

Mihnea Moldoveanu has been a true intellectual partner over the last five years. His notes have firmly tied the book's ideas to my many intellectual ancestors, and added a serious, scholarly, and practical spine to our sometimes playful book. Many of the concepts in the book arose through our struggles—Mike's and mine—to solve some daunting intellectual puzzles.

I also owe special thanks to John McArthur, former dean of the Harvard Business School, who lured me back to the school and gave me great freedom to pursue ideas, in whatever strange directions they took me. He provided necessary cover, and also the kind of constant encouragement that is so critical during the early stages of idea gestation.

And finally, special thanks to my wife, Fredi, who gave up so many of our few free moments together so that I could pursue this oddball passion. She has read each draft, given straight comments—I hope!—and made life fun all at once. I thank the Summer Search Foundation for allowing me to compete with it for Fredi's time.

Three colleagues at the Harvard Business School Press—Linda Doyle, Carol Franco, and Marjorie Williams—have provided the balance of encouragement and criticism needed to produce a final manuscript at a reasonable quality level. The copy editor did a thorough job of cleaning up my inconsistencies and making sure I was saying what I wanted to say. (Thank you for winking at all those Odd Initial Caps.) Working with these people makes me proud to be part of the Harvard Business School Press family and the larger Harvard Business School Publishing Company.

On to all those friends and colleagues who have spent many hours reading drafts and telling us gently what didn't (as well as what did) work. True, not all of the problems they identified have been cleared up. Nevertheless, this book would not be what it is without their generous investment. I'm still amazed at the generosity of these good friends, each of whom is just as busy as the next, but all of whom found time to help me. It is impossible to acknowledge their individual contributions, so I'll list them alphabetically. They include:

Robert Ackerman	President, Sheffield Steel
Teresa Amabile	Professor, Harvard Business School
Joseph Badaracco	Professor, Harvard Business School
Amar Bhide	Associate Professor, Harvard Business School
Joseph Bower	Professor, Harvard Business School
Adam Brandenburger	Professor, Harvard Business School
C. Roland Christensen	Professor Emeritus, Harvard Business School
Michael Crow	President, Spencer Entertainment
John Davis	Senior Lecturer, Harvard Business School
	Founder and President, Owner Managed Business Institute
Linda Doyle	President, Harvard Business School Publishing Company
Thomas Eisenmann	Former Partner, McKinsey & Co.
	Assistant Professor, Harvard Business School
Myra Hart	Cofounder and former Vice President, Operations, Staples, Inc.
	Assistant Professor, Harvard Business School
James Heskett	Professor, Harvard Business School
Steven Karol	President, Watermill Ventures
	President-elect, Young Presidents Organization
Seth Klarman	President, The Baupost Group
Nancy Koehn	Associate Professor, Harvard Business School

Walter Kuemmerle	Assistant Professor, Harvard Business School
Ellen Langer	Professor, Department of Psychology, Harvard University
Joseph Lassiter	Former Executive Vice President, Teradyne Corp.
	Former President, Wildfire, Inc.
	Senior Lecturer, Harvard Business School
Paul Lawrence	Professor Emeritus, Harvard Business School
John Lefler	President, Gulf States Steel
Warren McFarlan	Professor, Senior Associate Dean, Harvard Business School
James McKenney	Professor Emeritus, Harvard Business School
Pierre Mornell, M.D.	Practitioner and consultant
Kent Plunkett	President, Bumblebee Technology
Stephen Pond	Chairman, The Education Center
William Poorvu	Adjunct Professor, Harvard Business School
	Chairman, The Baupost Group
Stephen Robbins	Independent consultant
Michael Roberts	Vice President, Finance, Baldini's Pizza
William Sahlman	Senior Associate Dean, Professor, Harvard Business School
Malcolm Salter	Professor, Harvard Business School
Edward Schifman	President, Interconnect Devices, Inc.
Leonard Schlesinger	Professor, Harvard Business School
Eileen Shapiro	President, The Hillcrest Group
Richard Tedlow	Professor, Harvard Business School
Patty Toland	Associate, Kohn-Cruikshank, Inc.
Judy Weil	Executive Director, Northeast Human Resources Association

| Yeoh Poh Seng | Chairman, Sportma-Malaysia |
| Gerald Zaltman | Professor, Harvard Business School |

The final group of contributors includes many who taught me at one point or another during my life. Some had formal teaching responsibilities. Others taught and led by their example, which in many cases embodied predictability in action. To these individuals, who have been so much a part of my life and learning, I owe special thanks:

Margaret Ackerman, Kenneth Andrews, Carol and Isaac Auerback, Harold Bacon, George Baker, Carliss Baldwin, Fritz Balmer, Louis "By" Barnes, George Barton, Jordan and Rhoda Baruch, Frank Batten, John Bishop, Michael Boland, Norm Berg, Pier and Renee Borra, Jo-An Bosworth, Robert McAfee Brown, Roberta Brown, Keith Butters, William Bygrave, Paul Camell, Alfred Chandler, Clayton Christensen, Charles Christenson, Kim Clark, Raymond Clark, Raymond Corey, Howard Cox, Dwight Crane, Loretto Crane, Ian Cumming, Robert Danforth, Gregory Dees, Philippe and Nan-b de Gaspé Beaubien, Eileen Delasandro, Paula Duffy, James and Ruth Faust, Richard Floor, Ronald Fox, Robert and Sandy Freeman, Thomas Furman, Sumantra Ghoshal, William and Sharon Gould, H. Irving Grousbeck, William Guth, Janet and Richard Hanna, Howard Head, James Healy, James Henderson, Nancy Hsiung, Barbara Jackson, Ralph James, José Carlos Jarillo-Mossi, Michael Jensen, Richard Johnson, Dan Jorgensen, Alice and Auguste Juillard, Anne-Marie and Louis Juillard, Robert Kaplan, Mitch Kapor, Andrea Larson, Donald Levi, Jay Light, Patrick and Dagmar Liles, Thompson Little, Harry Lynch, Myles and Bunny Mace, Ian MacMillan, Costas Markides, Robert Marini, Paul Marshall, John Matthews, Deborah Mauger, David O. McKay, Linda Mornell, Dan Muzyka, Ashish Nanda, Adriano Olivetti, Sharon Daloz Parks, Andrall Pearson, David Perini, Thomas Piper, Lia Poorvu, Henry Reiling, Robert and Grace Reiss,

Arthur and Toni Rock, John Rosenblum, Richard Rumelt, Marge and Walter Salmon, Thomas Schelling, Benson Shapiro, Matthew Simmons, Wickham Skinner, Carl Sloane, George Albert Smith, Jr., Robert Stobaugh, Nan Stone, John and Sally Stopford, John Timberlake, Jeffry and Sara Timmons, Eldon Tolman, Joseph Torras, Susan and Thomas Tureen, Bert Twaalfhoeven, Michael Ullman, Hugo Uyterhoeven, Paul Vatter, Raymond Vernon, Harris Ware, Douglas Weil, William Wiggins, Peter Wilde, Frederick and Mary Wolfe, Sarah Wyatt, John Wynne, Hansjoerg Wyss, Abraham Zaleznik, Ed Zschau—and, of course, all of the students, executive participants, associates, and audiences with whom I worked to refine these ideas.

Seemingly at the end of this long list of people who have taught me so much about the virtue of predictability—but actually at the very top of that list—are the members of my always interesting family: father and mother, aunts and uncles, sister and brother, in-laws, grandparents, and the troops (Fredi's and my children, their spouses, children, and significant others: Michon, Van, Hib, Trevor, Michael, Olivia, Devin, Adam, Cavan, Willie, Rika, Charley, Kate, and Andy). Thanks to you, especially.

notes

Introduction

1. Many species of bees launch suicidal attacks on intruders or passersby. Some small birds feign injuries in order to lure would-be predators away from the group, at some risk to their own lives. Sociobiologists such as Wilson ascribe such altruistic acts (damaging to oneself but of potential benefit to the group) as the behavioral correlates of a genetically determined predisposition toward the maximization of the inclusive fitness of the individual; that is, the chance of survival of the individual's genetic content. See E. Wilson, *On Human Nature*, Cambridge, MA: Harvard University Press, 1978.

2. Biologist Richard Dawkins argues (*The Selfish Gene*, New York: Oxford University Press, 1976) that people, like cells and viruses, are survival machines. In nature, the stable system survives. The unstable system decays. Atoms are relatively stable forms of energy. Cells are relatively stable forms of life. Stability and survival are linked, in the sense that stability through time *means* survival. An organism that cannot survive a particular period of time is no better (from a survival perspective) than an unstable organism. Survival and predictability are also linked, in the sense that an organism that can predict the consequences of its own actions may survive longer than an organism that cannot do so—assuming that the former also has the intention, or the will, to survive.

A suggestive parallel can be made between stable systems and predictability. Stable systems have at least some features that are stationary or periodic. Homeostasis, for instance, maintains key physiological variables at a set of optimal levels, through constant adaptation to the environment. Therefore, stable systems (genes or organisms, say, to follow Dawkins) "predict themselves," in the sense that their past states are good indicators of the nature of their future states.

3. The focus of the enormous literature on corporate planning and strategy testifies to this proposition. Early models of corporate planning focused on the current goals and current states of corporations, and helped managers synthesize feasible paths for getting to the desired states of the organization from the current state of the organization. They led to predictions about the behavior of the organization given the goals of its managers and their opinions about the current endowments of the business. One current approach to strategic management, based on the market structure of the firm's industry and the ability of the firm to extract supernormal profits in this market (M. Porter, *Competitive Strategy*, New York: Free Press, 1980), is another predictive instrument for the structurally minded manager. It allows for the prediction of corporate performance on the basis of a small set of observable parameters of the firm's current situation: the number and characteristics of competitors in its industry, the number and bargaining power of its suppliers and buyers, and the characteristics of potential entrants in the industry or of potential substitutes for the products of the firm.

4. See, for example, "Don't Go Away Mad, Just Go Away," *New York Times*, 13 February 1996, D1.

5. Ibid.

6. "The Shredder: 'Chainsaw Al' Dunlap Pulled Off a Stunning Turnaround at Scott Paper . . . or Did He . . . ," *Business Week*, 15 January 1996.

Chapter One

1. M. Moldoveanu (*Information, Prediction and Coordination*, draft, 1996) has argued, following Hayek ("The Uses of Knowledge in Society," in F. Hayek, *Individualism and Economic Order*, Chicago: University of Chicago Press, 1991), that the function of any economic organization, such as a firm or a market, is to process and distribute information to its participants so that they can form expectations (which they can use to make predictions) about the consequences of their actions. When the future is unknown, an action feels like a choice between lotteries. If a person values predictability, then he or she will choose a lottery with lower uncertainty over a lottery with higher uncertainty. It is then possible to make conjectures about how people will act (because actions are represented by choices among lotteries) if we can find a suitable representation for the uncertainty associated with a lottery.

Claude Shannon—an information theorist who laid the foundations of the digital representation of information (in C. E. Shannon and D. Weaver, *The*

Mathematical Theory of Communication, Champaign-Urbana: University of Illinois Press, 1949)—constructed a mathematical function that increases with the uncertainty of a lottery and showed that this function is functionally equivalent to the quantity of entropy, a concept used by physicists to describe the amount of disorder in a physical system. This result is intuitive: a system with greater disorder implies a lottery with a higher uncertainty for someone who lays a bet on an output of the system. M. Moldoveanu ("Uncertainty, Verisimilitude, Choice and Preference," Harvard Business School mimeo, 1997) has argued that the concept of entropy can also be used to measure the discomfort we feel when faced with an ambiguous lottery—one in which we know neither the probabilities of the various outcomes nor the outcomes themselves—such as proceeding alone in complete darkness in a strange place. The intolerability of this situation corresponds nicely to an asymptote of the entropy function (at infinity).

Moldoveanu ("Production Cost Economics," Harvard Business School mimeo, 1996) used the concept of entropy to formulate a description of the function of an economic organization: to process and transfer information about the world to its participants in such a way as to allow each of them to form expectations about the future. In the language of entropy minimization, the function of an economic organization is to process and transfer information to its participants in such a way as to allow them to calculate the entropy of the lotteries they are facing, in a finite amount of steps. Each participant then acts to minimize the entropy associated with the lottery that his or her actions have selected. The function of the economic organization is to map an ambiguous lottery (the world lottery) into a finite-uncertainty mixture of lotteries (the organizational lottery) from which individuals choose according to their tolerance for ambiguity and uncertainty. The organization performs this function by means of a coordinative mechanism that provides a scheme for mapping states of the world into states of the organization.

The more complex the organization, the lower the uncertainty faced by its individual participants, because a more complex organization can "encode" a higher number of states of the world than can a simple organization. Fewer states of the world will be unforeseeable or inconceivable to a participant in a more complex organization, which maps a greater number of logically possible states of the world into physically possible states of its participants.

Moldoveanu ("Production Cost Economics") shows that markets and organizations are different means of processing information about the world and transferring it to their participants. Whereas markets rely on an arbitrage mechanism for pooling and transferring information, organizations rely on a mechanism of data gathering and reporting to a central intelligence unit—its executive management, which then makes decisions and transmits them back to the managers and employees. In the absence of coordination costs or increasing returns to a personal history of interactions, organizations and markets compete with one another on equal footing as information processing and transfer structures. Coordination costs—such as those imposed by politically motivated distortions of information by managers in large organizations—can make large organizations considerably less efficient information-procesing structures than markets. When agent-specific memory of past interactions is important, then organizations have an informational advantage over markets.

For instance, if I send you a signal that you can interpret on the basis of having seen me act before (presenting you with a low-entropy lottery), but that is meaningless to you otherwise (presenting you with a high-entropy lottery), then committing to a stream of subsequent mutual interactions may be efficient for both of us. This information-based theory can be used to understand the effect of various administrative measures designed to improve the performance of the firm and to critically assess their impact on the function of the firm as an information-processing and transfer unit.

2. Redefining the functions and protocol practices of people in an organization often implies doing without the precedents of past interactions that give organizations an informational advantage over markets. For example, I may redefine the function of a sales department and redistribute tasks, according to the new definition, among the members of that department. On paper, the new solution seems to lead to higher sales for the company. In practice, however, the solution requires the creation of a new set of coordination patterns among the members of the reconfigured department, which were implicit in the old system.

Coordination patterns are based on actions, not on words. I may say that I will visit a customer tomorrow, but what matters for the people who must coordinate with me is whether or not I will visit that customer tomorrow, as I had indicated. I may say that I will reward you on the basis of your performance, but what matters to you is the way I measure your performance, the way I map my observation of your performance into a compensation package—and eventually into what you get for your efforts.

Actions on which coordination patterns rest are part of the collective memory of an organization. When coordination depends sensitively on established, unspoken precedent, *de jure* changes in the function of the various units of the firm will sharply raise coordination costs in the short term. Business process reengineering involves redefining (in words) the criteria by which successful individual action will be recognized. The recognition of an action is itself an action, which people will try to predict. The success of reengineering therefore depends on the credibility of the management team that is implementing changes.

3. "Reengineering: Beyond the Buzzword," *Business Week*, 24 May 1993.

4. "Reengineering: What Happened?" *Business Week*, 30 January 1995.

5. Georgetown Steel, "Continuous Improvement," http://www.gscrods.com/improve.htm

6. *Continuous Improvement Bulletin: The Newsletter of the HHS Continuous Improvement Program* 1, no. 3 (1994).

7. Because the informational efficiency of an organization depends on the efficiency of the coordination between the activities of various independent agents, changes in these activities can have significant consequences for the way the organization as a whole processes information.

To see how this could happen, envision a chess game in which the pieces of each color play independently, according to their general knowledge of the rules of chess, on the basis of their local observations and communications with one another, and with the common goal of winning the game. They might, however, disagree about how to go about winning. When the repertoire of moves of each piece is fixed, the coordination task of the team depends on the efficiency with which they signal their observations to one another and on the level of agreement they share about what the right collective strategy is. But in a continuous improvement environment, the repertoire of moves of each piece would be slightly modified at every move. Knights, for example, could increase the range of their L-shaped moves by one or two squares. The queen could diversify its repertoire to include L-shaped moves.

The problem of coordination must be solved *ab initio* with every move. Each piece must take into account not only what the range of moves of the other pieces is, but also what it could become. If each of the 32 pieces can make one of 3 changes to its move repertoire, then the number of configurations of the entire ensemble of teams is 332, without taking into account the various possible locations and strategies each team might have. Even within a 5-piece neighborhood, a piece would have 243 possibilities to consider, excluding geographical considerations. It would not be possible, in such a situation, to "think ahead."

But this may be what membership in an organization (or a chessboard) is all about—the ability to predict one's future with more confidence than one could have while trying to produce and exchange by oneself. This is accomplished in organizations by decreasing the range of possible alternative futures that each individual faces. A model of human choices based on an aversion to a large spread of different futures is shown to account for many observed choice patterns in Moldoveanu, "Uncertainty, Verisimilitude, Choice, and Preference" (Harvard Business School mimeo, 1997). The idea of aversion to uncertainty dates back at least to the paper by D. Ellsberg, in which he refers to it as "ambiguity" ("Risk, Ambiguity and the Savage Axioms," *Quarterly Journal of Economics* 75 [1961]).

8. From a discussion by Baldrige Award winners about continuous improvement.

9. Ibid.

10. For a fun and insightful summary of recent developments in management binges, see Eileen Shapiro's *Fad Surfing in the Boardroom* (Reading, MA: Addison-Wesley, 1995).

11. We can think of matrix management as a process of coordination by which one executive agent exchanges signals with two supervisory agents. This structure of communication enables the executive agent to "manage" his or her own workload by sending different signals to his or her different managers.

For example, an employee skilled at the matrix game can use a matrix management structure in order to always look busy for whichever of the two managers happens to need his or her efforts. The system is also susceptible to inefficiencies because of exploitation by its managers, who have the capability of exaggerating the resources at their disposal when bidding for a desirable project, or presenting these resources as inadequate when wishing to avoid a project.

On the live chessboard, think of a communication structure in which the king and the queen are overseeing different aspects of the strategy: board position and number of the opponent's pieces taken. Notwithstanding any benefits, a matrix-managed chess game will produce two effects: (1) an increase in the communication overhead for the individual pieces, and (2) an increase in the time required for the king and the queen to reach understanding about the overall strategy. The entire coordination game is susceptible to the failure of the bargaining game between the two leaders.

12. "Europe Unilever: If at First You Fail Miserably . . . ," *Business Week*, 4 December 1995, international editions.

13. "President's letter to our stockholders, employees, customers, and partners," 1 September 1994.

14. From a press release issued by Unisys, 6 October 1995.

15. "Can Jim Unruh Stop the Unisys Slide?" *Business Week*, 3 June 1996.

16. Bob Palmer's keynote address to DECUS Europe, Cannes, France, 13 September 1994.

17. From a study by the American Management Association, reprinted (in summary form) in *Harper's*, May 1996, 40.

18. "Does America Still Work?" *Harper's*, May 1996, 35.

19. In informational terms, strategic restructuring resembles business process reengineering. It involves a radical change in the structure of the firm and therefore in the structural correlates of the process of information transfer between people within the firm. If the information transfer process itself is not dependent on the structure of the firm, then one could argue that the strategic restructuring exercise has achieved no result from an informational perspective. If it achieves no result from an informational perspective, then it would be difficult to argue that it has achieved any result at all. The reason why we think that people act differently after the change is that they have new information to act on, such as new incentives, new perspectives, and new insights.

If the information transfer process does change, then the accompanying loss of precedents on which organizational coordination patterns are based may increase coordination costs in the short term. Consider again the metaphor of the chess game played by independently minded, communicating pieces. Strategic restructuring can be thought of as a change in the repertoire of moves of a subset of the pieces, followed by a broadcast of these move changes to the rest of the pieces. Assuming that the broadcast message is clear, each piece must now (1) calculate its own optimal move strategy; (2) wait to see how the other pieces have interpreted the broadcast message; (3) recalculate its own optimal move strategy in view of its observations; and (4) iterate on steps (1) through (3) until it is confident of its predictions about the moves of the other pieces.

This process of coadaptation is well described by the mathematical biologist Stuart Kauffman: "Agents persistently attempt to predict optimally the behavior of other agents. To do so, each is driven to construct optimally complex models of the behaviors of the other agents. Inevitable disconfirmations of these models drive a coevolutionary process among the models adopted by the agents, as each agent replaces disconfirmed models with new hypotheses" (S. Kauffman, "Whispers from Carnot," in G. Cowan, D. Pines, and D. Meltzer, eds., *Complexity: Metaphors, Models and Reality*, Santa Fe Institute Studies in the

Sciences of Complexity, Reading, MA: Addison-Wesley, 1994). The success with which mindful chess pieces attempting to win a game together (or people trying to make a product and sell it to other people) coordinate their actions depends, in this view, on the success with which they can predict one another's actions. In turn, this will depend on the rate of change of the null hypotheses, which they test when observing one another's actions. It is not clear, Kauffman hints later (on the basis of a private communication with J. M. Grammont), that the agents in question can converge on a set of stable mutual predictions, if they take all of their historical pattern of interaction into account. By changing the known rules of the game, strategic restructuring therefore raises coordination costs at least in the short term, but also possibly in the long term as well.

20. Changing management practices according to the latest price commanded by the equity of the firm in the capital markets can be understood in an informational framework by a direct coupling of the informational activities of the firm to the informational activities of the market. Even if the market were an efficient information-processing mechanism, such a strategy would be costly because organizations optimally process information differently than markets: on the basis of precedents, which take time to build up. An explicit model of this sort of information transfer in organizations and the political mechanisms by which this transfer of information takes place is given in M. Moldoveanu and H. Stevenson, "Path-Dependence in Organizational Resource Allocation Processes," Harvard Business School mimeo, 1996.

Efficient markets are "memoryless": past realizations of the price of a company's share are not correlated with the current realization of this price. This is not the case in organizations. Current realizations of a strategy are intimately related to past realizations, because people, as uncertainty minimizers, take action based on their observations of past actions of other people, not on current promises. It is irrational to expect the realized strategy of the firm to change with the current realized stock price of the firm, because markets, which determine stock price, process information differently than organizations, whose value that stock price represents. In addition, stakeholders in the organization will become involved in a guessing game regarding the consequences of their own actions within the firm, in which they try to predict the way managers will interpret the next change in the firm's stock price, the way they (the managers) will react, and the way other employees will react to the proposed changes.

In the chess game metaphor, suppose that the king is responsible for surveying the situation after each move, evaluating the position of its team, and prescribing a new course of action. This situation corresponds to the hierarchical information transmission network proposed by Kenneth Arrow (*The Limits of Organization*, New York: Norton, 1974) as a characterization of a firm. Internally evolved codes of communication allow different pieces on the chessboard to understand what is being communicated to them. It would be naive, however, to think that the code used to transmit messages back and forth does not depend on the kind of message that is being transmitted. Certain codes are simply not complex enough to transmit certain messages (just try representing the number 9 using two bits in the memory of a computer).

Therefore, if the king is memoryless—if it is just following the latest trend in chess strategies and is keeping up with the latest chess journal—then there will be no stable code of communication. The same word could have different meanings today and tomorrow. Each piece's ability to understand a signal, to predict its consequences, breaks down when the king "manages by the stock price."

21. "Does America Still Work?" 35.

22. "It's Not Only Rock 'n' Roll," *Business Week*, 10 October 1994.

23. For an eloquent first-person commentary on the virtual organization and similar trends, see "Welcome to the Company That Isn't There," *Business Week*, 17 October 1994.

24. The virtual organization implies the placement of a technological constraint on the communication channel between different members of the organization. Communications between some members of the organization are to be carried out over artificial channels (such as videophones, telephones, fax machines, and email) using codes that may or may not adequately represent the same organizational reality that a member of a "real" organization would see. Therefore, verifiable agreement between a telecommuter and a real commuter will be more difficult to accomplish. If the information relevant to solving the problem of coordination is readily transmissible through a low-bandwidth channel, then the virtual organization will not necessarily carry higher coordination costs than a real organization.

If, however, the "code" by which incumbents signal each other is incomplete or inefficient, then the information transfer capacity of the virtual organization will be inferior to that of a real organization. To understand what is at stake, consider again the chess game with independent pieces, and assume that some pieces are playing the game with blinders on (simulating a virtual channel). Each piece will rely on a set of signals from other pieces for determining its own next move. These signals may or may not be adequate substitutes for what the piece itself would have deemed relevant information for its actions. Nonverbal behavior, for example, has been shown to repeatedly account for the outcome of interactions between people and to play a significant role in the way people see each other and interpret each other's words (B. DePaulo, "Non-Verbal Behavior and Self-Presentation," *Psychological Bulletin* 111, no. 2 [1992]: 203–243).

The information that a piece on the board receives is filtered or distorted relative to the information received by a piece not wearing blinders. This information distortion introduces uncertainty for each piece wearing blinders (it must construct a model of the process generating the information and of the biases of the transmitter). If people facing an unpredictable situation are themselves unpredictable, then the uncertainty faced by those with blinders on translates into a higher uncertainty for the rest of the team. Organizing a firm using virtual communication channels may therefore entail a higher level of unpredictability for all members of the firm.

Chapter Two

1. Details on the Caterpillar-UAW situation are from "Strike Appears Ready to End at Caterpillar," *Wall Street Journal*, 28 September 1995, A4; and "Union Capitulation Shows Strike Is Now Dull Sword," *New York Times*, 5 December 1995.

2. From "Cummins Contract Long on Wealth for Each Side," *Columbus Evening Republic*, 9 May 1993.

3. From a front-page news brief in the December 3, 1996, edition.

4. Jeffrey L. Cruikshank and David B. Sicilia, *The Engine That Could*, forthcoming from Harvard Business School Press.

5. Magical rites may serve very practical functions in making competent predictions about the future. Writing about the prehunt rituals of the Montagnais-Naskapi, Omar Moore advances the thesis that "some practices which have been classified as magic may well be directly efficacious as techniques for attaining the ends envisaged by their practitioners. . . . The shoulder blade of the caribou is held by them to be especially 'truthful.' When it is to be employed for this purpose the meat is pared away, and the bone is boiled and wiped clean; it is hung up to dry, and finally a small piece of wood is split and attached to the bone to form a handle. The shoulder blade, thus prepared, is held over hot coals for a short time. The heat causes cracks and burnt spots to form, and these are then 'read,'" sometimes to determine the direction in which the tribe will set forth to locate game. Moore argues that the ritual serves a useful purpose, because it eliminates personal or group bias in the selection of a direction to carry out the hunt. This randomizing strategy prevents the Naskapi from "being victimized by their own habits," which might, for example, lead them to overhunt certain herds of animals, causing the animals to become more suspicious of human presence and leading to less successful hunts ("Divination, a New Perspective," *American Anthropologist* 59 [1957]: 69–74).

6. Ken Andrews, in his book *The Concept of Corporate Strategy* (Homewood, IL: Irwin, 1971), asserts that the statement of a clear corporate purpose must be the first step in any chief executive's position. Without a corporate purpose that is intelligibly communicated to other employees, the strategy of the firm as a system of mutually coherent planned actions cannot exist, because there is no way to measure their internal consistency.

Chapter Three

1. Some philosophers call something that could have happened but did not, or was not observed, a "counterfactual." For instance, "If I had consumed a bottle of vodka, I would not now be sober" is a counterfactual, involving a prediction: "If I drink this much alcohol, then I will become intoxicated." Counterfactuals give us ways of reconstructing the past, given what we know about the present ("I am not intoxicated; therefore, I have not consumed a bottle of vodka"). Predictions give us a way of constructing the future, given our knowledge of past and present ("If I drink a bottle of vodka . . .").

2. Karl Popper, who proposed a method by which science should approach the creation of knowledge, argues that the fact that a model was verified by several past observations does not mean that it will predict accurately in the future (see *The Logic of Scientific Discovery*, London and New York: W. B. Routledge, 1934). The scientist's proper role is that of seeking *disconfirming* evidence for the models he thinks up or receives from other thinkers of models. The chief aim of the scientific method is the creation and preservation of a critical stance toward theories and models of the world.

By this measure, when attempting to predict the course of their lives on the basis of models of themselves and the world, people are not acting like scientists. Were they to act like scientists, they would have to detach themselves completely from their own opinions and actions, to the point of not caring whether or not they would take any particular action in the next instant. Actions would depend strictly on their observations about the validity of their models of the world.

Psychologist Daniel Gilbert differentiates between Cartesian and Spinozan systems for formulating beliefs ("How Mental Systems Believe," *American Psychologist* [February 1991]). Cartesian minds (named after the French philosopher René Descartes, who proposed this model of the mind) can hold a belief or an image while withholding judgment about it until further deliberation or subsequent observations. They can comprehend a statement without accepting it to be true. Spinozan minds (named after the philosopher Baruch Spinoza, who held this view of the mind) cannot comprehend a statement without lending it some credence. Cartesian minds can be critical and skeptical. Spinozan minds cannot; they embrace fact and fiction alike.

Gilbert points out that the modern experimental record in cognitive psychology suggests that people's minds behave as Spinoza thought they would. People on whom cognitive experiments are performed show themselves to be credulous, or gullible. They accept statements uncritically (from sources they do not trust), and they are willing to assign truth values to sentences about nonsensical subjects (such as a "glark").

3. Economists and statisticians use probability as a measure of one's certainty about a prediction. Probabilities are defined either by long-term statistics of repeated experiments, or by repeated states of nature (these are objective probabilities), or by the "gut feeling" or "personal opinion" or "best judgment" of the decision maker (subjective probabilities). See David Kreps, *Notes on the Theory of Choice*, Underground Classics in Economics, Boulder and London: Westview Press, 1988.

In economics, the link between individuals and the outcomes of actions is the utility which those individuals have for any given outcome, or the preference for one outcome over another. It is assumed that people know how they will evaluate a certain outcome—that they know their preferences and utilities—and have only to predict the consequences of their actions correctly. See the collection of essays on rational choice contained in John Elster, ed., *Rational Choice*, New York: New York University Press, 1986.

4. Francis Fukuyama argues that spontaneous sociability, rather than some optimal market or institutional mechanism, is behind the prosperity of developed countries today. By spontaneous sociability he means the extent of mutual trust and grounds for agreement that exist in a society at a given time. See F. Fukuyama, *Trust*, New York: Free Press, 1995.

5. And the way I interact with the world is itself subject to change, according to moral development psychologists. The individual's view of the world evolves from one based on reactions to constraints and compulsions, through an understanding of constraints within the norms and practices of one's group, to the development of a private code of morality that functions apart from socially constructed rules. See Lawrence Kohlberg, *Collected Papers on Moral Development and Moral Education*, Cambridge, MA: Center for Moral Education, 1976.

6. A recent article on the economics of envy (V. L. Mui, "The Economics of Envy," *Journal of Economic Behavior and Organization* 26 [1995]) shows that the state's powers to deter those who, out of envy, destroy the products of others who are more successful are limited. For, if the state punishes envious destruction, the envious will be able to more credibly commit to not taking destructive action, and innovators will have a greater incentive to produce. But instances of envious destruction will increase with the higher opportunities for envy, if the envious are indifferent between levels of punishment.

7. Raymond Boudon paraphrases Alexis de Tocqueville thus: "As they become more equal, individuals find their inequality harder and harder to bear." As people see that those around them have things that they think they *could* have, they become envious and subsequently frustrated, whereas, if people see others in possession of situations that they do not realistically aspire to, they will not feel frustration to the same degree ("The Logic of Relative Frustration," in J. Elster, ed., *Rational Choice*, New York: New York University Press, 1986).

8. Details about Matsushita's vision, and the history of the company it guided, are from *Matsushita*, a special issue of the Harvard Business School *Bulletin*, © 1983, President and Fellows of Harvard College.

9. And this aversion to risk seems to be imprinted on the way we process probabilistic information. Kahneman and Tversky, two psychologists from Stanford University, have found that individuals are sensitive to the transitions from "possible" to "probable" and from "probable" to "almost certain," given choices between outcomes with preassigned probabilities of occurrence (D. Kahneman, P. Slovic, and A. Tversky, *Judgments Under Uncertainty: Heuristics and Biases*, New York: Cambridge University Press, 1982).

10. The scientific method sometimes suggests a view of the world that overlooks the imperative to act. According to Popper, the scientist should always adopt the position of a skeptic relative to his or her theories and always look for disconfirming evidence. The scientist should avoid reasoning by induction; that is, by assuming that a law, having been verified by past experience, will predict future events. But this is exactly what people (including scientists) do when they are required to take action: they make predictions based on past experiences, inferring that the greater the frequency with which they have observed an event in the past, the more likely it is that they will observe it in the future. Attribution and imputation from daily experience fall short of the standards of the scientific method. But then, perhaps it is those standards themselves that err in distancing themselves from our intuitive understandings of the world and our need to act in the face of uncertainty.

11. The problem of changing opportunity sets should feel familiar to anyone who has toyed with a Rubik's cube. The sequence in which rotations of the various columns of the cube are performed critically affects the outcome of an entire set of rotations. Unless you remember the exact sequence you pursued, you cannot get back to where you were a few moves ago. For the more strategically minded, a game of chess also illustrates path dependence. The disastrous situation in which you find yourself finally reveals its causes—in the form of your opponent's strategy—but the key to preventing that strategy from succeeding lies a few moves back, in the inaccessible past.

Chapter Four

1. Stephen J. Gould, in *Full House* (New York: Harmony Books, 1996), argues that even the complexity of the human organism may be a disadvantage in the survival game, compared to the variety and adaptability of bacteria. He argues that highly complex organisms are the small twigs on the highly differentiated evolutionary tree. If Gould's thesis is true, the only real survival advantage we humans have is our capacity for coordinated action.

2. The desire for variety can also be interpreted as a desire for personal freedom. Some have argued that individuals value freedom for its own sake, rather than as a means to a particular end or set of ends. Imagine that I found out which one of several flavors of ice cream you prefer above all others (and therefore would choose the next time you buy ice cream) and then told you that you could get *only* that flavor of ice cream. You might consider this unpleasant or undesirable, *even though you would have chosen that ice cream flavor in any case.* If you would consider it undesirable, then you are placing a value on the freedom to choose, which is quite separate from the value you are placing on the ice cream itself. See A. Sen, *Inequality Reexamined*, Cambridge, MA: Harvard University Press, 1984.

3. Although firms do not seem to be very good at adapting to new market conditions. Fully one-third of the Fortune 500 companies of 1970 are no longer around today. See Peter Senge, *The Fifth Discipline*, New York: Free Press, 1993.

4. For an interesting discussion of the interaction of society with those with different ways of thinking, see Julian Jaynes, *The Origins of Consciousness in the Breakdown of the Bicameral Mind*, Boston: Houghton Mifflin, 1976.

5. Social psychologists caught on a while ago to humans' propensity to conform and to give in to the rule of the majority. Solomon Asch observed that individuals modify their stated perceptions of the length of objects in obviously incorrect ways, when these objects are repeatedly declared to be of a certain (false) relative length by a (paid) set of (fake) coparticipants in an experiment. Some of the individuals in question sweated profusely and were evidently uncomfortable with their choices. Nevertheless, most of them did not deviate from the stated majority opinion. See S. Asch, "Opinions and Social Pressure," *Scientific American* 193, no. 5 (1955).

6. Even so, English language is about 40 percent redundant, according to Jeremy Campbell (*Grammatical Man*, New York: Simon & Schuster, 1982). Is redundancy a means for increasing predictability? Quite possibly, if we consider redundant letters, syllables, and words to be "error-correcting codes," which allow us to ascertain what was said, just in case we misunderstood it in the first place. "Wtr" is most likely to code for "water," but might also code for "weather" or "waiter." So we introduce the vowels and silent consonants, which guide our understanding of the word to its properly intended meaning.

7. You may think that the use of an orchestra as an example of an organization is too self-serving. Orchestras, after all, follow scripted behavioral patterns, the script being the musical score and the gestures of the conductor. But how is a gesture to be interpreted? Should the strings come in right on the beat, slightly after the beat, or slightly before the beat? What does "slightly" mean? Who says what "slightly" means? What does "a beat" mean? Is it measured within one-thousandth of a second? one-hundredth? one-tenth? Or, for that matter, how is a quarter note on a sheet of paper to be understood? How much time should it last, precisely? Should it trail off gently, or end suddenly? Can conducting even begin in an uncoordinated orchestra? If not, can any algorithmic description of the coordination process suffice to cause coordination to take place? Can any script be detailed enough?

8. Merlin Donald summarizes much of the interaction between culture, language, and the mind in his *Origins of the Modern Mind*, Cambridge, MA: Harvard University Press, 1991. He provides an extensive bibliography for the reader who wishes to delve more deeply.

9. One of the most powerful forms of culture that is aimed squarely at predictability is the culture of science. Thomas Kuhn has argued that scientific progress has much to do with the psychology and sociology of the people doing scientific research. He defined paradigms as ways of thinking about the world, which shape the scientist's design of experiments, the choice of which data are relevant, and interpretation of the data. Paradigms can be challenged or overturned by discoveries that cannot be explained within their world of ideas, but this process takes time and only brings about new paradigms. One therefore cannot escape paradigms in general; one can only move from one paradigm to another (T. Kuhn, *The Structure of Scientific Revolutions*, Chicago: University of Chicago Press, 1970).

Chapter Five

1. See Alfred D. Chandler, *The Visible Hand*, Cambridge, MA: Harvard University Press, 1977.

2. Hobbes's conception of the state as the Leviathan that orders human interactions lest the passions of men turn society into a raging bloodbath can be understood through the lens of predictability. According to Hobbes, people need a covenant in order to live together in a state of interaction. Covenants, in order to be enforceable, must bestow power on some person or group of persons. The covenant is not between individuals and their government; it is between people themselves. In the case of a freely elected assembly, the covenant therefore binds together not only those in the majority of voters, but those in the minority as well. Hobbes's covenant between citizens of a state is akin to the covenant between drivers on the public ways of a region. They all obey a set of rules, not out of commitment to the rules themselves, but rather due to the simultaneous commitment to *some* set of rules (which will make the consequences of their actions predictable), coupled with the existence of that *specific* set of rules. It is not insignificant that Hobbes considered the individual's will for self-preservation to be the only interest that takes precedence over the individual's commitment to the laws of the state. If the laws of the state, in other words, mandate the self-destruction of the individual, then the individual is at freedom to disobey and fight these laws. This is because self-preservation is the reason why someone is bound to obey the rules of the state in the first place. Extending his argument, if the laws of the state legislate anarchy, rendering individuals incapable of predicting the consequences of their actions, then they are free to disobey them, because securing predictability is the reason why someone would submit to a set of rules in the first place. See Bertrand Russell, *A History of Western Philosophy*, New York: Simon & Schuster, 1945.

3. The *New York Times* reprinted a transcript of Khrushchev's address and the subsequent question-and-answer session (17 September 1959, 18).

4. *Winston S. Churchill: His Complete Speeches, 1897–1963*, ed: Robert Rhodes James, New York: Chelsea House Publishers, vol. 6, 1974, 6220.

5. In Greek mythology, men going to war, embarking on heroic quests, or seeking the meaning of their lives often consulted oracles before setting off. The ensuing battles and conflicts were portrayed as the results of the direct intervention of the gods in the affairs of humans. The Trojan War, we are given to understand, would not have started had it not been for Paris's decision to award a golden apple to Aphrodite, over Athena and Hera, in a staged beauty contest. Aphrodite then helped Paris abduct Helen, Menelaus's wife, and bring her with him to Troy. Menelaus went to war against Troy, bringing with him all of the armies of Greece, led by his brother Agamemnon, but also the implicit endorsement of the two goddesses who were injured by Paris's ruling. Each side had its own champions among the gods, and each trusted in the timely intervention of the gods at critical moments. One comes to think that neither side would have acted had it known that all of the gods would be against them. In this case, one wonders why neither side realized that winning the war would mean the defeat of at least a subset of Olympians, which in turn would have had to undermine their belief in the remaining gods. See Robert Graves, *The Greek Myths*, London: Penguin Books, 1955.

6. "The leaders of the barons in 1215 groped in the dim light towards a fundamental principle. Government must henceforward mean something more than the arbitrary rule of any man, and custom and the law must stand even above the King. It was this idea, perhaps only half understood, that gave unity and force to the barons' opposition and made the Charter which they now demanded imperishable" (Winston Churchill, *A History of the English Speaking Peoples*, New York: Dorset Press, 1990 [1956]).

7. Churchill describes the scene at Runnymede very suggestively: "On a Monday morning in June, between Staines and Windsor, the barons and Churchmen began to collect on the great meadow at Runnymede. An uneasy hush fell on them from time to time. Many had failed to keep their tryst; and the bold few who had come knew that the King would never forgive this humiliation. He would hunt them down when he could, and the laymen at least were staking their lives in the cause they served. They had arranged a little throne for the King and a tent. The handful of resolute men had drawn up, it seems, a short document on parchment. Their retainers and the groups and squadrons of horsemen in sullen steel kept at some distance and well in the background. For was not armed rebellion against the Crown the supreme feudal crime? Then events followed rapidly. A small cavalcade appeared from the direction of Windsor. Gradually men made out the faces of the King, the Papal legate, the Archbishop of Canterbury, and several bishops. They dismounted without ceremony. Someone, probably the Archbishop, stated briefly the terms that were suggested. The King declared at once that he agreed. He said the details should be arranged immediately in his chancery" (Winston Churchill, *A History of the English Speaking Peoples*, New York: Dorset Press, 1990 [1956], 253–254).

8. There is a significant difference between predictions and explanations, which is related to the arrow of time. Explanations refer to the past. They purport to show why something happened as it did, usually by offering up a set of causal connections between events that are already known. The simplest form of explanation is the connection of two points on a graph with a line. We do not *know*, of course, that, had there been another point, it would also have fallen on that line. We are simply guessing. If the experiment that generated the two points is adjustable so as to generate other points, we might try to refine our guess by running it again under identical conditions. This is often possible in physics, chemistry, and biology, but not in the social and behavioral sciences, which confront us with a variety of new contexts and experiences.

Another form of explanation is that of establishing a causal connection between two point events: *A* caused *B*. This means that, had it not been for the occurrence of *A*, *B* would not have been observed to occur. Again, we need experiments to figure out whether a sequence of events reflects a causal connection or simply an association. The repetition of a sequence of events over time does not by itself imply a causal connection between events. To use an example of the philosopher Robert Nozick, are you willing to say that a singer's rendition of the national anthem has *caused* the start of a baseball game?

It seems, therefore, that experiments are required in order to make social explanation rigorous in the same way that explanation in the natural sciences is. The philosopher Karl Popper, in summarizing the arguments against the application of the scientific method to social investigation, mentions that social systems are constantly evolving in time and therefore do not permit the replication of experimental conditions in the same way physics and chemistry seem to (*The Poverty of Historicism*, London and New York: W. B. Routledge, 1976). (Popper subsequently defends the use of the scientific method in social inquiry, for reasons taken up below.)

Prediction, on the other hand, has to do with the future. You run an experiment and *predict* the outcome, on the basis of some *a priori* knowledge of the experimental conditions and of the laws that govern the behavior of the system investigated and of the experimental apparatus. The difference between the scientific method and historicist narratives can be understood as the difference between prediction and explanation. The scientific method (see K. Popper, *The Logic of Scientific Discovery*, London and New York: W. B. Routledge, 1934) relies on the use of falsifiable hypotheses as a basis for understanding the world. A hypothesis is falsifiable if it can be proven false by an empirical finding; that is, if its prediction can be shown to be incorrect by subsequent observations of the world. Hypotheses themselves can come from anywhere: a hunch, a well-established theoretical framework, and so forth. What makes investigation scientific in the Popperian sense is the bias for prediction (rather than explanation).

Kuhn, on the other hand (*The Structure of Scientific Revolutions*, Chicago: University of Chicago Press, 1970), argues that scientific inquiry is conducted through the intermediation of paradigms, which Hilary Putnam (in R. Boyd, P. Gasper, and J. D. Trout, eds., *The Philosophy of Science*, Cambridge, MA: MIT Press, 1991) defines as "a scientific theory together with an example of a successful and striking application." Kuhn defines *normal science* as the sort of investigative activity that takes place when a paradigm has been established (by an impressive instantiation of a theory) and is followed up on by a coterie of young scientists who hope to build their careers on the respective body of ideas.

The Kuhn-Popper debate can be understood again by the difference between prediction and explanation. By predicting, you make explicit what will happen in the future, on the basis of your knowledge in the present. The nature of the theory that you use to make a prediction is irrelevant in Popper's view; it is only its empirical falsifiability that counts toward its rigor. In Kuhn's view, on the other hand, that theory is crucially tied to the explanation of past events—it *is* the explanation: "Novel theories are not born *de novo*. On the contrary, they emerge from old theories and within a matrix of old beliefs about the phenomena that the world does and does not contain" (Kuhn, ibid.). We generate predictions from our explanation of the past events, and therefore we make our predictions only as good as are our explanations. This leads to a false illusion of control, because there are innumerably many explanations that will account for a sequence of events, just as there are innumerably many curves that pass through two data points. A line is only the simplest polynomial that can be fitted to two points. Therefore, there should be innumerably many predictions that we could make based on our knowledge. This will obviously not do for an action-oriented individual (a manager or an engineer, for instance), who must answer questions such as "How shall we act? What direction shall we take? Which prediction shall we count on and base our decisions on?" In such circumstances, the question then becomes, "Which explanations produce good predictions? How do we choose them out of the [infinite] set of all *possible* explanations?"

Kuhn's view (in Putnam's interpretation; see Boyd, Gasper, and Trout, eds., ibid.) is that paradigms can be overthrown only by paradigms—and not by one or two instances in which the paradigm leads to a false prediction (as it does in Popper's conception of science). To an action-oriented practitioner, Kuhn's idea makes sense: better to have a theory that predicts accurately the outcomes of most situations and fails in some isolated instances than to have nothing—randomness—and the accompanying anxiety of not knowing what to do and who we are. We choose the former without much hesitation. This phenomenon can be understood from a psychological standpoint as a deeply rooted desire for predictability in our individual lives—a feature that psychologists have identified and called the "illusion of control" (Ellen Langer, "The Illusion of Control," *Journal of Personality and Social Psychology* 32, no. 2 [1975]). Repeatedly, individuals exhibit the belief that they control systems (roulette wheels, dice) that "objective measurements" would indicate that they cannot control. Our need for predictability, it seems, makes us into poor Popperians. One might ask, "Is not the scientific method just a device for allowing us to convince ourselves of the predictability of our universe?"

9. In what sense, you might ask, was Karl Marx's conception of history "scientific"? Scientism, one could argue, is the process of building knowledge by independently generating theory and testing that theory on data sets that were generated by evolving processes or phenomena. Thus I am doing science if I generate my own recipe for a soufflé that must grow to a particular height and, following the recipe precisely and repeating the experiment several times,

I observe whether or not I achieved the desired height with consistency. I am not doing science if, having concocted the recipe, I then proceed to adjust all of the relevant parameters (ingredients, oven temperatures) upon realizing that the recipe cannot possibly give me the desired effect. Nor am I doing science if, having (randomly) gotten a soufflé to be the right height, I am now writing down an explanation for what must have happened for the soufflé to grow. Nor am I doing science if, having baked a lot of soufflés according to my recipe, I then discard all of those that did not come out right, retain the few that did, and conclude that my recipe was optimal. (See J. W. Pratt, H. Raiffa, and R. Schlaifer, *Introduction to Statistical Decision Theory,* Cambridge: MIT Press, 1995.) Marx did not have a fully equipped kitchen to experiment with; nor were experiments possible with the subject matter of his interest: the history of all societies. His approach failed the test of scientism because he picked out those characteristics and episodes of human societies that could be explained by his concepts of class divisions, class consciousness, and class warfare. In other words, he retained only the best soufflés and threw out the instances of history that challenged his theory or did not fully support it. If there is value to a Marxist critique of society, it lies not in the power of the theory to explain the past, but rather in its power to predict future phenomena.

Another interpretation of Marx (due to Peter Railton, in Boyd, Gasper, and Trout, eds., ibid.) might go like this: if "the ideas of the ruling class are, in every epoch, the ruling idea," as Marx says—that is, if all ideas serve some personal (and in some sense political) purpose—then what does that make Marx's ideas? Is scientific objectivism possible at all, if it has been classified as an ideological tool *ex ante*? As Railton puts it, "Is [Marx] to defend his view using a piece of bourgeois ideology about the objectivity of science of which his own theory tells him to be suspect? Or is he to renounce the claim of scientific objectivity, and the special epistemic status associated with it?" Railton's argument is then that the fact of the use of scientific explanation for ideological purposes (the advancement and stability of the monied class) does not in itself undermine the objectivity of scientific inquiry. In fact, if objectivity has to do with the recognition of the distinction between what is "out there, in the world" and what is "in our minds," then it could be that the use of scientific inquiry to advance the interests of the monied class (by the creation of new forms of capital) is a force that works for scientific objectivity, and not against it, regardless of the use to which the scientific method is put. To crudely paraphrase the argument, I may use my head as a burrowing instrument, but if burrowing is an activity that stimulates me to think, then it will not make my head into less of a thinking instrument, but perhaps more so. Now consider the argument from a predictability perspective. If I can generate useful predictions of future events using Marx's theory of class consciousness and the ideological use of the scientific method, that does not in itself make me a Marxist, nor does it corrupt the objectivity of my world view; but it may, if my predictions are correct, make Marx into more of a scientist.

10. Even more simple than closing or correcting genetic defects, suppose that you could take a drug that would induce you to be happy, in a preadolescent, naive, and ignorant sort of way (like the population of Aldous Huxley's *Brave New World*). Furthermore, when you are in that state, you would have no recollection of your "past self"—indeed, there would no "other self" for you to worry about. You will have forgotten what the world felt like before you took the drug. Would you take it?

One argument goes like this: "Well, I would like to feel good, and the fact that I will have forgotten about my former self means that I will have no opportunity for regret. Therefore, I will take the drug." Another argument might run as follows: "What makes me what I am is not the state that I am in, but rather the set of states that I *could* be in. By taking the drug, I will lose my freedom to become something other than what I am right now. Because I value this freedom, I will not take the drug." Does the fact that you value your freedom to become mean that your actions are unpredictable to others? Is it that, as Hayek has pointed out, freedom is a good in itself, independent of the likelihood of someone choosing the more unusual actions that make up the option set that defines freedom instrumentally?

11. Sun-Tzu, *The Art of War*, London: Oxford University Press, 1977, 84.

12. China has now instituted governmental control over the dissemination of economic and technical information. All news must be cleared by a central agency, in order to ensure that it does not contain information that negatively impacts the interests of the Chinese state (*Wall Street Journal*, 18 January 1996). The Chinese government, to use an old cliché, has realized that "information is power."

But in what sense *is* it power? Using accurate information, individual citizens can predict the consequences of their actions, which enables them to act without taking into account the wills of a set of bureaucrats in Beijing, whose power, it seems, rests particularly on the inability of the citizens of China to predict the consequences of their own actions. In a competitive market, one knows that producing a good at a lower marginal cost than the most efficient competitor will bring monopoly profits in the short run. But what if the product must pass through regulatory hurdles whose definition and meaning is in the hands of people who are themselves connected to other people, and so forth? Information is power because it enhances predictability for those who have it and decreases predictability for those who do not have it.

13. Proposition 2½, as our Massachusetts law is called (it's Proposition 13 in California), was fueled in part by a yearning for predictability. Before its passage, people didn't know whether they would be able to hold onto their houses in the face of rapidly escalating taxes. Now, perversely, we are finding that these laws simply substitute one kind of uncertainty for another. As things now stand, we put issues of great local consequence on the ballot for a simple up-or-down vote. Will our schools prosper or languish? Who knows?

Chapter Six

1. Models in general have to yield easily computable results in order to be useful in real-world applications. In the field of telecommunications engineering, for example, the Fourier Transform, which maps a function in the time domain onto a function in the frequency domain, has been known as a mathematical entity since the work of Jean-Baptiste Fourier in the eighteenth century. But it was not until fast algorithms for computing the Discrete Fourier Transform were designed (in the 1960s) that the Fourier Transform found widespread use in telecommunications, where it is used for analyzing the frequency content of signals and as a modulation technique. Even more generally, the axioms of plane geometry were known since the time of the Greek mathematician Euclid. But it was not until the French mathematician Monge used them to show three-dimensional objects in cross-section that these mathematical abstractions enabled the replicable production of complicated three-dimensional objects (such as guns). And it was not until modern digital computers enabled the representation of arbitrarily complex surfaces that the full potential of plane geometry could be utilized for engineering design and manufacturing applications. The computational complexity of concepts and models often limits their applicability in real situations, at least until adequate computational tools are developed.

2. David Hilbert proposed the following problem at the beginning of the century: Given a logical system and any arbitrary proposition, is it possible to show that the proposition is true or false, starting from the axioms of the logical system? Kurt Gödel showed that this was not possible. He showed that any logical system (any system of mutually consistent propositions) is incomplete. Alternatively, the system must be internally inconsistent. For a discussion, see John Casti, *Reality Rules*, New York: Wiley, 1991.

3. Rational choice theory insists that people's preferences are transitive, or at least acyclical. If I prefer A to B and B to C, then I cannot prefer C to A, regardless of the option sets from which I have chosen A, B, and C. Let A, B, and C denote apples, bread, and cheese, respectively. Consider an individual who chooses A from the bundle (A, B, X) and B from the bundle (B, C, Y), where X and Y are oranges and pears. Rational choice theory would predict that he would choose A over C, from whatever bundle is available. But suppose the third bundle contains the object Z, which is "receiving a brochure describing the beneficial effects of eating various cheeses." Now he might pick C over A, simply in light of the fact that the third alternative *informs* his choice, or helps him frame it in a particular fashion. For a formal discussion of these problems, see Amartya Sen, "Internal Consistency of Choice," *Econometrica* 61, no. 3 (May 1993): 495–521.

Chapter Seven

1. Kant held that our experience of external objects, although caused by these objects (in their form as objects-in-themselves) is possible only through the existence of *a priori* concepts or ideas in our minds. One such *a priori* is the concept of "space," in its Euclidean form. "Space" says Kant, "is not an empirical concept abstracted from external experiences. For in order that certain sensations may be referred to something outside me (i.e., to something in a different position in space from that in which I find myself), and further in order that I may be able to perceive them as outside and beside each other, and thus as not merely different, but in different places, the presentation of space must already give the foundation" (*Critique of Pure Reason*, 1787, translated by J.M.O. Meiklejohn, Buffalo, NY: Prometheus Books, 1990, 23–24). Kant's project, therefore, is to ascertain what we can, in principle, experience, before attempting to understand our experiences; and what we can experience is something that is a feature of our minds, and not of the world.

2. You could argue that categorization comes before simplification—in other words, that you give things names before you begin thinking of discarding them from your model of the world. Alternatively, you could argue that simplification is performed unconsciously—that we more or less automatically focus on a narrow range of stimuli—and then give these names and fit them into a model or cognitive scheme. If you take the first view, then you might also think that conscious moral judgment is a means of simplification, through the labeling of particular observations as instances of good or evil. If you take the second view, then you might also think that (unconscious) cognition has built within it a means for simplification of our field of observation based on an *a priori* model of what matters in the world. This is one view cited by neo-Darwinians as the account for intelligence (see M. Donald, *Origins of the Modern Mind*, Cambridge, MA: Harvard University Press, 1991).

3. Jake may have been a more profound thinker than he would seem. One of the central problems of the philosophy of science is that of mapping things-in-the-world to things-in-the-mind. Suppose that I call "round" anything that can be represented by a circle when drawn in at least one cross-section. A circle is defined in its turn as the locus of all points that are equidistant from one fixed point. You might feel justified, by this definition, in calling a bicycle wheel, a truck wheel, a coin, a ball, and a tree all "round." Closer inspection will reveal that none of these objects can be represented by circles that conform precisely to the definition of a circle. Their (instantaneous radii) will differ from a fixed value by a (multiplicative) amount X, which is (preferably) small in comparison to the average value of the radius. If we furthermore define an instantaneous radius as the distance between the center of mass of the object's cross-section and the farthest point away from the center of mass in a particular direction, which is still on the cross-section, then we arrive at the undesirable conclusion that a square is also a circle, to within approximately $X = 0.71$. If, on the other hand, we define instantaneous radius as the reciprocal of instantaneous curvature, then a circle will differ from a square by an amount equal to infinity. At the other end of the spectrum, there is no object in the real world for which $X = 1$ exactly. Things are round to different degrees, indexed by a numerical value whose definition is itself at our discretion. Objects-in-the-mind are precise in ways in which our representations of objects-in-the-world are not. Declaring a potato to be bad on the basis of a definition of a good potato can be a tricky problem and a fabulously complicated undertaking: bad-potatoes-in-the-world do not map precisely into bad-potatoes-in-the-mind.

4. AT&T and Motorola may, on any given day, be simultaneously interacting as competitors, strategic partners, and suppliers and clients of each other.

5. Having observed and experienced, we make attributions and predictions. Our beliefs about causation underlie both forms of understanding. In order to predict that B will always follow A, it must be the case that we believe that

A causes *B*, or figures in some way (possibly as a necessary concomitant) in a causal chain of which *B* is the endpoint. British philosopher David Hume subjected our intuition about causation to a critique from which it has never recovered. Hume argued that the perception of causation is a feature of the mind, and not of the world. An event exhibiting a consistent pattern of occurrence need not follow that same pattern in the future. A phenomenon that behaves according to a theoretical prediction need not behave similarly next time around.

Causal attribution, in other words, is simply our willingness to believe that the world behaves in an organized fashion. Observation, Hume argued, cannot be a proper logical basis for induction. "The supposition, that the future resembles the past, is not founded on arguments of any kind, but is derived entirely from habit. . . . When I am convinced of any principle, 'tis only an idea, which strikes more strongly upon me. When I give the preference to one set of arguments over another, I do nothing but decide from my feeling concerning the superiority of their influence. Objects have no discoverable connexion together; not is it from any other principle but custom operating upon the imagination, that we can draw any inference from the appearance of one to the existence of another" (*An Equiry Concerning Human Understanding*, 1739). Nevertheless, we proceed to make predictions and to organize our lives on the basis of past experiences and the regularities that we infer from them.

6. Or, perhaps, stop generalizing from limited observations of complex phenomena with such ease. Social psychologists (see R. Nisbett and L. Ross, *Human Inference: Strategies and Shortcomings of Social Judgment*, Century Psychology Series, Englewood Cliffs, NJ: Prentice-Hall, 1980; and S. T. Fiske and S. E. Taylor, *Social Cognition*, New York: McGraw-Hill, 1988) have validated the hypothesis that people easily make dispositional attributions (generalizations) to explain isolated observations of the behavior of others, when in fact much of concrete human behavior is influenced by the context of the action and not by the personality of the actor.

7. Most of our acquired problem-solving skills are algorithmic in nature. An algorithm is a set of rules or instructions for processing and combining input data in such a way as to produce a desired output, or an answer. The simplest general representation of a machine that executes algorithms is a Turing machine: a machine that accepts input data, moves from one internal state and output configuration to another internal state and output configuration on the basis of the input data, and stops when it reaches the desired output (see J. Casti, *Reality Rules*, New York: Wiley, 1991).

8. Emotions and desires that we would rather not have can make calculation even more difficult, and self-discipline can be regarded as a reduction in the difficulty of this calculation. Suppose that I want to lose some weight, but every time I go by the cookie jar I feast on the buttery morsels until I feel sick. Any rational choice theory that I apply after postulating my preference for losing weight over not losing weight would deem me irrational: my actions and my preferences do not fit together. If I throw out the cookie jar—thus removing the temptation—I simplify the task of recalculating my preference every time I am in the kitchen. A functionalist interpretation of the mind (which maps mental states into the states of a computer) was proposed by the philosopher Hilary Putnam. (See H. Putnam, "The Nature of Mental States," in *Art, Mind and Religion*, ed. W. H. Capitan and D. O. Merrill, Pittsburgh: University of Pittsburgh Press, 1967.) In such an interpretation, desires and preferences, and not only cognitions, are the results of computations, or sequences of different machine states. Weakness-of-will, or *akrasia*, as rational choice theorists call it, can then be interpreted as a computational difficulty: the computation that is supposed to yield a set of preferences that is decisive over a given menu of options does not converge to a unique final state, but rather to different final states at different times, depending on which of the contending multiple selves wins out the battle (or comes ahead in the negotiation) for the control of the body. See also Antonio R. Demasio, *Descartes' Error*, New York: Grosset-Putnam, 1994.

9. One might ask whether or not an algorithm is computable; that is, whether or not a computing machine programmed using that algorithm will ever converge to an answer. The computability of an algorithm depends in turn on the complexity of the internal states of the machine. If, for instance, the machine is capable of only two-bit representations of numbers, it will not be able to compute the product 3×3. The mathematician and computer scientist Gregory Chaitin was the first to formalize the computability properties of algorithms and strings of data, and to show the link between computability and computational complexity. Chaitin's most significant result was that an algorithm of a given computational complexity cannot calculate a number of a greater computational complexity. Chaitin defined computational complexity as the length of the shortest string of bits that can be used to exactly represent an algorithm or a number.

Chaitin's results imply that, if one is attempting to predict the behavior of a system (or a person), one needs an algorithm for predicting that behavior that is at least as complex as the algorithm actually used by that system (assuming that the system in question is algorithmic in nature). Even if you do not agree that people can be modeled algorithmically, you will note that many of the relations between people and people, and people and things in the workplace, have an algorithmic nature: "If X happens, do Y, except when Z also happens, in which case do W." As long as the complexity of these algorithms is manageable, the behavior of hierarchical structures is predictable from above. As soon as production tasks become very complex, alternative forms of organization may become necessary in order to maintain the same level of predictability (M. Moldoveanu and H. Stevenson, "Production Cost Economics," Harvard Business School mimeo, 1996). See also Ivar Ekeland, *The Broken Dice*, Chicago: University of Chicago Press, 1993, for a discussion of how we attempt to glean predictive power from observations of apparently random behavior.

10. Pattern recognition is far more efficient than deductive reasoning. It takes $(2^9 + 2^8 + 2^7 + 2^6 + 2^5 + 2^4 + 2^3 + 2^2 + 2^1 + 1 = 2047)$ calculations to verify the internal self-consistency of 10 propositions, and only 10 comparisons to determine which of 10 elements of a set another element is most similar to. You will need considerably more memory if you are relying merely on pattern recognition, however. For instance, suppose that you know the axioms for the real numbers, and therefore that you know how to multiply any two numbers, from first principles. If you were to memorize the multiplication table up to 100, you would need $(100 + 99 + 98 + 97 \ldots + 1 = 5050)$ elements of memory if you wanted to rely merely on pattern recognition for finding an answer to a multiplication problem. Using the rules for multiplication and addition, however, you need only a memory partition of a few elements (enough to store the rules in question, together with some representative examples).

11. Indeed, the "scientific method" has nothing to say about the source of the hypotheses that are tested. They could just be guesses, or they could be propositions that are implied logically by a set of axioms that formalize a model of the world. See Karl Popper, *The Logic of Scientific Discovery*, London and New York: W. B. Routledge, 1934.

12. Or, oddly, that we share the same cognitive biases. Kahneman and Tversky (see D. Kahneman, P. Slovic, and A. Tversky, *Judgments Under Uncertainty: Heuristics and Biases*, New York: Cambridge University Press, 1982, for a review; see also R. Nisbett and L. Ross, *Human Inference*, for a broader discussion of cognitive biases) have uncovered cognitive biases that people asked to make judgments under uncertainty reveal through their choices, which represent deviations from choices prescribed by normative theories of rational choice. For example, participants in one experiment estimated the probability that a person drawn from a group with a known proportion of lawyers and engineers was a lawyer. They made their estimate for a person fitting a stereotype of a lawyer, on the basis of the resemblance of the description to the stereotype, rather than on the basis of the objective probabilities given. This choice is in violation of the prescription of expected utility theory. Kahneman and Tversky have suggested that a representativeness bias causes this behavioral pattern. Other people participating in an experiment estimated the chances of a particular event occurring to them in the next year on the basis of their knowledge of similar events occurring to people with whom they were familiar. Kahneman and Tversky have suggested that an availability (of private information) bias causes this behavioral pattern. A very complete and readable discussion of risk and human beings dealing with it is Peter L. Bernstein's *Against the Gods*, New York: Wiley, 1996.

13. In spite of the care we take to reason about the future and to observe the present, there is an irrational component in any action, because the ends to which reason is applied cannot be deduced using reason alone. Aristotle, for example, suggested that humans take action for some good, and set out to describe the good that is the proper end of human actions, which he calls happiness. Aristotle divides the self into a rational self and an irrational self, and the irrational self is further divided into an appetitive self and a vegetative self. But for the appetitive irrational self, Aristotle believes, people would not act, because reason by itself is pure contemplation and cannot supply the motive for action. See Bertrand Russell, *A History of Western Philosophy*, New York: Simon & Schuster, 1945.

14. A formal model of the relationship between entropy—which measures the uncertainty of a situation—and choice is given in M. Moldoveanu and H. Stevenson, "Path-Dependence in Organizational Resource Allocation Processes," Harvard Business School mimeo, 1996. The model is trying to capture the intuition that we attempt to avoid ambiguity and uncertainty (jointly captured by the concept of entropy) when choosing between alternative courses of action with unknown consequences. The model predicts that we will choose a risky course of action (one in which we can predict the odds of success) over an uncertain course of action (one in which we cannot); that we will choose a course of action with fewer possible outcomes over a course of action with more possible outcomes; and that we will choose a course of action for which the possible outcomes are fully defined, over a course of action for which the outcomes are not fully defined. We may also choose to either restrict the scope of our choices so as to minimize ambiguity, or we might choose (if we are self-deceived) to simplify a choice in our mind to the point where we can decide.

15. Economic theorists assume that people project themselves into the future through their preferences, which determine their choices. Some of them do not consider queries about the origin of preferences relevant to their trade, as some social psychologists, for instance, do. Social psychologist Daryl Bem has argued that people observe themselves choose, and then infer their preferences from the content of their choices and the context of those choices. If someone perceives, for example, that he or she was forced to become a doctor, rather than a lawyer, then he or she will not make a strong inference about the preference for medicine over law. If, on the other hand, a person has freely chosen one profession over another, then he or she will infer that he or she prefers to function in that profession.

Mihnea Moldoveanu ("A Nonlinear Theory of Decisions Under Uncertainty and Ambiguity," Harvard Business School mimeo, 1996) has formalized Bem's argument and constructed a theory of choice in which people infer their preferences for a choosable object from a pattern of past decisions. Preferences, in this theory, are more like addictions or habits than like immutable psychological quantities. By understanding their own propensity for addiction, people can learn to predict their own preferences over time, by understanding the effects of their choices in the present over their choices in the future.

Ellen Langer has built a theory of decisions in which people collect information about alternatives until the decision is identical in their minds to a decision between a large sum of money and a small sum of money, at which point the decision is already made. We collect information until, looking back, we find out that we have already chosen. Langer calls mindless those decisions that do not involve an active consideration or redefinition of the available alternatives. Mindful decisions, on the other hand, involve active reformulations of the decision problem (E. Langer, "The Illusion of Calculated Decisions," Harvard University mimeo, 1992).

Chapter Eight

1. Early English theories of political economy—such as that of John Locke, on which much of the currently accepted view of property and individualism is based—assume that property rights are given and absolute. In this view, what is on my property is mine, what is on your property is yours, and I have no standing to object to your cutting down a magnificent maple tree in the middle of your yard. This view assumes *ab initio* that we cannot reach agreement about what we want our respective futures to be like: property rights therefore appear to be a social disaggregation mechanism. At the opposite end of the property rights spectrum, we could declare the area around the maple tree one in which neither of us has individual property rights—we jointly own it. I cannot do something to it without your agreeing to the same measure. This arrangement will be satisfactory unless neither of us values his ownership of the maple tree enough to care for the area surrounding it. In this case we run into what economists call "the tragedy of the commons" (T. Schelling, *Micromotives and Macrobehavior*, Harvard University Press: Cambridge, MA, 1978), which relates to the gradual degradation of a pasture owned in common by the sheepherders of a village who do not individually have the incentive to care for its upkeep. The pasture decays over time and becomes unusable. Some economists have used the commons example (which is really a thought experiment) to argue against joint property rights in general. The alternative they propose—namely, individual and absolute property rights—falls short of encouraging efforts to come to agreement about the long-term consequences of actions undertaken in the scope of self-interest maximization alone; it seems therefore to resolve the commons problem only in the short term.

2. Another way to think about this is to go back to the distinction between deduction and induction. Since there is no logical basis for induction, we might say that where logic fails, trust or agreement must exist if we want to predict accurately what someone else will do. Building trust is analogous to an inductive process. A person forms beliefs about another on the basis of her observations of the latter's behavior over a period of time. There is therefore no logical basis for trust.

3. Sociologist J. D. Thompson has also spoken of these two dimensions of agreement in his *Organizations in Action*. He writes: "Assessment inevitably involves some standards of desirability against which actual or conceivable effects or causal actions can be evaluated. Assessment also requires determined evaluation of what those effects actually are or would be. In the abstract, these two problems in assessment are easily solved. In reality, this is another matter. There is nothing automatic about standards of desirability, nor is knowledge of effects easily come by" (*Organizations in Action*, New York: McGraw-Hill, 1967, 84).

Though he recognizes the problem that is raised by the necessity to define collective standards of achievement, Thompson does not proceed to examine the way in which people actually and actively go about solving this problem. Rather, he represents standards of desirability as already built into the organization, via the culture of the incumbents, and understanding of cause/effect relationships as a static property of the organization as a whole. "In simple, closed systems, knowledge of cause/effect relationships may be complete. In the complicated open system, however, causal actions often have multiple effects which ramify in different directions and varying distances into the future." Thus, the organization as a whole is represented as capable of "understanding."

Thompson does not seem to realize that "we" cannot understand anything. We can only attempt to agree on an understanding of something. We may never know, in many cases, whether or not we truly agree, and must therefore repeatedly test this agreement by undertaking tasks that require the coordination of our individual actions.

4. In physical science, definitions can be thought of as the outcomes of an agreement-building process. Definitions—reductions of one set of concepts to another set of concepts—must be coordinated, or mapped, to observable actions and events, which are in turn determined by the properties of the measurement apparatus used to acquire them. We cannot detect, therefore, a force that affects the measured quantities and the measurement apparatus to the same extent. All measurements—including those of space and time—are to be understood relative to our frame of reference, which includes the properties of our measurement apparatus, and relative to the properties of our minds. See Hans Reichenbach, *The Philosophy of Space and Time*, London: Dover, 1958.

5. A persuasive argument about both the need for agreement and the value created through those agreements is given by Frederick Reichheld in *The Loyalty Effect*, Boston: Harvard Business School Press, 1996. He focuses on the opportunities inherent in managing the process of creating flexible and enduring bonds.

Chapter Nine

1. Self-knowledge, however, should not be taken for granted. As Confucius has pointed out, the hardest thing of all is knowing oneself. In more recent times, social psychologists have documented many self-enhancing and cognitive biases that make self-knowledge difficult. People make dispositional attributions about themselves that are quite often inconsistent with their behavior (E. E. Jones and R. E. Nisbett, "The Actor and the Observer: Divergent Perceptions of the Cause of Behavior," in *Attribution: Perceiving the Causes of Behavior*, ed. E. E. Jones et al., General Learning Press, 1971); and they profess to adhere to rules of behavior that are contradicted by a narrative of their actions. They make self-enhancing attributions about their own observed behavior and downgrading attributions about their observations of the behavior of others. It is doubtful that people know their own preferences over arbitrary sets of objects, and it is possible that preferences, like habits and addictions, evolve over time. (A theory of self-definition over time based on the principle that "the more one does X, the greater the chance that one will do X in the future because one comes to think of oneself as an X doer" can be found in Mihnea Moldoveanu, "A Nonlinear Theory of Decisions under Uncertainty and Ambiguity," Harvard Business School mimeo, 1996. But predictability gives one a test of one's self-knowledge: "If you know thyself, then predict thyself." Such a test could lead to a higher level of knowledge of the self by the self. The reader is encouraged to take this test.

2. Sociologist and scholar of business administration J. D. Thompson, introduced in Chapter 8, also wrote about the need for consensus prior to the pursuit of a task requiring coordination (such as a task within an organization). He wrote, "Only if the organization's claims to domain are recognized by those who can provide the necessary support, by the task environment, can a domain be operational. . . . The specific categories of exchange vary from one type of organization to another, but in each case, as noted by S. Levine and P. E. White, in 'Exchange as a Conceptual Framework for the Study of Interorganizational Relationships,' *Administrative Science Quarterly*, v. 5 (March 1961): 583–601, exchange agreements rest upon *prior consensus regarding domain*. The concept of domain consensus has some special advantages for our analysis of organizations in action, for it enables us to deal with operational goals without imputing to the organization the human quality of motivation and without assuming a 'group mind,' two grounds on which the notion of organizational goals has been challenged. Domain consensus defines a set of expectations both for members of an organization and for others with whom they interact, about what the organization will and will not do. It provides, although imperfectly, an image of the organization's role in a larger system, which in turn serves as a guide for the ordering of action in certain directions and not in others. Using the concept of domain consensus, we need not assume that the formal statement of goals found in charters, articles of incorporation, or institutional advertising is in fact the criterion on which rationality is judged and choices of action alternatives are made. Nor need we accept such ideologies as that which insists that profit is the goal of the firm. The concept of domain consensus can be clearly separated from individual goals or motives. Regardless of these, members of hospitals somehow conceive of their organizations as oriented around medical care, and this conception is reinforced by those with whom the members interact. Members of regulatory agencies likewise conceive of a jurisdiction for their organizations, and members of automobile manufacturing firms conceive of production and distribution of certain kinds of vehicles as the organization's excuse for existence" (J. D. Thompson, *Organizations in Action*, New York: McGraw-Hill, 1967). Thompson believes, therefore, that the purpose of the firm is defined by whatever the members of the firm are already agreed upon. The point made in this book is that the purpose of the firm is defined by whatever the members of the firm can and do agree upon. Agreement must often be discovered by a process akin to mining. The arguments in this book aim at providing some of the mining technology for this task.

3. Specialization of individuals could lead to lower standards of agreement for a group. If I am a specialist, then I have made a cognitive commitment to a particular way of looking at the world—in particular, at the problems I am paid to solve. If I am faced with a concrete problem that must be resolved through collaboration with another person who is not a cospecialist, the requirement that I coordinate with him or her poses a problem. If I remain committed to the particular way of looking at the world subscribed to in my field, then we may not be able to agree on how the world works. If I abandon my commitment to a particular viewpoint, then my contribution to the solution of the problem may be limited. Resolution of this conundrum requires the use of tools identified in this chapter.

4. And the most compelling rationale for a hierarchical structure is based on a coordination-oriented argument (K. Arrow, *The Limits of Organization*, New York: Norton, 1974), rather than on individual people's need to control others in order to enhance their self-image. Arrow's argument for the hierarchical organization of work is that it is optimal, from an information processing and transfer perspective, for a central "node" ("the leader") to gather information from subordinates, distill this information into a set of executive decisions, and convey only relevant decisions to each subordinate. The alternatives entail far greater information processing costs. Either subordinates individually process information and make decisions without knowledge about one another, in which case coordination between them becomes difficult and perhaps impossible, or the chief executive conveys back to each subordinate all of the information he uses to make decisions, along with the relevant decisions (in which case the information transfer process becomes lengthy and expensive).

Arrow's argument presupposes that agreement between agents making up a hierarchy already exists. A separate theoretical argument (M. Moldoveanu, "Coordination Cost Economics," 1996) shows that hierarchies are inefficient when subordinates don't trust their superiors and therefore have incentives to give their bosses false or fuzzy information. In this case, superiors must become sleuths and spend most of their time figuring out which of their subordinates' statements are true and which are false. If they are themselves subordinates, then their time is further taken up by figuring out how to give false information to their superiors without being found out. In the absence of agreement between subordinates and superiors, hierarchies are inefficient structures for the organization of work.

5. The standard argument one finds in economics textbooks is that every equilibrium between suppliers and consumers in which there is perfect competition among suppliers (i.e., every competitive equilibrium) is such that you cannot make any participant in the market better off without making another participant worse off (i.e., is Pareto-optimal). See, for instance, Andreu Mas-Collel, Michael Whinston, and Jerry Green, *Microeconomic Theory*, New York: Oxford University Press, 1995. The abstract notion of perfect competition one finds in economics textbooks may, however, not correspond to a particular scenario one encounters in the real world. Perfect competition as defined in a textbook implies that products are undifferentiated, in either price or quality. As Hayek points out, this definition has the paradoxical effect of portraying competitive activities (such as advertising and research and development) as taking one away from perfect competition, and not toward a more competitive market, by the textbook definition of the term. See Friederich Hayek, *Individualism and Economic Order, Collected Essays*, Chicago: Chicago University Press, 1991.

6. Markets and hierarchies can be distinguished from each other at least on the basis of the fact that some market mechanisms do not work in a hierarchical structure (they do not enhance survivability of the exchange structure). Suppose that a hierarchical organization has hired a number of workers and lower-level managers at wages that clear the "prices" determined by the market for their services (the labor market). Suppose also that a number of tasks, deemed highly undesirable by the members of the firm, are deemed by top management to be necessary to the survival of the firm. It is then necessary to think of a way of apportioning these tasks among the workers in a way that will not antagonize them, lead them to sabotage the firm's activities, or become so apathetic as to stop caring about the quality of their work. Top managers may even wish to preserve the trust of the workers in the fairness of the processes by which the organization allocates tasks to people.

The "market" solution to the task allocation problem is to hold an auction among the workers, which requires them to bid their willingness to perform various tasks for a preannounced sum of money (which decreases as more and more tasks are allocated). Managers can employ various auctioning strategies to head off collusions between the workers. However, this allocation strategy leads to personal dilemmas for the workers, which they may resolve by making moral judgments about the firm's top managers. For instance, a worker who "won" a particularly undesirable task for a large sum of money may, on spending this money, come to resent his situation when he looks upon the more desirable tasks performed daily by other workers. He may also make denigrating moral judgments about other workers who did not bid in the lottery and are now seemingly having a good time at their original tasks. These workers in turn may resent the firm's policy to reward someone's willingness to trade his own time and enjoyment for money and feel therefore that they are disfavored by such a compensation policy.

A pay-for-performance system in which the difficulty/unpleasantness of the task is part of the performance measure applied to a worker in determining compensation will accomplish essentially the same thing as will a lottery, except that it will create an incentive for all workers to portray their own tasks as difficult or unpleasant over time, and therefore the allocation system will run down or become very expensive to implement. A pay-for-performance-based task allocation scheme is furthermore subject to the same economics-of-envy dynamics that undermine the cohesion of the organization as a whole.

An alternative task allocation scheme is provided by a fair division protocol (S. J. Brams and A. D. Taylor, *Fair Division*, New York: Cambridge University Press, 1995), which emphasizes agreement among workers about the difficulty or unpleasantness of various tasks. A fair division protocol works on the same principle used by two children to divide a piece of cake between them without further conflict: one cuts the cake, and the other chooses a piece for himself. With three people, the protocol works as follows: person 1 cuts the cake into three slices, person two adjusts what she perceives to be the largest slice by cutting away one piece from it, person three chooses from among the four resulting slices, person two chooses from among the remaining slices, and person 1 chooses from among the remaining two slices. The last slice is divided again according to the same protocol. The protocol can be applied to the division of an unpleasant task or set of tasks among workers. In this case, however, each worker attempts to minimize her share of the "pie" rather than maximize it. Because workers will also have an incentive to minimize the average "slice" and therefore to prolong the process for as long as possible, top management will need to impose a time limit on the partitioning of the tasks. The resulting allocation protocol is more expensive in the short term from an organizational point of view (time and energy need to be invested in enforcing the protocol, and a protocol with N participants takes $2N - 2$ rounds to complete). However, if the protocol is successful, each worker will walk away with the feeling that she has "crafted" her own task and is likely to feel better about the outcome than will a worker who has participated in an auction.

7. Oliver Williamson (*Markets and Hierarchies*, New York: Free Press, 1975; *The Economic Institutions of Capitalism*, New York: Free Press, 1985) has proposed that transactions will be carried out either through firms or through markets, depending on the costs that the two different modes of exchange impose on the transactors. Transaction costs depend on the specificity of the assets involved in carrying out the transaction (specific capital investments in real estate and machinery, for instance), on the expected frequency of future interactions between contractors, and on the likelihood of perverse incentives for either of the transactors. Transaction cost economics can be understood as the calculus of minimizing the costs of failures of prediction. If one transactor incorrectly predicts the actions of the other (because the other has lied, for instance), then the structure of the transaction will serve to mitigate the loss to the wronged party. Focusing on increasing predictability can then be understood as a preventive form of transaction cost economics: it acts by decreasing the likelihood of transaction failures, rather than by minimizing the costs associated with the worst-case scenario.

8. But force may lead to unpredictability in the not-too-distant future. Robert Frank tells the story of repeated, bloody feuds between the Hatfields and the McCoys, two American families who lived in the mountains on the border between Kentucky and West Virginia. The feuds took place over a thirty-five-year period, more than a hundred years ago. "To this day, no one is sure how it actually started. But once under way, its pattern was one of alternating attacks, each a retaliation for the one preceding, and thus also the provocation for the one to follow. On New Year's night of 1888, the Hatfields attempted to end the feud once and for all by killing the remaining members of the main branch of the McCoy family. Led by James Vance, they set fire to the McCoy farmhouse, planning to shoot the McCoys as they were trying to escape" (R. Frank, *Passions Within Reason*, New York: Norton, 1988, 1). They killed most of the McCoy family, but some escaped and dedicated much of their time and energy to killing people whose last name was Hatfield.

The will to avenge a wrong or an injustice places the individual who uses force in perennial danger. He can never be sure of what will happen to him next. This is because the memory of an injustice or an atrocity has an uncontrollable effect on the mind that remembers it. It may be rational to forego the opportunity for revenge, but the mind may demand revenge nonetheless, with a force which the body is bound to follow.

9. Agency theorists speak of pay-for-performance contracts in terms of subjective and objective performance measures. They call "objective" those measures of performance that do not require a personal judgment or interpretation on the part of the principal or the agent; any other performance measures are subjective. An example of an objective performance measure is the stock market performance of the value of a firm, measured at a time interval agreed upon by both principal and agent. An example of a subjective performance measure is the principal's evaluation of the contribution of the agent to the intellectual capital of the firm. The distinction between objective and subjective, although seemingly clear, is subject to interpretation and therefore must be governed by interpersonal agreement between principal and agent. If the principal wants to maximize the stock price of the firm over a particular time interval and the agent believes that as agent can achieve the increase in value with an aggressive product strategy, then the agent will accept a nonlinear pay-for-performance contract that rewards modest appreciations in value scantily, and steep appreciations in value steeply. If, however, the agent had formed her expectations about possible actions in ignorance of information about the firm's product development group that the principal had, which showed the agent's assumptions about the firm to be invalid, then the performance measure is subjective, not objective, because the acceptance by the agent of the contract depends on information that the principal had, but the agent did not. A more meaningful distinction, therefore, between different performance measures is that between *subjective* and *intersubjective* measures. The former rest on some informational asymmetry between principal and agent, whereas the latter rest on the reduction of such asymmetry to areas lying outside the scope of the contract.

Chapter Ten

1. Graph of tax rates and Reiling quote are both from Harvard Business School teaching note 1-288-050, © 1988 by the President and Fellows of Harvard College. Reprinted with permission. I'm indebted to Hank Reiling for his quick and lively answers to my tax-related and legal questions.

2. Oliver Wendell Holmes, in *The Common Law*, poignantly makes the point that a criminal's predictions about the consequences of her actions should be taken into account when handing out the sentence. He treats the judicial sanctioning of murder (defined by Sir James Stephen as "unlawful homicide with malice aforethought" in *Digest of Criminal Law*) in terms of what the murdered predicts would happen to the victim as a consequence of her actions. He writes, "For instance, a newly born child is laid naked out of doors, where it must perish as a matter of course. This is none the less murder, that the guilty party would have been very glad to have a stranger find the child and save it."

Foresight of consequences, according to Holmes, is "a picture of a future state of things called up by knowledge of the present state of things, the future being viewed as standing to the present in the relation of effect to cause. . . . If the known present state of things is such that the act done will very certainly cause death, and the probability is a matter of common knowledge, one who does the act, knowing the present state of things, is guilty of murder, and the law will not inquire whether he did actually foresee the consequences or not. The test of foresight is not what this very criminal foresaw, but what a man of reasonable prudence would have foreseen."

In Holmes's view, the proper application of the law seems to rest upon a delicate agreement (between people who have a stake in discharging the authority of the law) on what "reasonable prudence" might actually be. This requirement highlights the relationship between mutual predictability and prior agreement about the facts that constitute the bases for prediction. The law and its administration are therefore only as predictable to its subjects as the subjects themselves are to one another. If there is no mutually (and perhaps universally) agreeable definition of what one means by "reasonable prudence," then what one person would call a crime, another would call an accident. The law creates an overarching incentive for people to get to know and learn to predict each other, so as to form some impression of the acts that can be understood by others (perhaps members of a jury) in a court of law.

3. See, for example, "Dispute Resolution: The Explosion in Private Justice," *Business Week*, 12 June 1995.

4. Ibid.

5. "High-tech Hype Should Carry a Disclaimer," *USA Today*, 24 July 1996, B1.

6. Steve Case's 7 August 1996 letter to AOL subscribers. See also "System Crash Signs America Online Off" and "Blackout Could Raise Question of Reliability," *USA Today*, 8 August 1996.

7. Clifford Stoll, *Silicon Snake Oil*, New York: Doubleday, 1995, 64.

8. Edward Tenner, *Why Things Bite Back*, New York: Alfred A. Knopf, 1996, 195.

9. "Regulation—Fewer Strings Attached," *Business Week*, 13 May 1996.

10. "Small Business Gets Regulatory Relief," *Inc.*, 20 May 1996. It's worth noting that the boxed "trailer" to this article begins, "So will YOU sue the government now?"

11. "Are Regulations Bleeding the Economy?" *Business Week*, 17 July 1995.

Chapter Eleven

1. C. Bartlett and S. Ghoshal, "Changing the Role of Top Management: Beyond Systems to People," *Harvard Business Review*, May–June 1995, 132–143.

2. Through specialization, an individual becomes more predictable to others with whom he is interacting in his role as a specialist. What constitutes a specialty is a body of specialized and codified knowledge that is transferred to a person by a process of education, accreditation, and apprenticeship. This knowledge to a great extent defines the "role" the specialist will play vis-à-vis other people who approach her in her capacity. Phil Zimbardo, a social psychologist at Stanford University, has shown that individuals easily fall into prescribed roles, even when the role contradicts what the "actor" believes about herself. Zimbardo was surprised to find that Stanford undergraduates easily adopted the roles of prisoners and prison guards in an experiment lasting several days; the prison guards displayed a level of zeal and sadism that was not compatible with their belief that they were "just taking part in an experiment" (P. Zimbardo and M. Leippe, *Psychology of Social Influence and Attitude Change*, New York: McGraw-Hill, 1991). Thus, if we know the characteristics of a role (a specialty) and also the fact that an individual has invested a significant amount of time in learning that role, then we may be confident in our predictions of her behavior, when we interact with her on a professional level.

3. This is one of the basic principles behind the theory of games. A game is defined by a set of players, an information set for each player, and a set of strategies for each player. Players gain insight into the game by putting themselves in the shoes of the other players and asking themselves what they would do if they were in their competitors' positions. It is then reasonable for a player to assume that another player will proceed in the same way that the player herself would. Therefore, an opponent's strategy is made transparent by an act of introspection, guided by calculation and based on observation. This argument was first developed by Thomas Schelling (*The Strategy of Conflict*, Cambridge, MA: Harvard University Press, 1961).

4. Therefore, it is not only what we do that counts, in isolation, but rather the correlation between what we say and what we do. The economic importance of words is explored in Mihnea Moldoveanu, *The Economics of Verbal Behavior*, in preparation, 1996. If one is interested in making one's behavior inscrutable (impossible to judge according to standards of predictability) then one will use language that is ambiguous and capable of supporting many meanings, and be reluctant to answer questions about one's own area of competence and personal circumstances, because to do so would entail enabling someone else to predict one's behavior. A hierarchy made up of expert obfuscators may be inefficient, because middle managers will spend most of their playing signaling games with their superiors and trying to see through the signaling games of their subordinates.

5. A person who believes that game theory can explain most of human behavior might argue that lying is against the liar's own best interests, because if she is found out, then her reputation will suffer, the market for her services will be reduced, and the expected future value of her earnings will also go down. This, however, is not an argument against lying. Rather, it is an argument for lying well enough for the lie to go undetected during the time period in which the agent is interested in maintaining an operation that depends on reputation. If the probability of getting caught is very low, then the expected value of the agent's loss will also be very low. If the expected gains from lying are high, then a cost-benefit calculation will lead the agent always to lie. However, every other agent will apply the same reasoning, and all agents will lie to each other. Gains from lying will be diminished in the long run, because there is no one to count on for delivering the gains. This way of reasoning can only explain why so *few* people lie only by assuming that agents are farsighted enough to take into account the consequences of similar behavior by every other agent in society.

The predictability-based argument, by contrast, focuses on why so *many* people lie, even though their lies destroy predictability for themselves as well as for others who depend on their actions. The agent's choice between lying and not lying hinges, in this argument, on the effect of the lie (discovered or undiscovered) on the person to whom the lie is told. Let us say, for instance, that I discover that what you told me is false, but I do not know whether you are a liar, an incompetent, or were yourself given false information by someone you had reason to trust. The reputation-based argument suggests that all you have to do is properly hide your own motives for telling a lie and your competence level. Optimally, you should find someone whom you could credibly blame for the falsehood. The predictability-based argument says that making someone else's life unpredictable, either through lying or through incompetence, will make your own life unpredictable if your future actions depend on the actions of that person.

Because the search for predictability is common to all agents, it implies a rudimentary sort of system of justice: in the long run another agent seeks predictability, just like you would. If you cannot offer it to her, she will search for someone else who will, until she finds him.

6. Again, there is at least one game-theoretical argument in favor of cheating. When all of your possible strategies will lead to your "losing the game," and the expected payoff to cheating or starting a different game is much greater than that of staying in the game, it is rational for you to cheat, or to play "outside of the rules," assuming that you find another game that gives you a better chance of succeeding. If you pursue this strategy, your payoff will materialize. However, the other players in the game (who were expecting to win) will lose not only part of their expected payoff, but also their ability to predict the outcome of the next game. Therefore, if they care about predictability, it is rational for them to increase the expected payoff of the dominated strategy (your strategy) in order to keep you in the game. Whereas a purely self-maximizing argument would point toward playing to win everything, a predictability-based argument would argue for leaving some money on the table.

7. The boss might invoke a standard economic argument for his decision: "Capital is the scarce resource, not labor. For any job, no matter how demanding, I can have ten applicants at my front door tomorrow. Therefore, it is rational for me to ask you to leave town on Sunday and return on Thursday, if the expected benefits of my doing so outweigh the costs of replacing you with someone else, multiplied by the probability of your quitting." A predictability-based argument would caution the boss that he or she does not know *a priori* the costs of replacing the worker in question, because hiring another worker involves making a *prediction* about the latter's competence and honesty. Furthermore, the probability of the worker's quitting her job has just increased because of her decreased perceived ability to predict the boss's next request. The predictability of the boss's own life will in the short run depend on another, yet unknown, person, and his reaction to the new environment. In the long run, it will depend on a workforce that is increasingly reluctant to live up to a standard of predict-ability, if other bosses act in similar ways.

Chapter Twelve

1. Linguist Deborah Tannen ("The Power of Talk: Who Gets Heard and Why," *Harvard Business Review*, September–October 1995) has pointed out several differences in the linguistic styles of men and women that can lead to misunder-standings that undermine the process of reaching substantive agreement and that make men and women distrustful of each other in subsequent exchanges.

Tannen writes, "Communication isn't as simple as saying what you mean. How you say what you mean is crucial, and differs from one person to the next, because using language is a learned social behavior: How we talk and listen are deeply influenced by cultural experience. Although we might think that our ways of saying what we mean are natural, we can run into trouble if we interpret and evaluate others as if they necessarily felt the same way we'd feel if we spoke the way they did" (p. 138). This sort of false projection of one's motives and dispositions onto the utterances of another person is at the heart of many misunderstandings between men and women that can be traced to consistent differences in expressive style that lead one to incorrectly interpret the words of the other.

Tannen first argues that linguistic style is inescapable: "Everything that is said must be said in a certain way—in a certain tone of voice, at a certain rate of speed, and with a certain degree of loudness. Whereas often we consciously consider what to say before speaking, we rarely think about how to say it, unless the situation is obviously loaded—for example, a job interview or a tricky performance review. Linguistic style refers to a person's characteristic speaking pattern. It includes such features as directness or indirectness, pacing and pausing, word choice, and the use of . . . jokes, figures of speech, stories, questions, and apologies. In other words, linguistic style is a set of culturally learned signals by which we not only communicate what we mean but also interpret others' meaning and evaluate one another as people" (p. 139).

Next, Tannen presents evidence that the linguistic style of men is on average different from that of women and shows that these differences emerge early in the socialization of men and women as children. She claims that whereas girls "use language to negotiate how close they are and tend to downplay ways in which one is better than the other and to emphasize ways in which they are all the same," boys, by contrast, "learn to use language to negotiate their status in the group by displaying their abilities and knowledge, and by challenging others and re-sisting challenges" (p. 140).

Because men and women learn their respective conversational skills in child-hood play groups, they "tend to have different habitual ways of saying what they mean, and conversations between them can be like cross-cultural communication: you can't assume that the other person means what you would mean if you said the same thing in the same way." The linguistic styles developed in childhood play groups lead to detectable interpersonal dynamics between men and women in business contexts. "Men tend to be sensitive to the power dynamics of interac-tion, speaking in ways that position themselves as one up and resisting being put in a one-down position by others. Women tend to react more strongly to the rapport dynamic, speaking in ways that save face for others and buffering statements that could be seen as putting others in a one-down position."

Tannen proceeds to inventory the consequences of the sexual differences in linguistic style. She argues that getting credit in a "man's world" may require a linguistic assertiveness that women habitually lack, whereas men do not. "What-ever the motivation, women are less likely than men to have learned to blow their own horn. And they are more likely than men to believe that if they do so, they won't be liked" (p. 141). Furthermore, women may not enjoy the "grabbing game" that governs the quest for personal rewards in organizations made up of mostly male collectives.

Men and women have different ways of representing their opinions about the same piece of information. "Women are likely to downplay their certainty; men are likely to minimize their doubts" (p. 142). When managers make judg-ments about allocating resources on the basis of their perception of the relative confidence of the proponents of the respective projects, they stand a good chance of overestimating the projects proposed by men and underestimating the projects proposed by women. Women are likely to ask more questions of a speaker. Men are likely to ask fewer questions and to see asking questions as a sign of incompetence or of lack of self-confidence. Women give feedback in a way that is designed to protect the self-esteem of the person to whom they are giving it. Men can misinterpret such feedback, paying attention only to the positive comments and ignoring or devaluing the criticisms that follow the praise. Tannen observed that women pay more compliments than do men, who are less likely to ask open-ended questions about their own performance, for fear that it might be criticized.

These differences all lead to misunderstandings: Men say what they mean to women, who hear what a woman (like them) would have meant had she said it; and women say what they mean to men, who hear what a man (like them) would have meant had he said it. In turn, such misunderstandings undermine the potential for real agreement between men and women—and, more generally, between any persons with differing expressive styles. The substance of a message—that which both interlocutors would presumably be able to agree on had they had access to an artifact-free medium of representation—is not separable from the medium of the message. One person cannot ask another to express herself expressionlessly, and not all information that is expressed (such as self-reported levels of enthusiasm or confidence) can be represented in an artifact-free form. Tannen's article therefore has pessimistic implications for the ability of people to reach agreement by transcending their own expressive idiosyncracies. However, it highlights the importance of trying to represent the information required to reach agreement on coordinated action in the most objective, evaluation-free form possible.

select bibliography

Andrews, Kenneth. *The Concept of Corporate Strategy*. Homewood, IL: Irwin, 1971.

Aron, Raymond. *Main Currents in Sociological Thought I*. Garden City, NY: Anchor Books, 1969.

Arrow, Kenneth. *The Limits of Organization*. New York: Norton, 1974.

Asch, S. "Opinions and Social Pressure." *Scientific American* 193, no. 5 (1955).

Bartlett, Christopher, and Sumantra Goshal, "Changing the Role of Top Management: Beyond Systems to People," *Harvard Business Review*, May–June 1995, 132–143.

Bernstein, Peter L. *Against the Gods*. New York: Wiley, 1996.

Boyd, Richard, Philip Gasper, and J. D. Trout, eds. *The Philosophy of Science*. Cambridge, MA: MIT Press, 1991.

Brams, Steven J., and Alan D. Taylor. *Fair Division*. New York: Cambridge University Press, 1995.

Campbell, Jeremy. *Grammatical Man*. New York: Simon & Schuster, 1982.

Casti, John. *Reality Rules*. New York: Wiley, 1991.

Chandler, Alfred D. *The Visible Hand*. Cambridge, MA: Harvard University Press, 1977.

Churchill, W. *A History of the English Speaking Peoples*. New York: Dorset Press, 1990 (1956).

Cruikshank, Jeffrey L., and David B. Sicilia. *The Engine That Could*. Boston: Harvard Business School Press, forthcoming.

Dawkins, R. *The Selfish Gene*. New York: Oxford University Press, 1976.

DeMasio, Antonio R. *Descartes' Error.* New York: Grosset-Putnam, 1994.

DePaulo, Bella. "Non-Verbal Behavior and Self-Presentation." *Psychological Bulletin* 111, no. 2 (1992): 203–243.

Donald, Merlin. *Origins of the Modern Mind.* Cambridge, MA: Harvard University Press, 1991.

Ekeland, Ivar. *The Broken Dice.* Chicago: University of Chicago Press, 1993.

Ellsberg, Daniel. "Risk, Ambiguity and the Savage Axioms." *Quarterly Journal of Economics* 75 (1961).

Elster, Jon, ed. *Rational Choice.* New York: New York University Press, 1986.

Fiske, Susan T., and Shelley E. Taylor. *Social Cognition.* New York: McGraw-Hill, 1988.

Frank, Robert. *Passions Within Reason.* New York: Norton, 1988.

Fukuyama, Francis. *Trust.* New York: Free Press, 1995.

Gilbert, Daniel. "How Mental Systems Believe." *American Psychologist* (February 1991).

Gould, Stephen J. *Full House.* New York: Harmony Books, 1996.

Graves, Robert. *The Greek Myths.* London: Penguin Books, 1955.

Hayek, Friederich. *Individualism and Economic Order.* Collected Essays. Chicago: University of Chicago Press, 1991.

Holmes, Oliver W. *The Common Law.* Boston: Little, Brown, 1881.

Hume, David. *An Enquiry Concerning Human Understanding* (1739). Indianapolis and Cambridge: Hackett Publishing Company, 1977.

Jaynes, Julian. *The Origins of Consciousness in the Breakdown of the Bicameral Mind.* Boston: Houghton Mifflin, 1976.

Jones, E. E., and R. E. Nisbett. "The Actor and the Observer: Divergent Perceptions of the Cause of Behavior." In *Attribution: Perceiving the Causes of Behavior,* edited by E. E. Jones, D. E. Kanouse, H. H. Kelley, R. H. Nisbett, S. Valins, and B. Weiner, 79–94. General Learning Press, 1971.

Kahneman, Daniel, Paul Slovic, and Amos Tversky. *Judgments Under Uncertainty: Heuristics and Biases.* New York: Cambridge University Press, 1982.

Kant, Immanuel. *Critique of Pure Reason* (1787). Translated by J.M.D. Meiklejohn. Buffalo, NY: Prometheus Books, 1990.

Kauffman, Stewart. "Whispers from Carnot." In *Complexity: Metaphors, Models and Reality.* Santa Fe Institute Studies in the Sciences of Complexity, edited by George Cowan, David Pines, and David Meltzer. Reading, MA: Addison-Wesley, 1994.

Khayam Moore, Omar. "Divination, a New Perspective." *American Anthropologist* 59 (1957): 69–74.

Kohlberg, Lawrence. *Collected Papers on Moral Development and Moral Education.* Cambridge, MA: Center for Moral Education, 1976.

Kreps, David. *Notes on the Theory of Choice.* Underground Classics in Economics. Boulder and London: Westview Press, 1988.

Kuhn, Thomas. *The Structure of Scientific Revolutions.* Chicago: University of Chicago Press, 1970.

Langer, Ellen. "The Illusion of Control." *Journal of Personality and Social Psychology* 32, no. 2 (1975).

Levine, S., and P. E. White. "Exchange as a Conceptual Framework for the Study of Interorganizational Relationships." *Administrative Science Quarterly* 5 (March 1961): 583–601.

Marx, K., and F. Engels. *The German Ideology.* Part I (1846). Translated by W. Lough, edited by C. J. Arthur. New York: International Publishers, 1970.

Mas-Collel, Andreu, Michael Whinston, and Jerry Green. *Microeconomic Theory.* New York: Oxford University Press, 1995.

Mui, Vai-Lam. "The Economics of Envy." *Journal of Economic Behavior and Organization* 26 (1995): 311–336.

Nisbett, Richard, and Lee Ross. *Human Inference: Strategies and Shortcomings of Social Judgment.* Century Psychology Series. Englewood Cliffs, NJ: Prentice-Hall, 1980.

Popper, Karl. *The Logic of Scientific Discovery.* London and New York: W. B. Routledge, 1934.

———. *The Poverty of Historicism.* London and New York: W. B. Routledge, 1976.

Porter, Michael. *Competitive Strategy*. New York: Free Press, 1980.

Putnam, Hilary. "The Nature of Mental States." In *Art, Mind and Religion*, edited by W. H. Capitan and D. D. Merrill. Pittsburgh: University of Pittsburg Press, 1967.

Reichenbach, Hans. *The Philosophy of Space and Time*. London: Dover, 1958.

Reichheld, Frederick F. *The Loyalty Effect*. Boston: Harvard Business School Press, 1996.

Russell, Bertrand. *A History of Western Philosophy*. New York: Simon & Schuster, 1945.

Schelling, Thomas. *The Strategy of Conflict*. Cambridge, MA: Harvard University Press, 1961.

———. *Micromotives and Macrobehavior*. Cambridge, MA: Harvard University Press, 1978.

Sen, Amartya. *Inequality Reexamined*. Cambridge, MA: Harvard University Press, 1984.

———. "Internal Consistency of Choice." *Econometrica* 61, no. 3 (May 1993): 495–521.

Senge, Peter. *The Fifth Discipline*. New York: Free Press, 1993.

Shannon, Claude E., and Dennis Weaver. *The Mathematical Theory of Communication*. Urbana-Champaign: University of Illinois Press, 1949.

Shapiro, Eileen C. *Fad Surfing in the Boardroom*. Reading, MA: Addison-Wesley, 1995.

Stoll, Clifford. *Silicon Snake Oil*. New York: Doubleday, 1995.

Sun-Tzu. *The Art of War*. London: Oxford University Press, 1977.

Tannen, Deborah. "The Power of Talk: Who Gets Heard and Why." *Harvard Business Review* (September–October 1995).

Tenner, Edward. *Why Things Bite Back*. New York: Alfred A. Knopf, 1996.

Thompson, James D. *Organizations in Action*.New York: McGraw-Hill, 1967.

Williamson, Oliver E. *Markets and Hierarchies*. New York: Free Press, 1975.

———. *The Economic Institutions of Capitalism*. New York: Free Press, 1985.

Wilson, Edmund O. *On Human Nature*. Cambridge, MA: Harvard University Press, 1978.

Zimbardo, Philip, and M. Leippe. *Psychology of Social Influence and Attitude Change*. New York: McGraw-Hill, 1991.

index

Accountability, 11

Action. *See also* Consequences
  in art of prediction, 129–32
  effective, components of, 135–38
  models and, 131–32

ADR. *See* Alternative dispute resolution

Advanced Micro Devices, 195

Agency theory, 272*n*9

Agnew, Spiro, 39

Agreement
  concept of domain consensus and, 267*n*2
  dimensions of, 149–54, 158–63, 176–77
  domains for creation of, 176–84
  elimination of, 171
  grounds of, 157
  impact of change on, 165–66, 188
  modes of exchange and, 158–64
  need for, 156–57
  predictive perspective and, 143–48
  reducing the need for, 171–72, 174–76, 184–87
  tools for increasing, 172–74
  tools for reducing need for, 174–76, 184–87

Agriculture, development of, 81

Algorithms, 260*n*7, 261*n*9

Alliances, 160–61, 162–63. *See also* Business relationships

Alternative dispute resolution (ADR), 195–96

Ambiguity, 275*n*4

America Online (AOL), 197

Amos (book of the Bible), 142

AOL. *See* America Online

Apple Computer, 170

Apprenticeship, 179–80

Arbitration, 195–96

Argonne National Labs, University of Chicago, 131

Aristotle, 86–87, 262*n*13

Arrow, K., 268*n*4

The Art of War (Sun-Tzu), 90–91

Asch, Solomon, 249*n*5

Asset depreciation, and regulation, 203

AT&T, *xv-xvi*, 70

Autocracy, 92–93

Automobile industry, 3–4, 224–25

Baldrige Award, 10

Bartlett, Chris, 11

Beliefs. *See also* Cults; Religion; Tribal thinking; Values
  collective, 148–49
  effective projectability and, 140–41
  incentives and, 174
  systems for formulation of, 246*n*2

Bem, Daryl, 263*n*15

Biology, and predictability, 34–36, 44–45

Blackwell, Ronald, 14

Boole, George, 127–28

Boudon, Raymond, 247*n*7

Brass Tacks Fasteners Company, 169, 171

Howard H. Stevenson is the Sarofim-Rock Professor of Business Administration at Harvard Business School and Chairperson of the Entrepreneurial Management Unit. He returned to Harvard in 1982 to revitalize the program in entrepreneurship. He has published in the field of entrepreneurship, including a bestselling text (now in its fourth edition), a book of readings, and numerous articles. In addition, he served as a Senior Assistant Dean for Financial and Information Systems.

In his business life, he has helped found several companies, including Quadra Capital Partners and The Baupost Group, Inc. He has served as the chairman and president of these two companies, respectively, as well as vice-president, finance and administration, of Preco Corporation. He has served on the board of directors of more than 25 companies, ranging from hopeful start-ups to NYSE-listed organizations. He has been active in land conservation and other community efforts.

Jeffrey L. Cruikshank is a writer, editor, and business consultant. He is a cofounder of Kohn Cruikshank Inc., a Boston-based communications firm, and has authored or coauthored numerous books on topics of interest to managers. He is the coauthor (with David B. Sicilia) of *The Engine That Could*, a history of the Cummins Engine Company, forthcoming from the Harvard Business School Press.